501 Baseball Books Fans Must Read before They Die

RON KAPLAN

University of Nebraska Press   Lincoln & London

Library of Congress Cataloging-in-Publication Data

Kaplan, Ron, 1957–
501 baseball books fans must read before they die /
Ron Kaplan.
p. cm.
Includes bibliographical references and index.
ISBN 978-0-8032-4073-5 (pbk.: alk. paper)
1. Baseball—Collectibles—Handbooks, manuals,
etc. 2. Baseball—Collectors and collecting—
Handbooks, manuals, etc. 3. Book collecting—
Handbooks, manuals, etc. I. Title.
GV875.2.K36 2013
796.357—dc23   2012043518

Set in Scala by Laura Wellington.

501 Baseball Books Fans Must Read before They Die

To Faith, who always believed I could do it even when I didn't believe it myself.

And to Rachel, to show that anything is possible.

Contents

Acknowledgments

One of my favorite quotes comes from the memorable TV character Benjamin Franklin "Hawkeye" Pierce of *M*A*S*H*. When asked what one book he would want if stranded on a desert island, he replied, "The dictionary, because it has all the other books in it."

Along those lines, a project like this would not have been possible without all the hard work of the hundreds of authors who have written about the national pastime for the past 150-plus years. So, to paraphrase another famous character, Yogi Berra, thanks to them for making this book necessary.

Many thanks also to the fine folks at the University of Nebraska Press—Robert Taylor, Courtney Ochsner, Tish Fobben, Roger Buchholz, Tyler Holzer, Acacia Gentrup, Laura Wellington, and Rosemary Vestal—for guiding this rookie through the process.

Introduction

In his introduction to *The Norton Book of Sports*, George Plimpton described his "small ball theory" of literature. Plimpton, who served as editor for the anthology, believed there was "a correlation between the standard of writing about a particular sport and the ball it utilizes—that the smaller the ball, the more formidable the literature" (13). Accordingly, since the national pastime employs one of the smaller pieces of sporting equipment, there have been "very good books about baseball," he wrote.

Sure, it's a cliché to say that baseball is a metaphor for life (and points off for the unimaginative author who insists on including the Jacques Barzun line, "Whoever wants to know the heart and mind of America had better learn *baseball*," in his book), but precisely that notion *is* reflected in the wide range of genres from fiction to philosophy, statistics to science, and biographies to business, among others.

Perhaps it's the leisurely pace of the game, stretched out over several hours and played during the languid days of summer, that lends baseball to the printed word. The Hall of Fame Library in Cooperstown boasts a collection of more than ten thousand volumes dating back to the early nineteenth century, and the Library of Congress has similar holdings.

I make no claim that the five hundred (or so) titles you will find herein are necessarily the *best* baseball books; that's too subjective. But I hope they will provide an entry into the fascinating world of baseball literature, with its connections to other areas one might not normally associate with the game: fiction, history, science, the arts, music, and many more.

Just as there are the David McCulloughs, Stephen Kings, John Clancys, and Agatha Christies in the so-called real literary world, there are similar staples of baseball lit: W. P. Kinsella in fiction; Peter Golenbock for team and oral histories; Donald Honig for general history (with some fiction thrown in for a change of pace); Harold Seymour and David Q. Voight for their multivolume histories of the national pastime; and John Thorn, appointed as official historian for Major League Baseball in 2011, who's been a bit of a polyglot, with volumes of history, statistics, analyses, reference, and even a children's book.

The books listed here represent some of the best, most well-produced, and quirkiest examples of the various departments within the grand department store that is baseball. Of course, you might disagree. What's baseball without a good debate? If you think I left out one of your favorites or have some other bone to pick, drop me a line at RonKaplansBaseballBookshelf@gmail.com. Maybe I'll consider it for the second edition.

Some books fit into more than one category. For example, Jonah Keri's *The Extra 2%: How Wall Street Strategies Took a Major League Baseball Team from Worst to First* is located in the business section of my local Barnes and Noble, rather than with the rest of the baseball titles. Similarly, a biography of necessity crosses into history, while volumes on statistics could also fit into the area of analysis. They are offered here based on the most appropriate category with additional notation of other crossover themes where appropriate.

A note on formatting: Because of their popularity, many titles have been reissued over the years, often by different publishing companies. The dates, sources, and notes herein are from editions I have either in my own library or have read elsewhere. Similarly, the identifications for the authors are based on the information given within their books at the time of publication.

3. *The Baseball Fan's Companion: How to Watch a Game Like an Expert,* by Nick Bakalar. New York: Macmillan, 1996.

The phrase is *"play* ball," not *"work* ball." Baseball is a game; it's supposed to be fun (although there are those curmudgeonly types who would disagree). This means that books like *The Baseball Fan's Companion* should not strive to be taken too seriously, and fortunately, that's exactly Bakalar's route.

He mixes his primer with bits and pieces that make no pretense of being a textbook as he delivers his lessons in almost a stream of consciousness. Bakalar follows only the loosest organization in his discussions of such items as offense, defense, pitching, and rules. (The least-enforced rule: opposing players shall not fraternize on the field while in uniform. Yeah, right.)

Of particular interest are several diagrams mapping out defensive positioning for specific situations and a too-short section on baseball chatter, in which the author offers a detailed "translation" of what a broadcaster might say and what it actually means in terms a rank beginner can follow.

Other categories: History, Pop Culture, Reference

4. *The Beauty of Short Hops: How Chance and Circumstances Confound the Moneyball Approach to Baseball,* by Sheldon Hirsch and Alan Hirsch. Jefferson N C: McFarland, 2011.

There are several books that propound the concepts of sabermetrics and the *Moneyball* approach to the game, but few titles actually come out *against* the theories that became so popular after the publication of Michael Lewis's book in 2003.

This father-and-son writing team takes a more old-fashioned approach. They want to show that not everything comes down to slide rules and computer printouts. That is, all the planning in the world can't foresee the little quirks of fate that make sports (and life) so interesting. Statistics, they claim, can be tweaked to support your purposes and desires. As evidence, they offer a number of games from 2009 that were full of bad hops, balls deflected by birds in flight, and baserunning blunders. Lewis and Billy Beane, the Oakland A's general manager on whom *Moneyball* is based, certainly couldn't have accounted for such circumstances in their equations.

But this is the beauty, according to the Hirsches, who write from the point of view of the fans who watch the game, as opposed to general managers with a business plan on how to put together a ball club, whether as a front-office professional or as an ersatz GM drafting a fantasy team.

Who's the audience for this book? It's certainly not a scholarly treatise, but it *is* a reminder of what baseball has always been and should be again, at least according to the authors: a game played by human beings, warts and all.

5. *The Bill James Baseball Abstract*, by Bill James. New York: Villard, 1985.

There have always been books on statistics and books of commentary, but before James came along, the two sides of the same baseball coin were rarely presented in one volume. James—who created the first of his annual *Abstracts* while working as a night watchman at a pork-and-beans company and sold them by mail order through advertisements in the *Sporting News*—used a newly developed system of "runs created" to prove who the best players really were. The first *Abstracts* were self-published from 1977–81, but once word about his theories and amusing presentation spread to a wider audience, James produced his work through established publishing houses from 1982–88. As word about his theories and amusing presentation spread, he signed on with Ballantine Books to distribute the *Abstracts* throughout the 1980s, after which he went on to author more diverse publications, in addition to consulting for the Boston Red Sox and other baseball outlets. Subsequent annual editions would concentrate on a specific theme—the 1982 edition looked at the effects of aging on production, for example—in addition to team analysis.

His seminal work has earned him a place in baseball lore and American pop culture: James has been profiled on *60 Minutes*, and he also appeared as a guest voice on *The Simpsons*.

Other categories: History, Pop Culture, Statistics

6. *The Book on the Book: A Landmark Inquiry into Which Strategies in the Modern Game Actually Work*, by Bill Felber. New York: Thomas Dunne/St. Martin's Press, 2005.

7. *The Book: Playing the Percentages in Baseball*, by Tom M. Tango, Mitchel G. Lichtman, and Andrew E. Dolphin. Dulles VA: Potomac, 2007.

"The book," as it has been traditionally regarded, is not really a physical book at all. Rather, it is a tradition, a time-honored way of doing things in a given discipline that's been accepted since time immemorial.

You'll often hear announcers say a manager is "going against the book," or, in other words, bucking long-held beliefs in an attempt to disrupt the opponent. When it works, the manager is a genius; when it doesn't, the announcers will either give him credit for trying something new or point to his faux pas as proof that the old system still works.

These two titles seek to break the mold, incorporating the ever-expanding universe of sabermetrics in an attempt to discern trends that should bring about a change in the standard approach. At the same time, they both take a broad overview of the game, asking questions about the personnel makeup of a team or deciding what a player is worth, either for trade value or at the negotiating table.

Felber's *Book on the Book* is a direct slap at the establishment. He divides his content into the game on and off the field. In the former, he doesn't attack the old so much as he offers new ways to interpret what he believes are misconceptions. The most interesting of these chapters is his assessment of general managers. After all, while the man in the dugout has to play with the cards he's dealt, the GM is the dealer.

Tango's *The Book* is an offshoot of his website (Tangotiger.net) where he, his coauthors, and their visitors discuss such matters as linear weights, base-out states, and run values. The print edition offers more than 140 charts and tables to illustrate their points. It takes a bit of effort to get through this one but, hey, Rome wasn't built in a day.

For those of you who are not on board the sabermetric train, I can practically hear your eyes rolling at all this. I was like you once. But after reading through these essays, I can say that they *can* change perceptions. Even if you don't want to become an expert on that side of the equation, these books can lead you to a new appreciation for the thought processes that go into making decisions. Such tactics are becoming increasingly in vogue as a younger generation of managers and GMs who have been brought up on this data nudge the old-timers aside.

Other categories: Business, History, Statistics

8. *Bullpen Diaries: Mariano Rivera, Bronx Dreams, Pinstripe Legends, and the Future of the New York Yankees*, by Charley Rosen. New York: HarperCollins, 2011.

No dynasty lasts forever. This is especially true in the world of sports, which has a tremendous turnover rate. Sure, you can sign stud free agents and make a few key trades here and there, but the building process must come from within, and you have to give your young players a chance to develop before shipping them off to another team. Rosen, a veteran journalist and longtime Yankees fan, follows the team in an unusual fashion by concentrating solely on the production of the relief corps during each contest of the 2010 season, grading the pitchers on each game's performance from spring training though the AL Championship Series against the Texas Rangers.

Mariano Rivera, who holds the all-time record for career saves, began his Yankee career on the same minor league teams as Derek Jeter, Jorge Posada, and Andy Pettitte. Now it's time for the new regime to step in, but according to *Bullpen Diaries*, it will be difficult to find someone to fill his shoes. One quickly notices how strategy has changed over the years and how many pitchers it takes to get through a game (even more if it goes into extra innings).

Rosen's style is somewhat repetitive, but he keeps things lively with plenty of filler, including historical trivia and interviews with the pitchers and other players, as well as a roundup of what was going on in the rest of the Majors and the Minor Leagues.

He wraps up *Diaries* with an assessment of what the Yankees have to do to move forward, including the unenviable task of finding a replacement for their future Hall of Fame closer.

Other category: History

9. *Clearing the Bases: The Greatest Baseball Debates of the Last Century*, by Allen Barra. New York: Thomas Dunne, 2002.

Almost as much as watching the game on the field, hardy baseball fans love a good argument: "who's better" (both team and individual player editions) and "what if" are perennial topics of discourse.

Barra, a sports columnist who has written for the *Wall Street Journal* and Salon.com, among other publications, brings up several compelling points in *Clearing the Bases.* Some are quantifiable, while others—such as why pitchers can't throw complete games anymore, or who is the greatest living player (asked at a time when Joe DiMaggio, who insisted on being introduced with that distinction, had recently died), or why the Mets couldn't maintain their winning ways in the mid-1980s—are not.

Some might disagree with his conclusions, but then that's just part of the greater theme, isn't it?

Also by the author: Barra followed up *Clearing the Bases* with *Brushbacks and Knockdowns: The Greatest Baseball Debates of Two Centuries* (2004). Guess he remembered a few additional items, such as "Sultan of Swat vs. Splendid Splinter: If Ted is the Greatest Hitter, Why is Babe the Greatest Player?"

10. *Fair Ball: A Fan's Case for Baseball*, by Bob Costas. New York: Broadway, 2000.

After the strike of 1994–95, the hot topic among baseball books was how to repair the game. Several experts — players, journalists, and broadcasters, among others — believed they had the answers to get the national pastime back on track.

Add Bob Costas to the list. His contribution is mostly a rant on the business and organization of the game. Among his suggestions is a new postseason system, even though he declared himself against a radical realignment that occasionally rears its ugly head and snaps at traditionalists. (Who knows — by the time you read this, it may have come to pass.)

Whether you love him or are put off by his almost pseudoreligious reverence for the game, you have to admit Costas has some good ideas, such as returning some postseason games to afternoon broadcasts and starting the night games at an hour that makes them actually watchable for fans on the East Coast who have to go to work or school the following morning. If Major League Baseball is serious about trying to counter flagging interest, they might want to give some of these proposals real thought. After all, this book did spend ten weeks on the *New York Times* best-seller list.

Other categories: Commentary, *New York Times* Best Seller

11. *The Game: One Man, Nine Innings: A Love Affair With Baseball*, by Robert Benson. New York: Penguin, 2001.

There are several books that put a single game under the microscope, examining it for various themes the author deems important. Benson takes it back a notch, looking at a Minor League contest between the Iowa Cubs and the Nashville Sounds in April 2000, a game with ostensibly even less on the line than an early season Major League affair. On the other hand, this may be the kind of game that represents the nostalgic ideal of baseball — a pleasant way to pass a warm summer's evening with family and friends.

Benson's *Game* combines several perspectives: those of a writer, a father, and, of course, a baseball fan. One can imagine hanging with the author as he sits back during the course of nine innings to ruminate on myriad topics. With writing that is both spare and reverential, Benson compares the plays of the game with the ups and downs of everyday life. At one point he allows that the national pastime is a collection of the routine; few plays, he suggests, are memorable on a long-term basis.

The Game is categorized as a sports book, but it's one more in the metaphor-for-life conceit: sometimes you hit a home run, sometimes you make an error. As the game winds down, the author hopes his children will one day recall the important life lessons it offers: "I wish for them that they will remember that there will be days when the best that can be done is to move the runner . . . that even the best of us . . . strike out a fair amount" (161).

12. *Inside Pitch: Life in Professional Baseball*, by George Gmelch. Washington DC: Smithsonian Institution Press, 2001.

Gmelch offers an excellent, if brief, overview of a ballplayer's life from cradle to grave, from auditioning before scouts in high school or college right up until the day he hangs up his spikes. The beauty is in its brutal honesty, so readers should beware lest their image of "the life" be shattered.

You can have all the talent in the world and still not make it to the Show due to factors outside your control, such as injury, organization indifference, or just plain bad luck. In fact, the majority of Minor Leaguers are just there so the high-priced upper-round draft picks have someone to play with. It's a sobering experience for a lot of these young men who were used to being the stars of their teams at every level. Some can't hack it; having been coddled since their tee-ball days, they're not used to hearing negatives or dealing with failure on any extended level.

But as the author points out, it's more than just the player who is involved in the hardships associated with the life. Two particularly interesting—disturbing, even—chapters deal with wives and groupies. With *Inside Pitch's* 2001 publication date, it seems an anachronism for Gmelch to write about wives and girlfriends as property of the players, compelled to always look their best since, obviously, these stud athletes are also judged by the company they keep. Infidelity is almost taken for granted, if not downright expected, and "clearly the baseball wife's primary goal is to support her husband and his career" (150). The groupies are described in even more disparaging terms, described as content to get "free tickets to the game and free beer afterward" (165).

Gmelch, who played in the Tigers' system in the 1960s, spent almost ten years working on this book. This lends him somewhat more credibility than other authors, having insider knowledge to help determine if what he's hearing from the players and others involved has the ring of truth to it.

Other categories: Behind the Scenes, History

13. *It Takes More Than Balls: The Savvy Girls' Guide to Understanding and Enjoying Baseball,* by Deidre Silva and Jackie Koney. New York: Skyhorse Press, 2008.

14. *The Cool Chick's Guide to Baseball,* by Lisa Martin. Salt Lake City: Gibbs Smith, 2003.

As a member of the male species, I have to tread carefully here. On the one hand, I think I would almost be insulted by a book that would try to explain the game based on my demographic (unless I was a child, perhaps). On the other hand, I'm all for anything that brings more fans to the baseball table.

The Cool Chick's Guide is the lighter of the two. While it does discuss the broader points of the game, such as offense, defense, and pitching, it offers a few sections that seem to appeal mostly to pre-feminist women, such as "Battling the Bulge: Your Ballpark Calorie Counter" (hey, guys could stand a few tips here, too) and "Seventh Inning Stretch: It All Comes Down to Shopping."

ting, base running, and fielding. Their graphs considered batting average, on-base percentage, runs and home runs, and RBIS per five hundred at bats. There were also "spray charts" indicating how and where they hit against righties and lefties.

One of several publications produced annually during the late 1980s and early 1990s that looked to cash in on the popularity of the *Bill James Baseball Abstracts, The Scouting Report* also featured a few of each organization's top prospects and others to watch, albeit to a lesser degree than the full-timers.

20. *Spalding Answers to Baseball's Most Asked Questions*, by A. Lou Vickery. Indianapolis IN: Masters Press, 1995.

The slim volume packs quite a punch, as it takes on quite a large responsibility.

From the simplest (What are the formulas for the standard statistics?) to the more difficult (Why is there an infield fly rule anyway?), Vickery, a former Minor Leaguer and coach, provides the answers in a manner that is neither patronizing to fans who already have a good knowledge nor too technical for newbies.

Categories in this volume include the finer points of batting, pitching, fielding, baserunning, and signs, as well as managerial strategy, umpires and rules, and records. There's also a separate glossary for quick reference.

And just to prove that baseball is still a game and not to be taken too seriously, Vickery thoughtfully concludes with a chapter on how baseball terminology has become a staple in everyday language and a transcript of Abbot and Costello's famous "Who's on First" routine.

Other categories: History, Pop Culture

21. *A Thinking Man's Guide to Baseball,* by Leonard Koppett. New York: Dutton, 1967.

A veteran sportswriter and columnist for several New York City newspapers, Koppett wrote one of the earliest (and still best, in my opinion) overviews of the wherefores and whys of baseball, mixing serious analysis with a gentle sense of humor.

Without the benefit of the Internet or modern analytics, Koppett—who received the J. G. Taylor Spink Award from the Baseball Hall of Fame in 1992—scrutinized the game, from offense to defense, business to broadcasting, and the Minor Leagues to marketing, to name only a few. This is not so much a history of baseball, which Koppett also wrote about in his usual pleasant manner, as it is a friendly conversation. You never get the feeling he's showing off, being in with the in crowd, or dropping names.

Koppett's *Guide* went through several revisions, including the most recent (and more politically correct in its title) *The Thinking Fan's Guide to Baseball,* published posthumously in 2004. Naturally, it includes topics that weren't on the radar when the original went to press, such as the designated hitter, free agency, and the increasing power of the Players Association.

In an article for TheColumnists.com published shortly after Koppett's death in 2003, his longtime friend and colleague, Maury Allen, described the first edition of the original *Guide* as "an intellectual look at the simple game."

Other categories: Classic, History

Also by the author: *Koppett's Concise History of Major League Baseball* (1998, revised in 2004); *The Man in the Dugout: Baseball's Top Managers and How They Got That Way* (1993); *The New York Mets* (1974)

22. *This Time Let's Not Eat the Bones: Bill James Without the Numbers*, by Bill James. New York: Villard, 1989.

For this anthology, James selected what he believed were the most informative and entertaining of his previous writings. Most of the pieces were extracted from his popular annual *Abstracts*, while other pieces appeared in *Esquire* magazine.

Some of the pieces are quite extensive, while others, such as this selection from the 1987 edition of the *Abstract*, are as brief as one line: "The Montreal Expos of Gary Carter's last years were a team with more holes than a porcupine's underwear" (47).

The comments are divided into five categories: teams; players; people (mostly managers and owners); essays (including a lengthy piece on James's love for the teams in his hometown of Kansas City); and research, in which the author revisits some of his favorite topics covered in previous *Abstracts*, the more unusual the better. All carry James's informative, offbeat, and thought-provoking style.

That's the great thing about James's work: having started out self-publishing, he doesn't give a hang for being commercial or popular. He writes what he wants and that's just fine with his fans.

Other categories: History, Statistics

23. *Three Nights in August: Strategy, Heartbreak, and Joy Inside the Mind of a Manager*, by Buzz Bissinger. Boston: Houghton Mifflin, 2005.

In this volume, Bissinger offers an in-depth examination of the national pastime, and he expands on the familiar theme of focusing on a game and microanalyzing what goes through a manager's mind.

In this case, the author chose a three-game series between Dusty Baker's Chicago Cubs and Tony La Russa's Saint Louis Cardinals in 2003. La Russa, who retired after the 2011 season and is a potential Hall of Fame candidate, won five pennants and two World Series titles between the Oakland A's and the Cards, so he was obviously an appropriate candidate for such a study.

Imagine watching a game with the ability to pause the action so the color commentator can provide an in-depth backstory on every player and event, then pressing the play button to resume the action. While that might get old after a while, a good portion of the audience would appreciate being privy to such inside dope.

Three Nights in August spent twenty weeks on *The New York Times* best-seller list.

Other categories: History, *New York Times* Best Seller

24. *Tim McCarver's Baseball for Brain Surgeons and Other Fans: Understanding and Interpreting the Game So You Can Watch It Like a Pro,* by Tim McCarver with Danny Peary. New York: Villard, 1998.

Baseball for Brain Surgeons offers plenty of examples and anecdotes drawn from nearly a half century of McCarver's experiences — a twenty-year playing career followed by many more seasons in the broadcast booth for the New York Mets and, later, for FOX Sports.

McCarver's book delves deeper into strategy and nuance than most introductions. It's an excellent source to gain understanding in all facets of the game: how a pitcher or, more frequently, a manager decides what to throw; what goes through a hitter's mind as he steps into the batter's box with the game on the line; how an outfielder positions himself according to who's on base; or how a speedy runner uses his savvy to know when *not* to steal.

Those who prefer watching the game from the comfort of their living rooms will cultivate a new appreciation for television broadcasts, as McCarver explains how the director pulls the action together, what he or she looks for, and what is not seen on the screen. Of course, media technology has advanced a bit since the book came out more than a decade ago, but the basics are still the same.

2

Autobiography, Biography, and Memoir

I've long been fascinated with memoirs, since they rely on, well, memory. The total recall athletes have for specific games—down to the count, the pitch they hit or threw, or the pretty blonde in the stands—never ceases to amaze me. But memory frequently proves faulty, especially with the advent of the Internet and sites like Baseball-Reference.com and Retrosheet.org, so active athletes and extant former ballplayers have to be a bit circumspect with their claims. Although there are obviously separate definitions for autobiography and memoir, I've put the two—together with biography—in one category for ease of organization.

Biographies also fall into a couple of camps: the popular, aimed at the everyday fan, and the scholarly, which are more attuned to so-called serious students of the game. Many authors pride themselves on research and include page upon page of notes, either out of a legal sense of obligation or just to show off. Be wary when a writer includes a "note on sources" in which he or she says something along the lines of, "Conversations and dialogue were based on years of association with the subject."

The student of the genre will also note the evolution in terms of theme, tone, and language. Earlier volumes were mostly written for younger audiences and had positive themes. More recent ones, while some still maintain that lesson-offering quality, are much more personal, covering topics that were never discussed prior to Jim Bouton's Ball Four, *which these days is almost considered quaint by comparison.*

27. *1947: When All Hell Broke Loose in Baseball,* by Red Barber. Garden City NY: Doubleday, 1982.

Few contemporary broadcasters have much in the way of influence. Go back to the days before television, however, and you will find a number of memorable radio personalities, primarily because the medium was the only way to tune in to the game. Red Barber was one of the greatest, an institution with three separate teams: the Cincinnati Reds, the Brooklyn Dodgers, and the New York Yankees.

For many fans, 1947 was Year One, the first time a black man took to a Major League field. The story has been told hundreds of times, but the fact that it's Barber doing the telling this time lends it a special quality, given his background.

Barber does not try to sugarcoat things; he was prepared to quit. His southern sensibilities made it too problematic for him to continue to do his job, but thankfully common sense (and perhaps a martini or two proffered by his wife) prevailed and he remained in the "catbird seat," one of his many colloquialisms. That Barber could overcome the barriers established by his deeply ingrained cultural sensibilities and accept Jackie Robinson and subsequent African American ballplayers adds an extra layer of depth to his already considerable reputation.

Robinson's arrival may have been the marquee event, but there was plenty of other action with the Dodgers for Barber to write about, including the ongoing feud between Branch Rickey and Larry MacPhail—a former Dodger executive and later coowner of the hated Yankees, and the man who gave Barber his first broadcasting job in 1935 with the Reds—and the suspension of Dodgers manager Leo Durocher for behavior deemed detrimental to the best interests of baseball.

Other categories: Broadcasting, Classic, History

28. *Aaron to Zuvernick: A Nostalgic Look at the Baseball Players of the Fifties,* by Rich Marazzi and Len Fiorito. New York: Stein and Day, 1982.

29. *Aaron to Zipfel,* by Rich Marazzi and Len Fiorito. New York: Avon, 1985.

32. *Ball Four*, by Jim Bouton and Leonard Schecter. New York: Dial, 1970.

Bouton was a solid pitcher for the New York Yankees in the mid-1960s; he won twenty-one games in 1963 and two games in the 1964 World Series. Arm trouble made him expendable, though, and he was traded to the expansion Seattle Pilots prior to the 1969 season. So he was in the nadir of his career, presumably with little to lose, when he decided to write about what he saw as the real world of baseball, with its pill-popping, lecherous players who wouldn't hesitate to close a bus window on a young fan begging for an autograph.

Working with New York sportswriter Leonard Schecter, the iconoclastic Bouton created what veteran baseball book editor Jeff Neuman described in an ESPN.com article as "if not the most famous baseball book, certainly the most important, and in good ways and bad. It changed the expectations of what not only sports books, but sports journalism could be."

Starry-eyed fans, teammates, opponents, and baseball's highest executives branded Bouton a pariah. Commissioner Bowie Kuhn called *Ball Four*—which spent seventeen weeks on the *New York Times* best-seller list—a detriment to the game and put pressure on Bouton to claim that his book was completely fictitious.

Where athletes and sportswriters had a fairly convivial relationship before, this new atmosphere post–*Ball Four* made many ballplayers suspicious of anyone with a pen, camera, or tape recorder, fearful of how they would be presented now that the bloom was off the rose.

For better or worse, Bouton opened the door for subsequent tell-all titles, the more serious of which are often compared to the original.

Other categories: Classic, History, *New York Times* Best Seller, Pop Culture
Also by the author: Bouton followed up his success with *I'm Glad You Didn't Take it Personally* (also edited by Shecter, 1971), which chronicles the fallout from *Ball Four*. In 2000 he released *Ball Four: The Final Pitch*, which includes the entire original text as well as revisitings from ten, twenty, and thirty years later.

33. *Baseball and the Cold War: Being a Soliloquy on the Necessity of Baseball in the Life of a Serious Student of Marx and Hegel from Rochester, New York,* by Howard Senzel. New York: Harcourt Brace Jovanovich, 1977.

This unusual memoir tells the story of a young man who believes he has outgrown the game, putting aside childish things to make room for more serious, adult reflection. But through an almost maniacal obsession, he returns to the sport of his youth, when playing pickup games and collecting cards was all there was in the world.

Senzel grew up in the 1950s and became part of the evolving student movement as young people became more aware of civil-rights injustices in the United States and Communist oppression in Eastern Europe and the Soviet Union. Politics replaced baseball as his major interest, but when he heard that a former Major Leaguer had been shot in the head during an exhibition game in Cuba between his beloved Rochester Red Wings and the Havana Sugar Kings, he embarked on a journey for knowledge about Communism's connections with America's national pastime and its export to the land of Fidel Castro.

Senzel's unemployed status gave him the opportunity to spend his days at the local library, searching through microfilm to confirm his suspicions. But his quest eventually brought into question his devotion to the Red Wings at a time when America was beset by troubles from within and without.

It is a hodgepodge tale, told in almost a stream-of-consciousness manner as he discusses his family, growing up with the strictures of being an observant Jew, and myriad other topics, which might confuse and frustrate more disciplined readers.

Other categories: History, Minor Leagues, Popular Culture

34. *Baseball As I Have Known It,* by Fred Lieb. New York: Coward, McCann and Geoghegan, 1977.

Lieb began covering baseball in 1911 and continued until the end of his life almost seventy years later, in the process becoming one of those journalists who knew everyone worth knowing. He was a pal to players like Lou Gehrig, Babe Ruth, and Ty Cobb, as well as to Commissioner Kennesaw Mountain Landis, among hundreds of others baseball personalities.

Think of all the events and innovations he witnessed since his first assignment: two world wars, the Black Sox scandal, night baseball, the debut of Jackie Robinson, and countless others. As one of the true media old-timers in the racket, Lieb embodied the curmudgeonly (or avuncular, depending on your point of view) gent who believes things were better in his time but is willing to listen to your opinions, if only to be polite. In fact, he could have been the model for the classic sportswriter you see in the movies — such as Sam Blake in *The Pride of the Yankees* — or as the narrator in baseball fiction — like Word Smith in Philip Roth's *The Great American Novel*.

The relationship between athletes and writers was certainly more convivial in his days, he claimed, since they spent so much time in proximity, whether traveling or dining together. Night games killed that, according to Lieb, since the players had later curfews and the writers had their deadlines. This was well before the widening gap in salaries caused further social separation.

Lieb, who received the Hall of Fame's J. G. Taylor Spink Award in 1972 in recognition of his contributions to baseball writing, published his memoir when he was eighty-nine, just three years before his death.

Other categories: History, Sportswriting

Also by the author: *Connie Mack: Grand Old Man of Baseball* (1945). Lieb also wrote several volumes in the Putnam series of team histories.

35. *Baseball Between the Lines: Baseball in the Forties and Fifties,* by Donald Honig. New York: Coward, McCann and Geoghegan, 1976.

36. *Baseball When the Grass Was Real: Baseball from the Twenties to the Forties Told by the Men Who Played It,* by Donald Honig. New York: Coward, McCann and Geoghegan, 1975.

To be honest, I don't need any more first-person accounts from superstars; they get plenty of ink. It's the good players who didn't quite break into that elite level that really interest me. How did they feel to come so close but not quite reach that next stage that might have made them household names?

For example, in *Baseball When the Grass Was Real,* we hear from Pete Reiser, one of the all-time great could-have-beens in any sport. If only he had dialed it down a bit and not run into walls in pursuit of fly balls, he might have avoided those injuries that cut short a promising career. Who knows how much better he could have been?

And what about Max Lanier, who, tired of not being paid what he thought was his due, jumped to the Mexican League in 1946? He realized his mistake too late and tried come return to the Majors, but Commissioner Landis suspended him for three years. Wouldn't you like to hear Lanier's side of the story?

These are just two of the eighteen players Honig interviewed for *Baseball When the Grass Was Real. Between the Lines* considered an additional nineteen ballplayers, including such seldom-heard-from guys like Ewell "The Whip" Blackwell; Johnny Vander Meer, author of back-to-back no hitters; and Herb Score, the Cleveland Indians pitcher who was hit in the eye by a line drive that basically ended his career.

One quibble, though: at least half of the players depicted on the dust jacket of each book are not interviewees, which seems somewhat misleading.

It would be cool if some publisher would reissue both volumes together, with a nice slipcase, since they are so similar in scope and form.

Other category: History

37. *Baseball Is a Funny Game*, by Joe Garagiola. Philadelphia: Lippincott, 1960.

What is it about mediocre catchers turning into court jesters? Perhaps it's a rebellion against the anonymity of being hidden behind a mask while you're working that turned guys like Bob Uecker and Joe Garagiola into gregarious raconteurs. Or maybe it's from being hit in the head by too many foul balls.

Garagiola, who played with some of the great Saint Louis Cardinals teams in the late 1940s before moving on to some lousy Pirates and Cubs teams in the 1950s, developed a reputation as a good story-teller. His amiable book, which spent thirteen weeks on the *New York Times* best-seller list, is a mix of locker room kibitzing, conversations on the mound, and self-deprecating stories.

After his playing career, Garagiola segued smoothly into the broadcast booth, and later had a long-running gig on *The Today Show* as well as stints as a game show host, where his bubbly personality was given a chance to shine.

> Other categories: Classic, Pop Culture, *New York Times* Best Seller
> Also by the author: Garagiola published *It's Anybody's Ballgame* in 1988, loosely a follow-up to *Funny Game* but with new stories. In 2007 he released *Just Play Ball*, a rejoinder to the trend of books that warned about the problems with the game in the poststeroids era.

38. *Baseball's Great Experiment: Jackie Robinson and His Legacy*, by Jules Tygiel. New York: Oxford University Press, 1983.

39. *Jackie Robinson: A Biography*, by Arnold Rampersad. New York: Knopf, 1997.

40. *Jackie Robinson: An Intimate Portrait*, by Rachel Robinson with Lee Daniels. New York: Harry. N. Abrams, 1996.

Plugging in the name Jackie Robinson into ABNER, the catalog for the National Baseball Hall of Fame Library, reveals more than 230 entries, second only to Babe Ruth (who has more than 400). You could argue, however, about which man had more of an impact. Some would say it was Ruth, who practically single-handedly saved baseball's bacon after the 1919 Black Sox scandal. But Robinson meant more to American society as a whole by breaking baseball's nefarious color line (with all due respect to Moses Fleetwood Walker).

With all those books, how is it possible to pick just a few to represent all that Robinson meant? Books aimed at kids teach the overarching lessons of tolerance and the injustices he helped dispel, but when it comes to more nuanced adult titles, it gets a bit tougher.

Several excellent books deal with the various stages of Robinson's life. Many were published to mark the twenty-fifth, fortieth, and fiftieth anniversaries of his first season with the Brooklyn Dodgers.

Tygiel, a professor of history at San Francisco State University who published three books about Robinson and his impact on baseball and society, was the first to mix the scholarly and the popular when he chronicled the steps leading up to Robinson's debut: how Branch Rickey orchestrated every step, picked the right man to have the honor—and burden—of being the first, and knew that if this experiment failed, it could be decades until it got another chance.

But Tygiel does not stop there, for Robinson's debut did not magically throw open the door for other African Americans to follow. By the time he retired in 1957, three teams had yet to have a black player on their Major League rosters.

Just as Tygiel was the first to publish an adult book about the machinations leading to Robinson's contributions, Rampersad was the first to offer a scholarly yet empathetic biography, encompassing the totality of the Hall of Famer's too-brief life. It is worth noting that the photo on the dust jacket features Robinson in street clothes instead of a baseball uniform, as if to emphasize that here was a man who would not be limited in his identity. After serving his "probation"—the agreed-upon time imposed by Rickey to take all the abuse that was meted out—Robinson indeed fought to maintain his pride on the field for himself and off the field for minorities across the country. Even in retirement, Robinson loaned his name to causes seeking social justice.

As the saying goes, behind every great man is a great woman.

Fans often overlook the fact that Robinson did not go through his travails alone. He was accompanied every step of the way by his ever-supportive and adoring wife, Rachel. She may not have been subjected to the same physical threats, but she certainly suffered the same indignities of prejudice and segregation. Yet she could only sit by and watch as her husband endured the taunts and worse.

In this richly illustrated coffee table book, Rachel Robinson shares her thoughts, joys, and sorrows about her husband's struggles and legacy through personal photos and recollections. Like any well-constructed family album, it marks the passage of time, from Jackie's college career at UCLA to his years in baseball and retirement.

Even the financial success brought about by his accomplishments on the field was no guarantee of acceptance off the diamond, as the growing Robinson family found out when they tried to move into traditionally white communities. Rachel recalls those times with sadness, but also with appreciation for the friends of all colors and ethnicities who stood by them.

Life after baseball had its joys, but more often it seemed laden with struggles. The quest for social and economic justice was never ending; Jackie was frequently called upon for a statement or to lead a committee. The death of their son, Jackie Jr., after a battle with drug addiction, was particularly painful. All of this no doubt contributed to Jackie's premature death at the age of fifty-three from complications of diabetes.

Other categories: Ethnicity, History

41. *Beaverball: A (Winning) Season with the MIT Baseball Team,* by Brooks C. Mendell. San Diego: Aventine Press, 2009.

Mendell, a senior on the MIT team in the mid-1990s, wants readers to know that eggheads play ball too. This fish-out-of-water tale serves to answer the common question: MIT has a baseball team?

In fact, the school has a proud, if unimpressive, record on the diamond since opening its program 1861. The term *student-athlete* really leans more toward *student* at MIT, and, as the author notes, the players don't feel they're expected to win, which no doubt removes a lot of pressure.

The nuances of Division III separates MIT from other college programs. Since D-III schools can't offer athletic scholarships, joining a team is a labor of love and commitment. MIT could be considered among the Major Leagues of the university set, so the classroom competition is sharp. Some athletes, carrying a substantial course load (in a few cases, it actually *is* rocket science), have little patience for losing and can easily find more productive ways to spend their limited free time.

Then why do they do it? Mendell tries to explain: "Time on the field took time away from in the library, which our professors didn't understand. However, we played on, with prospects of becoming little league coaches and softball players after MIT, not professional players. We just loved baseball" (137).

Mendell was prescient when he decided to write about the 1993 season. The team posted a 22-11 record, the best in school history, and won the Eastern College Athletic Conference championship.

And just FYI, two MIT students went on to enjoy very brief Major League careers. Jason Szuminski appeared in seven games as a pitcher for the San Diego Padres in 2004, which was six games more than Art Merewether, who made it into a single contest for the 1922 Pittsburgh Pirates.

Other categories: Academic, History

42. *The Big Bam: The Life and Times of Babe Ruth,* by Leigh Montville. New York: Doubleday, 2006.

In 1995 Robert Creamer published *Babe: The Legend Comes to Life,* which was considered a watershed in the genre of sports biography at the time. A heroic figure was presented as less than ideal, with flaws and appetites that would have rendered him unsuitable to younger readers a generation before.

Montville, a Boston-area sportswriter who wrote for the *Boston*

Globe and *Sports Illustrated*, introduces new material from earlier in Ruth's life, including the circumstances surrounding his residence at the Saint Mary's Industrial School for Boys and other items, employing heretofore-uncited interviews. To be honest, that in itself doesn't make or break this telling. Montville's narrative stands on its own, and it is a welcome addition to the pantheon of Ruthian literature.

Not much has changed since Creamer's publication. Montville does not bring much new information to light—how many ways can you tell the story of the stomach ache heard around the world, which may or may not have actually been an STD. But his 2006 biography of the man of a thousand nicknames is certainly the most stylish. That difference in the telling may just turn off some readers, but it would be a mistake to cast it aside without giving it a chance.

Other categories: History, *New York Times* Best Seller

Also by the author: Both *The Big Bam* and *Ted Williams: The Biography of An American Hero* (2004) appeared on the *New York Times* best-seller list.

43. *Branch Rickey*, by Jimmy Breslin. New York: Viking, 2011.

Breslin fans will enjoy this slim volume on the Mahatma, which was published as part of the Penguin Lives series featuring a wide variety of notable figures in the worlds of art, politics, music, and, now, sports.

Breslin broke his own rule when it came to his requirements for writing books: According to his code of ethics, he had to have first-person knowledge of his subject. But he had only met Rickey once, briefly and by accident, when he was a copy boy on a long-defunct Brooklyn newspaper.

Nevertheless, with his Pulitzer Prize–winning pugnacious style and journalistic skills, he put together this quirky little bio that focuses on a handful of highlights of Rickey's life and work.

This is not a traditional straight-line biography, but if brevity is the soul of wit, Breslin is one funny fellow.

44. *Branch Rickey: Baseball's Ferocious Gentleman*, by Lee Lowenfish. Lincoln: University of Nebraska Press, 2007.

At well over six hundred pages, Lowenfish's treatment of Branch "the Mahatma" Rickey would seem appropriate for a political leader, philosopher, scientist, or some other lofty profession. In a way, Rickey was all of those things. As a young executive for the Saint Louis Cardinals, he helped craft the Minor League farm system. Later, as president and general manager of the Brooklyn Dodgers, he had his eureka moment and paved the way for Jackie Robinson to break the nefarious color line. (An overlooked fact: Rickey also signed the first black Hispanic in Roberto Clemente.) He also had a hand in inventing the batting helmet and improving batting cages and pitching machines. Perhaps his most important innovation was using statistics as a tool for the ballclub, rather than a mere amusement for the fans.

Some of his critics said Rickey was an opportunist, that his reasons for signing Robinson were not totally altruistic, that he knew fully well what having a black player would mean to the Dodgers' income. Rickey would have been the first to ask, What's wrong with doing the right thing *and* making money?

Lowenfish presents the roller coaster that was Rickey's career with chapters bearing titles like "Years of Contention and Frustration," "That Championship Season," and "Another Championship and Then Decline." This serves to remind the reader that for all his successes, Rickey endured a lot of missteps along the way, but none of them could overshadow his efforts in righting a wrong that had been part of the American culture for centuries and baseball for decades.

Baseball's Ferocious Gentleman earned Lowenfish the 2008 Seymour Medal from SABR.

Other categories: Award Winner, History, Pop Culture

Also by the author: *The Imperfect Diamond: A History of Baseball's Labor Wars* (2011)

45. *The Bronx Zoo,* by Sparky Lyle and Peter Golenbock. New York: Crown, 1979.

Ever since Bouton published *Ball Four* in 1970, players have been trying to one-up him with their own outrageous revelations of what goes on in the locker room, on the field, and away from the ballpark. So much for the clubhouse motto "What you hear here, stays here."

Lyle, a Cy Young Award–winning relief pitcher who spent sixteen seasons in the Majors (1967–1982), never intended for his book to be as funny as Bouton's. Instead he writes candidly about what it was like to pitch on that 1978 team with all its colorful characters, including the volatile manager, Billy Martin; the egomaniacal Reggie Jackson; the curmudgeonly Thurman Munson; and the rest of the Yankee lunatics. Lyle is also brutally honest when he complains about having to share bullpen responsibilities with the Yankees' newest acquisition, fireballer Goose Gossage.

Like *Ball Four, The Bronx Zoo* follows a diary format and it makes for compelling reading as the season rolls along, with its ebbs and flows, its tensions and releases. (Lyle discusses all the idiosyncrasies of these so-called heroes, and you know what? They're just as normal and/or nuts as everybody else.)

The Bronx Zoo spent twenty-nine weeks on the *New York Times* best-seller List, the second-longest stint for a baseball title.

Other category: History/Team

46. *Campy: The Two Lives of Roy Campanella,* by Neil Lanctot. New York: Simon and Schuster, 2011.

All athletes have two lives: the first during their playing days, the (hopefully) longer one afterward, when they—or someone else—decide they can no longer do the job. The end of Campanella's career was especially sudden and tragic: he was rendered a quadriplegic in a car crash in January 1958.

The story that was circulated at the time was that he was driving home in the wee hours of the morning from the liquor store he owned and hit an icy patch on the road. That was the *circulated* story;

speculation held that he may have been coming back from a lover's tryst and perhaps fell asleep at the wheel. Of course, in the family-friendly fifties, the media kept such lurid notions off the pages.

For those familiar with the "Boys of Summer" canon, reading *Campy* is like waiting for the proverbial shoe to drop: you know what's coming, but not how it will be presented. The title of the chapter that introduces his accident is fraught with foreshadowing, like dramatic music in a movie. Nevertheless, Lanctot does a sober job condensing into a small portion of his book the years of suffering and small triumphs as Campanella was forced to adjust to his situation and the emotional and physical toll it took on him and his family.

Campanella was a three-time National League MVP and a Hall of Famer, yet aside from *It's Good to Be Alive*, his ghostwritten autobiography published in 1959, there have been no other adult titles written about him.

Other categories: History, Negro Leagues

Also by the author: *Negro League Baseball: The Rise and Ruin of a Black Institution (2008); Fair Dealing and Clean Playing: The Hilldale Club and the Development of Black Professional Baseball, 1910–1932* (1994)

47. *The Catcher Was a Spy: The Mysterious Life of Moe Berg,* by Nicholas Dawidoff. New York: Pantheon, 1994.

The oft-told joke about Berg was that he could speak seven (or eight, or a dozen) languages, but couldn't hit in any of 'em. Nevertheless, he managed to hang around the Major Leagues as a player for fifteen seasons.

Call him brilliant—he attended Columbia Law School and the Sorbonne—or call him eccentric—he would never touch a newspaper after someone else had read it—Berg was above all a colorful character and a worthy topic for a serious biography.

Dawidoff weaves a spellbinding take on Berg's service as a spy, both during his playing days and afterward, for the Office of Strategic

Services, the predecessor of the CIA. The author documents the catcher's daring exploits, among them the time when, as a member of an All-Star barnstorming trip to Japan in 1934, he disguised himself as a local (some feat, since Berg was well over six feet and quite swarthy) to take photographs of the Tokyo skyline that were used to plan the Doolittle Raid in World War II. Then in 1944, armed with a pistol and a cyanide capsule, Berg went to a lecture in Zurich by the German physicist Werner Heisenberg with instructions to assassinate him if it appeared the Nazis had atomic bomb capabilities, and to commit suicide if captured.

Following his retirement as a player, Berg couldn't seem to find anything worthy to do with his life. He went to a few ballgames, tried his hand at writing, and made a big deal about keeping his secret life secret—a sad coda to a fascinating life.

Other categories: Classic, History

48. *Clemente: The Passion and Grace of Baseball's Last Hero,* by David Maraniss. New York: Simon and Schuster, 2006.

The word *hero* is bandied about too much in the sports world. True, athletes frequently overcome economic, health, or other disadvantages, and there is always a risk of injury, but that's more of a personal issue; it doesn't really affect other people.

Clemente, on the other hand, was worthy of the designation according to Maraniss's excellent biography.

A perennial All-Star, Clemente had the double misfortune of coming into the Major Leagues as a person of color who did not speak the language. He overcame those challenges, however, to have a brilliant career.

On the field, Clemente brought joy to thousands of baseball fans, not just Pirates fans. Off the field, he was a loving family man who always thought of those less fortunate. It was this empathy that would cost him his life when he organized a humanitarian effort to deliver supplies to Nicaragua after an earthquake hit the nation in December 1972. Clemente's plane, overloaded with supplies, crashed into the ocean and he perished. He had stroked his three thousandth hit on the last day of the season, further adding to his legend.

Maraniss, who won the 1993 Pulitzer Prize for reporting, utilized his journalist's skills to present a compelling and ultimately tragic rendering of the life and death of a true hero.

Other categories: Classic, *New York Times* Best Seller

49. *Clowning Through Baseball*, by Al Schacht. New York: A. S. Barnes, 1941.

The author, known as the original clown prince of baseball (with all due respect to Max Patkin), was a pitcher with the Washington Senators from 1919–21, compiling a record of 14-10. Unfortunately, injuries curtailed his career, and he returned to the Minors for a couple of years before deciding to retire.

Throughout his playing days, Schacht loved to be the center of attention, even working out a comedy act with teammate Nick Altrock. He continued to entertain fans at the ballparks, but during World War II he gave servicemen a chuckle or two through his appearances with the USO.

Schacht wrote *Clowning Through Baseball* with "grammar and adjectives by Murray Goodman"—which gives you a hint of Schacht's sense of humor—and illustrations by Willard Mullin, famous for his Brooklyn Bums cartoons in the New York tabloids. Contrary to the title, the book covers more of Schacht's experiences off the field than on. The jokes are mostly self-directed and never mean spirited, providing a gentle look at the lighter side of baseball during a tough period.

Other category: Humor

Also by the author: *My Own Particular Screwball* (1955); *GI Had Fun* (1945)

50. *Cobb: The Life and Times of the Meanest Man Who Ever Played Baseball: A Biography*, by Al Stump. Chapel Hill NC: Algonquin Press of Chapel Hill, 1994.

51. *Ty Cobb: My Life in Baseball: The True Record*, by Ty Cobb with Al Stump. Lincoln: University of Nebraska Press, 1993.

With his health declining in 1960, Ty Cobb felt it was his last chance to offer the "true record," so he enlisted the help of Al Stump, a prolific sportswriter of the day with impressive national magazine credits.

In his memoir Cobb sought to justify a lot of his misanthropic activities and pass along the blame for every bad thing that ever happened to him, from poor ownership with the Tigers to being misunderstood by the press and fans. He displays the megalomania that Stump describes in his own biography of Cobb, almost bordering on paranoia as he battles — literally at times — opponents, fans, and umpires. Surprisingly, he makes no mention of his father, who died under mysterious circumstances. Given their relationship, this is quite strange and may, under a psychiatrist's study, explain a lot.

Cobb nevertheless had his admirers who marveled as his competitive drive and knowledge of the game. He was a proponent of "scientific baseball," the style of scratching out a hit, stealing bases, and sacrificing to bring in runs, before power hitters like Babe Ruth came along to save the sport in the wake of the Black Sox scandal.

Meanwhile, in his own biography on the redoubtable Cobb, Stump claimed the old buzzard was a pill to work with and that they often clashed about what to include and leave out. Free of that burden — though for some reason he waited almost thirty years — Stump came out with his own version of the Ty Cobb story, accusing his subject of some pretty heinous behavior.

Much of this information isn't new, but the juxtaposition of the two books is an interesting glimpse into the subject-coauthor relationship. The role of the collaborator naturally differs with each writer. Some believe they need to have a more hands-on approach, others think they should just transcribe what the subject puts on the tape recorder, while still others think they need to serve in some therapeutic capacity to draw out the details of the subject's life that he might not think are important.

52. *"Commy": The Life Story of Charles A. Comiskey,* by Gustaf W. Axelson. Chicago: Reilly and Lee, 1919.

"Occasionally, I have been charged with the crime of 'buying' pennants" (316). Gee, who does *that* sound like?

Charles A. Comiskey, aka the Old Roman, was the very model of a modern major ballclub owner, especially if he served as a model for the late George Steinbrenner.

Commy was a self-made magnate. He knew the game from all sides, spending thirteen seasons as a third baseman and manager in the Majors in the late 1800s before moving on to the executive office as owner of the Chicago White Sox in 1900.

Although the book was ostensibly an "as told to," it is written mostly in the third person and refers to its subject in mostly glowing terms, praising him as a tough, bright, progressive man who brought great changes to the game in its early years as a burgeoning profession and source of entertainment.

Comiskey did ostensibly take pen in hand for the final chapter in which he shares his opinions on why baseball is so important to America and, in an odd twist, warns that gambling has no place in the national pastime. Ironically, the book was published in 1919, the year of the Black Sox scandal. Imagine what Comiskey might have written a couple of years later, after the news broke.

Other categories: Business, History, Pop Culture

53. *Crash: The Life and Times of Dick Allen,* by Dick Allen and Tim Whitaker. New York: Ticknor and Fields, 1989.

Allen was one of white America's biggest nightmares: an angry black man. He was a Rookie of the Year, an MVP, and a seven-time All-Star, retiring with a career batting average of .292, 351 home runs and 1,119 RBIs. And yet he's never gotten close to being elected into the Hall of Fame. What's up with *that*?

In this compelling book, Allen shares his thoughts on the difficulties he had as an African American who grew up in an integrated town in the 1950s and later had to deal with the prejudice and hatred in the deep-South Minor Leagues and even in Philadelphia, the City of Brotherly Love. Plagued by injuries (he appeared in 140 or more games only six times in a fifteen-year career) and often at war with a press he considered condescending, Allen was not afraid to call out the hypocrisy directed against him: he received a standing ovation one minute, and was booed and called names the next. He would always wonder how much better he could have been had he just been left alone.

Crash—a nickname given to Allen because he took to wearing a batting helmet in the field to protect himself from fans who pelted him with batteries, coins, and other objects—was written a dozen years after he retired, but the sting evidently still lingered. Did he have flaws? Sure. Was he quick to take umbrage? Perhaps. Was he one of the most talented athletes of his generation? Certainly.

Credit goes to Whitaker, who didn't accept what Allen told him at face value, but sought confirmation or refutation from other sources. The result is nevertheless a sympathetic look at one of the underrated stars of the game, and *Crash* is one of the most underrated baseball books as well.

Other categories: Ethnicity, Underrated

54. *Diz: The Story of Dizzy Dean and Baseball during the Great Depression,* by Robert Gregory. New York: Penguin, 1992.

Jay Hanna "Dizzy" Dean was pure American folk hero. Or was the name Jerome Herman? That's just part of the legend of the larger-than-life pitcher who rose out of the poverty of his native Arkansas to become one of the most beloved figures not just in baseball, but in American popular culture. He was a source of pride for the average guy, a fly in the ointment of the swells who still managed to hang onto their property and enjoy the finer things in life while the rest were barely getting by.

Dean played just six full seasons in the Majors before injury cut his career short, but he was dominant during that time for the "Gashouse Gang" Saint Louis Cardinals. In that, he was like another Hall of Fame hurler whose star shone brightly for an abbreviated time: Sandy Koufax. But where Dandy Sandy was reticent to talk about his talents, Dean figured everyone knew how great he was, kind of like a Ring Lardner character from "Alibi Ike" or *You Know Me Al*. As Dean used to say, "It ain't braggin' if you can do it."

Although he was a country boy, Dean was no rube. He was the pitching equivalent of Babe Ruth in terms of popularity, and he was ahead of his time when it came to participating in barnstorming tours with Satchel Paige and other stars of the Negro Leagues in an era when such contests were illegal in parts of the country.

After he retired as a player, Dean remained in the game as a broadcaster, where he furthered his reputation as an eloquent, if grammatically challenged, raconteur.

Other categories: History, Media, Pop Culture, Underrated

55. *Ed Delahanty in the Emerald Age of Baseball,* by Jerrold Casway. Notre Dame IN: University of Notre Dame Press, 2004.

One of the charming qualities about baseball is that a fan from a hundred years ago would easily recognize the modern game. There are still nine innings, four bases, and three strikes, you're out.

Ed Delahanty is also recognizable—the stereotypical player who could have enjoyed even greater success had he been able to control his demons. Not only did the drink ruin his career; it no doubt contributed to one of most bizarre and storied deaths in sports and celebrity history. He was put off a train for rowdy behavior and was found dead the next morning, having fallen off a bridge to the rocks below.

Delahanty, who played at the turn of the twentieth century, was the Babe Ruth of his era, a power hitter before such a category even had a name. Accordingly, he was elected to the Baseball Hall of Fame by the Old Timers Committee in 1945. That his teams never lived up to expectations must have been frustrating for such a competitor, and he took up the bottle for solace.

Casway, a history professor and an expert on early-modern Irish history and nineteenth-century baseball, also examines the business complexities of the national pastime. Owners tried to take advantage of the players, who were often lacking in formal education, by keeping salaries low and binding them to the team through carefully worded contracts and tacit agreements between team executives.

And as the title suggests, the book also looks at the influence of the Irish on baseball in the Emerald Age, when men such as John McGraw, Dan Brouthers, and Connie Mack accounted for a disproportionately large percentage of the game's personnel.

Other categories: Business, Ethnicity, History

56. *Facing Roger Clemens: Hitters on Confronting Baseball's Most Intimidating Pitcher,* by Jonathan Mayo. Guilford CT: Lyons Press, 2008.

"If I knew then what I know now . . . "

I wonder how the hitters that Mayo—a senior writer for MLB.com—interviewed for this book might have revised their comments given the speculation that Clemens benefitted from pharmaceutical assistance. Can't you just hear them? "Sure, he struck me out eight out of ten times, but he was on the juice!"

The book includes conversations with batters of wildly divergent talents, including Dave Magadan and Julio Franco ("In the Beginning"); Cal Ripken Jr., Gary Carter, and Ken Griffey Jr. ("Legends"); four World Series opponents who had the additional disadvantage of not facing Clemens on any kind of regular basis; Phil Bradley and Torii Hunter ("Stats"); and Minor Leaguers Johnny Drennen and Clemens's own son, Koby, whom the elder statesman of the mound faced during Minor League rehab assignments.

While not on par with some of the other must-read titles listed herein, this one gets points for irony.

Other categories: Analysis, History

57. *A False Spring,* by Pat Jordan. New York: Dodd, Mead and Company, 1975.

Perhaps taking advantage of the precedent set by Bouton in *Ball Four,* Jordan followed a few years later with this bittersweet tale of promise unfulfilled.

You see, Jordan never made it to the Majors. Signed as an eighteen-year-old bonus baby by the Milwaukee Braves, he toiled in the Minors, trying to make his way both as an athlete and as a man.

The book is mostly about the fear and tyranny that often accompany talent. As an amateur, Jordan obviously had enough to attract the scouts and sign a contract. But ability alone is never enough, he learned; one needs a modicum of luck as well. Besides, you never know when that talent is going to abandon you, as it always does, sooner or later.

A False Spring is also about identity. For Jordan and his contemporaries—of any era—it's all about being recognized as a great athlete. He threw four no-hitters in little league, which no doubt added to his legend. But in pro sports, no one cares about your SAT scores or if you're good to your mother. For the majority who never get out of the first level of the Minors, it's a frightening prospect to think about what you're going to do when you get that tap on the shoulder indicating that the manager wants to inform you you're being released.

Other category: Classic

Also by the author: *The Suitors of Spring* (1973); *A Nice Tuesday* (1999)

58. *The Fifth Season: Tales of My Life in Baseball,* by Donald Honig. Chicago: Ivan R. Dee, 2009.

It's only fair that the man who has told the stories of so many baseball greats should get a chance to tell his own story in this sweet, nostalgic memoir.

Honig, who published his book at the age of 79, gives readers who have long enjoyed his oral histories, team profiles, and other compilations a chance to see how he came to his love for the game, which in some ways is similar to my introduction.

My father, a Russian immigrant who arrived in this country in 1916 as a child, knew nothing and cared nothing about baseball, so it was up to my uncle Dave, his American-born brother-in-law, to teach me; Honig's uncle Fendel served in that role.

As a young man, Honig hoped he might become the subject of someone else's baseball book. He was good enough to get a couple of tryouts with professional teams but didn't make the grade. He eventually came under the literary tutelage of Lawrence Ritter, the author of *The Glory of Their Times* who gave Honig his blessings to take over the business of interviewing all-but-forgotten ballplayers about their experiences in the game.

Honig has more than forty nonfiction and fiction baseball titles in his oeuvre (the latter consisting of *The Plot to Kill Jackie Robinson* and *The Last Great Season*), and there's not a bum in the lot.

The title of his latest book is at once mysterious and obvious, or at least it should be to fans of the national pastime. While everyone else has to settle for four seasons, we get an extra one: baseball season. And, according to Honig, it lasts all year long, if not on the field, then in our consciousness.

Other categories: History, Sportswriting

59. *Fleet Walker's Divided Heart: The Life of Baseball's First Black Major Leaguer*, by David W. Zang. Lincoln: University of Nebraska Press, 1995.

Baseball scholars love to refute the notion that Jackie Robinson broke organized baseball's color line in 1947. That honor, they point out, goes to Moses Fleetwood Walker, who caught for one season with the Toledo Blue Stockings of the American Association — then considered a Major League — in 1884; he also played on several Minor League teams over the next five years. Zang, a college teacher, presents his book as a combination biography and sociology treatise of race relations in the decades immediately following the Civil War.

Walker was the product of a mixed union, having a black father and white mother. He was a threat to some and a curiosity to others, despite coming into his own in the relatively enlightened environment of Oberlin College and the University of Michigan, where he became a star athlete. Advertisements for his teams' games highlighted Walker as a selling point: "See Walker, the great colored catcher" (33).

Yet his presence was not always welcome. He was refused restaurant and hotel services, and all-white teams often refused to take the field against him. Life after baseball proved even more difficult. Although Walker was relatively successful—he held a patent on an exploding artillery shell and applied for others for motion picture equipment—trouble had a way of finding him. He was arrested on suspicion of murder, for which he was acquitted, but he was later arrested and served a year in prison for mail robbery. It was during this period, Zang writes, that Walker became a race theorist, believing it might be better if blacks and whites lived separately.

Fleet Walker's Divided Heart received SABR's Seymour Medal in 1996.

Other categories: Award Winner, Ethnicity, History

60. *Foul Balls: Five Years in the American League,* by Alison Gordon. Toronto: McClelland and Stewart, 1984.

Gordon, an award-winning writer, came along at a time when women were still a novelty in the locker room. She was subjected to a sort of trial by fire, as some of the members of the all-male enclave played practical jokes and worse to see if she could stand the heat, which she did, admirably.

The difficulties didn't just come from the players, she notes, but from several of her fellow journalists, also a male-dominated profession. Since the sports world had heretofore been almost exclusively an old-boy network (*old* being the key word), she faced hostility, jealousy, and unwanted propositions as she struggled to prove herself professionally.

Gordon began covering the two-year-old Blue Jays for the *Toronto Star* in 1979. The team was still trying to find its way as one of the latest expansion teams, and, as is so often the case, the roster was made up mostly of players that other teams didn't want. Gordon managed to find the humor in an otherwise difficult situation, balancing her duties of covering the news with, like it or not, *being* the news. So *Foul Balls* also functions as a commentary on the sociological issues of women in the workplace.

The five-year narrative ends with Gordon moving on to greener pastures, away from the baseball beat. Regrets? Not really. After all, as boorish as the players, front office, and newsmen may have been, they did provide the fodder for her eye-opening book.

Other category: Women

61. *Good Enough to Dream*, by Roger Kahn. Garden City NY: Doubleday, 1985.

The popularity of Kahn's classic, *The Boys of Summer*, kindled his interest in trying a new topic: instead of writing about the players of the past, he would write about the players of the future.

There might be many ways to go about this, but Kahn found the one that worked best for him was to own a low–Minor League team and simply observe. He acquired the Utica Blue Sox, then an independent team in the New York–Penn League, for the 1983 season and got to see firsthand what it was like to enjoy watching a bunch of kids live out their dreams as pros, even if it was only in a small ballpark in upstate New York, and to deal with the headaches that come with running a franchise — even if it was only in a small ballpark in upstate New York.

Good Enough to Dream is filled with the usual material you'd find when you have a group of reasonably immature young athletes, many out on their own for the first time in their lives. But Kahn also reminisces about how he came to his own love for the game and the relationship with his father, and now his own teenage daughter, who joined him on his summer adventure.

That the Blue Sox just happened to have a great season was a bonus. It created an element of tension as they vied for the league championship. Kahn captures all the emotions in his usual subtle style, combining a look back with a look at what may lie ahead.

Other categories: History, Minor Leagues

62. *The Gospel According to Casey: Casey Stengel's Inimitable, Instructional, Historical Baseball Book,* by Ira Berkow and Jim Kaplan. New York: St. Martin's Press, 1984.

Where have all the colorful managers gone? As of this writing—and with the exception of Ozzie Guillen—the men who steer the baseball ships seem pretty interchangeable. They just don't make 'em like Casey anymore.

Stengel was a pretty fair country ballplayer from 1912–25 who went on to become a spectacularly successful manager with the New York Yankees from 1949–60, leading the Bronx Bombers to ten pennants and seven world championships.

But it wasn't just *what* he did; it was also *how* he did it. Stengel had his own language as he held court with the newspapermen, whom he called "my writers." In discussing past events, he would frequently say, "You could look it up," which coauthors Berkow and Kaplan have done, combing the Old Perfessor's most memorable quotes with comments from his players and associates. The results are offered under numerous subject headings: managing, pitching, fielding, batting, attitude, and ego. The chapter "Discourse on Stengelese" goes a long way in illustrating Casey's quirkiness better than descriptions from others.

One of the highlights of Stengel's storied career came as a result of his 1958 testimony before the Senate Anti-Trust and Monopoly Subcommittee Hearings; the transcript is presented as the book's concluding chapter.

Asked to briefly describe his background, Stengel, perhaps sensing a golden opportunity to shine on a different stage, went into one of his usual tangential meanderings before finally saying, in a one-word answer, that such legislation was unnecessary. Mickey Mantle followed his manager in the questioning. When asked for his observations, the future Hall of Famer answered, "My view is just about the same as Casey's" (160).

Other categories: History, Managers, Pop Culture

63. *Hank Greenberg: The Story of My Life*, edited and with an introduction by Ira Berkow. New York: Times, 1989.

There's no question that Greenberg was one of the premier sluggers of all time. Who knows how much better his statistics might have been had he not spent almost four full seasons serving his country in World War II. But he never complained; that's what was expected of the greatest generation.

Greenberg was also a source of pride to the Jewish people, a rejoinder to those who stereotyped them as bookish, unathletic, and worse. Unlike some of his coreligionists, the brawny outfielder did not shy away from his heritage by changing his name or trying to keep a low profile. His decision to refrain from playing on Yom Kippur, the holiest day in the Jewish calendar, won him the respect of fans across the baseball spectrum, even those who didn't necessarily follow the game.

As a member of a put-upon race, Greenberg had empathy for the underdog (his description of Jackie Robinson's travails is particularly compelling) but no patience for those ballplayers who constantly proved their ignorance through anti-Semitic comments. After he retired as an active player, he moved into the front office for the Cleveland Indians and Chicago White Sox, both of which enjoyed great success under his stewardship.

Greenberg's story is enhanced thanks to the editorial touch of Pulitzer Prize winner Ira Berkow's. Where Greenberg appears a bit reluctant to talk about himself, Berkow breaks in with his own commentary to put things into perspective. He also published *Hank Greenberg: Hall of Fame Slugger*, a book geared toward younger readers, through the Jewish Publication Society in 2001.

The autobiography was the inspiration for *The Life and Times of Hank Greenberg*, an award-winning film documentary produced by Aviva Kempner in 1998.

Other categories: Classic, Ethnicity, History, Wartime Baseball

64. *Have Glove, Will Travel: Adventures of a Baseball Vagabond,* by Bill "Spaceman" Lee with Richard Lally. New York: Crown, 2005.

Some guys just don't know when to quit, and Lee, one of baseball's truly fun characters, is one of them. Like fellow author Jim Bouton, Lee continued to look for opportunities to play wherever he could after retiring as a professional. Although he was disillusioned with the treatment of ballplayers during his time in the Majors, his love for the game in its purer stages remained undiminished.

Have Glove, Will Travel recounts his far-ranging journeys to small towns in such places as Canada, New England, Venezuela, Cuba, and Russia. It reads like both a travelogue and a memoir.

Credit Lee for admitting in an author's note that the stories are told as he remembers them, which opens the door for refutation and reinterpretation. Who could argue with that? Whether it's to cover his butt for legal reasons or simply to be honest, it's a fitting and refreshing testimonial to a man who has been known — and gotten in lots of trouble — for speaking his mind.

Also by the author: *Have Glove, Will Travel* marked the former ballplayer's second collaboration with Lally, who also worked on Lee's 1984 memoir, *The Wrong Stuff.*

65. *Hitter: The Life and Turmoils of Ted Williams,* by Ed Linn. New York: Harcourt Brace, 1993.

66. *My Life in Pictures,* by Ted Williams with David Pietrusza. Kingston NY: Total Sports Illustrated, 2001.

67. *Ted Williams: A Baseball Life,* by Michael Seidel. Chicago: Contemporary, 1991.

The tributes for Ted Williams came hot and heavy toward the end of his life and these biographies are representative of the wealth of material on Teddy Ballgame.

Some books focused on his role as a patriot and hero who answered his country's call not once, but twice, and lost almost five full seasons to military service in the process. Others take a psychobiographical approach, analyzing his childhood in an attempt to explain what drove him to succeed. For a good part of his career, Williams feuded with the Boston press and fans, outwardly disdaining their approval but left feeling unhappy when it wasn't given and when his conduct was questioned.

Linn, who collaborated on several baseball books including the autobiographies of Bill Veeck and Leo Durocher, takes a more personal approach in this, the last of his seventeen books. As a sportswriter, he knew Williams pretty well and, despite the prerequisite of journalistic objectivity, greatly admired the mythic figure.

Seidel, who admirably covered Joe DiMaggio's signature season in *Streak*, presents a straightforward examination of Williams's life and accomplishments.

Pietrusza worked with Williams on a coffee table scrapbook of his life, which serves as the next best thing to an audio or video interview. The reader can almost see the ailing ballplayer going over each photograph one last time, recollecting precious memories, from his youth to his final Major League appearance at the 1999 All-Star Game in Boston where Major League Baseball announced its All-Century team. The respect and affection the ballplayers and fans extended to the aging legend can still bring a lump to the throat and a tear to the eye.

In the concluding pages, Williams makes a plea to finally forgive Shoeless Joe Jackson for perceived crimes during the 1919 Black Sox scandal and put him in the Hall of Fame: "Come on in, Joe, I'd say, your wait is over. Let's talk hitting" (185).

No doubt that's what they're doing now.

Other categories: Coffee Table/Gift, History, Wartime Baseball

68. *I Don't Care If I Never Come Back: A Baseball Fan and His Game*, by Art Hill. New York: Simon and Schuster, 1980.

Hill, who describes himself simply as a lifelong Tigers fan, presents his observations on the 1979 season in a rough journal format. Most of the entries deal in one way or another with the Detroit team, both past and present. He also enjoyed following his editor's suggestion to round out the book by visiting other ballparks. His section on a trip to Olympic Stadium, then home to the Montreal Expos, creates a "stranger in a strange land" scenario: it *seems* like baseball, but the local twists make it a bit too foreign, as if their fans need supplementary stimulation in the form of ear-splitting music and a renegade Muppet for a mascot.

Hill is funny without appearing that he's constantly "on," and he obviously knows the game, which is evidenced through chats about his amazement and concern over strategies employed by players and managers. Even when he shares memories of his old favorites, like Hank Greenberg and Gates Brown (proving once again that an athlete needn't be a Hall of Famer to win a fan's affection), the reader can relate, even if she casts her lot with another team.

Before the ready availability of self-publishing, it was difficult for the average Joe to find a major house willing to publish his manuscript. So kudos to Hill and to Simon and Schuster for taking on this project.

Other categories: Classic, History, Pop Culture

69. *I Never Had It Made*, by Jackie Robinson as told to Alfred A. Duckett. New York: Putnam, 1972.

Much of the information in *I Never Had It Made* has appeared in other sources, but reading it from Robinson's perspective can almost move a reader to tears.

He divides his story into two sections: "The Noble Experiment" discusses his playing days, while "After the Ball Game" takes readers into his retirement from baseball and accounts for the bulk of the book. Neither Robinson's athletic skills nor his business and community accomplishments afterward ever gave him the feeling that he "had it made" as others (that is, whites) might have felt.

Robinson, who died shortly after the publication of the book, was expected to be a leading voice for civil rights, and he was, but not blindly or at the expense of others. He held some unpopular views — supporting Richard Nixon over John F. Kennedy in the

1960s presidential election and siding with Martin Luther King Jr. over Malcolm X before the latter denounced Islamist leader Elijah Muhammad's anarchic brand of black separatism.

In an afterword, Robinson made an impassioned case that racism was still a part of baseball, as demonstrated by the lack of African Americans in decision-making positions.

Other categories: Classic, Ethnicity, History

Also by the author: *Baseball Has Done It* (1964)

70. *Iron Horse: Lou Gehrig in His Time,* by Ray Robinson. New York: W. W. Norton, 1990.

71. *Luckiest Man: The Life and Death of Lou Gehrig,* by Jonathan Eig. New York: Simon and Schuster, 2005.

These two biographies serve as complementary commentaries on how the genre has changed over the last generation.

Robinson, a veteran freelance sportswriter, presents a straight-forward profile of the tragic ballplayer. Filled with facts, figures, and accomplishments, *Iron Horse* is representative of a certain style: unadorned and without academic scholarship, but, believe me, this is not meant as a knock.

Eig, on the other hand, offers more than twenty pages of notes in *Luckiest Man*; the introduction to that section, in which he explains his methods and procedures, has become de rigueur in recent scholarly biographies.

Anyone who knows Gehrig's fate understands that reading a book about him offers no surprises; we know he will die of the terrible disease that will one day bear his name. But how much do we want? Is it somehow an invasion of privacy, or do such things no longer matter in an era when every intimate detail is put out there for all to see? Your answer will determine which book you might prefer. It's not an issue of ghoulish interest; Eig is respectful and his work makes Gehrig an even more sympathetic figure.

Robinson—who saw Gehrig and his contemporaries play as a

youth — offers barely 30 pages (out of 300) on Gehrig's illness and passing. Eig fully devotes more than 130 (out of 420) from the onset of symptoms to diagnoses and the effects they had on Gehrig and his wife, the Yankees, and American culture.

Other categories: History, Pop Culture

72. *It's Gone . . . No, Wait a Minute . . . : Talking My Way into the Big Leagues at 40,* by Ken Levine. New York: Villard, 1993.

Unlike the case of field- or general managers, I don't think there are many people who listen to your average broadcaster and say, "I could do that job better than that clown."

Perhaps that's what set off Levine, an Emmy Award–winning writer whose credits include *M*A*S*H* and *Cheers.* At the age of forty, he decided he wanted to take the microphone for his beloved Baltimore Orioles.

But this isn't the George Plimpton–embedded journalist kind of thing; Levine had genuine radio and play-by-play chops, having worked in college ball and the Minor Leagues for a spell. So why not kill two birds with one stone and do the job *and* write about it?

Despite his previous experience, his was still a fish-out-of-water story, as he dealt with the errors any rookie might make: miscalls, *missed* calls, working with a whole new schedule and a more demanding skill set than earlier jobs, not to mention the time spent away from his family when the team was on the road.

Levine went on to do play-by-play for the Seattle Mariners and San Diego Padres. He returned to the Mariners in 2011 to help fill in after the death in 2010 of longtime broadcaster Dave Niehaus. Levine still writes about baseball, among other things, at kenlevine .blogspot.com.

Other categories: Broadcasting, Business, Humor

73. *I Was Right on Time,* by Buck O'Neil with Steve Wulf and David Conrads. New York: Simon and Schuster, 1996.

Timing is indeed everything. When Ken Burns included the eighty-something former Negro Leaguer in his watershed *Baseball* documentary series, no one could have anticipated how beloved a figure O'Neil would become.

The genial senior citizen told his story without bitterness or regret. If anyone had the right to be angry over decades of disrespect and mistreatment, it was he. But rather than complain, O'Neil became a philosopher of sorts and probably would have been great at authoring a self-help book or two.

O'Neil offers a fascinating array of anecdotes as he recalls experiences with some of the greatest players in baseball, black *and* white. In 1962, while working for the Chicago Cubs, he had the honor — if only for a day — of being the first African American manager in the Major Leagues (unofficially, of course). The Cubs were using their infamous rotating "college of coaches" while he served in as the de facto skipper with the team. He was also a scout and was credited with signing Lou Brock to his first professional contract and discovering Billy Williams, both of whom were eventually elected to the Baseball Hall of Fame, an honor that has eluded O'Neil at the time of this writing.

While this snub could have understandably clouded his outlook, O'Neil maintained in a Zen-like philosophy that he hadn't missed anything; he was right on time.

Other categories: Classic, Ethnicity, History, Negro Leagues

74. *Jocks and Socks: Inside Stories from a Major League Locker Room,* by Jim Ksicinski and Tom Flaherty. Chicago: Contemporary, 2001.

For many professional athletes, the locker room is a home away from home; they probably spend more time there than at their actual residences. Ksicinski, who managed the visitor's clubhouse at Milwaukee County Stadium from 1966 to 1997, offers an engaging behind-the-scenes account of life in the locker room.

A benefit of serving as the majordomo of the visitors' facilities is that you always have a new bunch of guys coming in, hence new material to write about, rather than the same twenty-five guys day in, day out. And since ballplayers are people too, you have a mix of nice guys, clowns, jerks, big tippers, and cheapskates (the tradition is to leave a gratuity for the locker room guys at the end of a series).

The work is grueling and nonstop. Cleaning up after each game is always a rush job to get ready for the next one. Then there's getting one team out while preparing for the next one's arrival. Still, Ksicinski manages to focus on the positive and funny in sharing his experiences.

The old saying goes that what happens in the clubhouse stays in the clubhouse, but Ksicinski manages to tell his stories—with the assistance of Flaherty, a veteran sportswriter for the *Milwaukee Journal Sentinel*—while undoubtedly keeping some of the more salacious material to himself. Who knows if *Jocks and Socks* might have been a bigger seller if he'd been more willing to dish the dirt.

Other category: Behind the Scenes

75. *The Jock's Itch: The Fast-Track Private World of the Professional Ballplayer*, by Tom House. Chicago: Contemporary, 1989.

Consider this a *Ball Four* for grown-ups. House—who pitched for the Braves, Red Sox, and Mariners from 1971–78—writes a frank account of baseball life on the way up, on the way down, and everywhere in between.

Without naming names, he relates stories mostly about the low points: the disillusionment with the parent ballclubs as they bring you along through the Minors on *their* terms; the variety of egos and ethics in the locker room, full of petty jealousies and insecurities; the infidelities, the drugs, the booze, and so on.

And then, just when you probably need the game most, the game no longer needs you. House, immortalized on video for catching Hank Aaron's 715th home run as a member of the Braves' bullpen, describes the anguish of being told your services are no longer required, and yet you refuse to believe your best days are behind you. So you try to go on despite the entreaties of your family, searching for some club somewhere willing to sign you for what just a year ago you would have considered an insult. Because even though you might have earned a handsome sum over your career, relatively speaking (remember this was back when the average salary was just over $400,000; today it's over $3 million), it's mostly gone by the time you hang 'em up.

House earned his PhD in psychology and did his dissertation in terminal adolescent syndrome in athletes. He wants you to understand that it's not all fun and games, literally. By the end of *The Jock's Itch*, you almost wonder why anyone would want to go into the profession in the first place.

Other categories: Analysis, Underrated

Also by the author: *The Diamond Appraised* (1989). House also published several instructionals about pitching, including *The Winning Pitcher* (1988).

76. *Joe DiMaggio: The Hero's Life*, by Richard Ben Cramer. New York: Simon and Schuster, 2000.

There are some things a faithful baseball fan won't abide, and one of those is the besmirching of a beloved hero.

When Ben Cramer published his biography of the Yankee Clipper, many readers—especially those who grew up following the Yankees of that era—were shocked. Sure, Babe Ruth might have been a boozer and womanizer, but Joltin' Joe, lauded in song ("Mrs. Robinson") and story (*The Old Man and the Sea*)? No way. He was too classy, too much of a perfectionist to sully himself with such issues as money, women, or boorish behavior.

But *The Hero's Life* shows that despite the buildup, celebrities are only human, with the same concerns as the rest of us. Their position in the public eye is both a hindrance (they have to be circumspect about their behavior off the field) and an advantage (use your imagination). Ben Cramer shows DiMaggio taking advantage of his status but paying a price for it in terms of the distance he kept with others, even—especially?—with members of his own family.

There is also the standard fare of any sports biography here: DiMaggio's humble beginnings as the son of a poor fisherman in San Francisco; his success on the sandlots and in the Minor Leagues; the fifty-six-game hitting streak; contract disputes; the various aches and pains that prevented him from being even greater; Marilyn; and, perhaps the most difficult portion of his life, retirement and falling out of the spotlight. DiMaggio was a proud man who lived in fear that he would be forgotten. Perhaps that's why he insisted on being introduced as the greatest living ballplayer, a title bestowed on him in a baseball centennial celebration in 1969. Pitchman for Mr. Coffee and the Bowery Bank? What an embarrassment, but at least they brought in a few bucks.

There were two schools of thought regarding *The Hero's Life*, which spent nine weeks on the *New York Times* best-seller list: many, especially those with only a middling knowledge of DiMaggio, appreciated it as an eye-opener. But for those who had their own memories of what the ballplayer meant to them personally and to America at a tenuous time in history, Ben Cramer didn't do any great service.

Other categories: History, *New York Times* Best Seller, Pop Culture

77. *Joe DiMaggio: The Long Vigil,* by Jerome Charyn. New Haven CT: Yale University Press, 2011.

Another in the popular genre of books that mark prominent anniversaries, *The Long Vigil* marked seventy years since DiMaggio established his fifty-six-game hitting streak as one of the most significant numbers in sports and a record believed to be unbreakable.

This not a hypercritical analysis of that streak, like Kostya Kennedy provides in his 2011 book, *56: Joe DiMaggio and the Last Magic Number in Sports*. Instead, Charyn concentrates on a much more melancholy topic: what happens to an athlete when the cheering stops.

The question is, Whose vigil is it? DiMaggio's, as he tends to the care and feeding of his mythology? Or is it America's, as it watches the decline of one of its last legends?

This brief volume is exceedingly sad. For all of the Yankee Clipper's accomplishments, he was never comfortable in his own skin. At once wanting the accolades but at the same time wishing to be left alone, DiMaggio became a hero first to the Italian community and later to the nation at large at a precarious time in history when it needed respite from the larger issues of the impending World War just months away.

A major theme of *The Long Vigil* is DiMaggio's complex relationship with Marilyn Monroe, another glamorous icon. They were America's royalty and the object of early-form paparazzi. But despite their mutual attraction and need, DiMaggio's jealous rages eventually ended their marriage, throwing him into further isolation and despair.

Other categories: History/Event, Wartime Baseball

Also by the author: Charyn, who followed the Yankees and DiMaggio as a youth, published a well-received novel, *The Seventh Babe*, in 1979. Baseball themes also run through several other pieces of his fiction.

78. *Judge Landis and 25 Years of Baseball*, by J. G. Taylor Spink. New York: Thomas Y. Crowell, 1947.

Landis serves as a prime example of the biographical styles prior to the 1970s. There is no mention of the Judge's feelings about African American players and his tacit policy of keeping them from the professional ranks. There is no index entry mentioning Jackie Robinson, or, using the vernacular of the day, "Negro" or the "Negro Leagues." How ironic is it then that one of the chapters is titled "Landis — The Great Emancipator" and covers his 1938 decision to make free agents of dozens of players buried in the Saint Louis Cardinals system?

But this isn't surprising given that the book was written by Spink, a longtime Landis ally, who writes with overwrought dramatic language that seems better suited to almost a half century prior to the book's publication.

As founder of the *Sporting News*, the so-called Bible of Baseball, Spink was privy to a lot of inside dope. While he was also a friend of American League president Ban Johnson, with whom Landis clashed, Spink makes no bones about either objectivity or his lack of research. It would not be surprising if he took a healthy chunk of his material from the pages of his own paper or the notes of his writers; this was an era when full disclosure wasn't on the journalistic ethics radar.

Other category: History

79. *Juiced: Wild Times, Rampant 'Roids, Smash Hits, And How Baseball Got Big*, by Jose Canseco. New York: William Morrow, 2005.

There's no denying Canseco—a former Rookie of the Year, Most Valuable Player, six-time All-Star, and poster boy for better living through chemistry—has played a role in keeping baseball on the level.

Canseco named names, and as a result—like Bouton following the release of *Ball Four*—he was shunned by many of his contemporaries, fans, and baseball executives who preferred to bury their heads in the sand. Not only had *he* taken performance enhancing drugs, Canseco claimed, but he spread the wealth, lauding their benefits to teammates like Alex Rodriguez and other potential Hall of Famers whose accomplishments have since fallen under suspicion.

Steroid use was baseball's dirty little secret by the end of the twentieth century. There had been widespread rumors that some of the biggest stars were juicing, including Mark McGwire and Sammy Sosa, his buddy in the 1998 home run race. McGwire's new mark of seventy was broken three years later by Barry Bonds, another suspected doper.

As odious as some may find Canseco motives for publishing this self-serving memoir, he raised some legitimate issues, not the least of which was whether baseball's hierarchy and club owners actually knew what was going on but chose to turn a blind eye, realizing that all that extra offensive power was putting more butts in the seats. Other names emerged, congressional hearings were held, and Canseco came out looking first like a pariah but later like a Cassandra.

Juiced was one of only three baseball titles to reach number one on the *New York Times* best-seller list.

Other categories: History, New York *Times Best* Seller, Scandal, Underrated
Also by the author: Like Bouton, Canseco published a second book — *Vindicated: Big Names, Big Liars, and the Battle to Save Baseball* (2008) — which served as commentary on *Juiced* as well as a big "told you so" to all those who didn't believe there could be such widespread abuse and shame in the national pastime.

80. *The Last Boy: Mickey Mantle and the End of America's Childhood,* by Jane Leavy, New York: Harper, 2010.

How sad it is to be faced with the realization that childhood is over. It's even more sad when it turns out you have to write about your own personal hero from those years and he turns out to be a jerk.

This is the scenario Leavy faced in 1983 when she was assigned to do a profile on the retired Yankee legend for the *Washington Post.* What she found — a bitter alcoholic with no regard for anyone else — must have been heartbreaking, a wake-up call that her childish images of the Mick were misplaced, her innocence—and, by extension, the rest of that generation that grew up worshipping him — gone.

Mantle had his greatest years during the 1950s, when America was enjoying a postwar calm. By the time he was heading into retirement in the late 1960s, the country was deep into the Vietnam era and full of antiestablishment anger. Young people had no time or patience for baseball; there were more pressing issues.

Leavy — who conducted more than five hundred interviews for *The Last Boy*—alternates between tales of Mantle's glory years and her disillusionment with seeing the Yankee icon at his worst, boozily palling around with fans who would pay for the privilege of golfing or drinking with him. How the mighty had fallen. And with him,

our childhood memories have tarnished as well, leaving us with
... what?

Yes, he did make a dramatic turnaround toward the end of his
life, apologizing to America and serving as the poster boy for organ
donation. But he did force his boomer fans to grow up at last.

The Last Boy spent twelve weeks on the *New York Times* best-
seller list.

Other categories: History, *New York Times* Best Seller, Pop Culture

81. *The Lip: A Biography of Leo Durocher,* by Gerald Eskenazi. New York:
William Morrow, 1993.

82. *Nice Guys Finish Last,* by Leo Durocher with Ed Linn. New York: Simon
and Schuster, 1975.

The poet Robert Burns's lines — "O would some Power the gift to
give us / To see ourselves as others see us!" — gave me the impetus to combine these two books about Leo the Lip. How does he see
himself in comparison with how he was perceived by others? Would
he agree with the overall consensus that he was an egotistical fill-
in-the-pejorative-of-your-choice? Or would he try to alibi away his
poor treatment of players and his penchant for gambling and hanging with a rough crowd? How would he describe his courtship of
and marriage to actress Laraine Day, whom he evidently wed under
spurious circumstances?

Eskenazi starts off his profile, published two years after Durocher's
death, with a derivation of one of the Hall of Fame skipper's favorite
four letter words. Now *that's* the Durocher we know and love — or
hate. Granted, it was written almost fifteen years after Leo's own,
more genteel, version, but the sentiment is the same: Durocher was
one tough SOB who wanted to win more than anything else. He had
no patience for mistakes, especially from rookies, which is why he
played his regulars practically to death.

The juxtaposition of Durocher's and Eskenazi's books makes for
interesting coreading. Just think of them as college texts for a class
on baseball management skills.

Durocher was suspended for Jackie Robinson's first season for consorting with gamblers, but before he left he was the ballplayer's biggest supporter. When a faction of the team threatened to take up a petition saying they would not play with a black man, Durocher told them in no uncertain terms what they could do with their piece of paper.

It didn't hurt Durocher's legend that he had not one but two of the premier black players of all time in Robinson and, later, as manager of the hated rival New York Giants, Willie Mays. If there was anything redeeming about the feisty Leo's otherwise contentious career, it was how he helped players such as these make the difficult adjustment into the big leagues at a time when they weren't always welcome.

By the way, the title of Durocher's autobiography—which made the *New York Times* best-seller list—refers to a quote that had long been attributed to Leo regarding Mel Ott, his opposite number on the Giants. Whether those were the actual words he uttered is still a matter of debate, kind of like the apocryphal "Say it ain't so, Joe" for Shoeless Joe Jackson following the 1919 Black Sox scandal.

83. *The Long Season*, by Jim Brosnan. New York: Dell, 1961.

Before there was Bouton, there was Brosnan, a pitcher who spent nine seasons in the Majors and wrote about the day-to-day life of a big leaguer his 1961 memoirs.

Like Bouton, once word got out about his project, Brosnan quickly branded as an oddball, basically because he had an interest in literary pursuits. Unlike Bouton, however, he did not fill his pages with salacious stories or icon-busting descriptions of his fellow ballplayers. Still, there were those who believed Brosnan should stick to playing the game and leave the writing to Shakespeare.

Brosnan wrote about issues facing the average ballplayer in the years before free agency and $350,000 minimum contracts: being released, sent to the Minors, or traded to another team with no regard for the disruption of family life; trying to cope with injury without the availability of the medical advances yet to come; and simply enduring the day-to-day boredom that naturally comes with a long season.

Brosnan was surprisingly candid in his observations, including the boys-will-be-boys entitlement philosophy of the professional athlete, so there *is* a modicum of locker-room talk and after-hours recreation, although it's couched in PG-13 terms.

The Long Season appeared on the *New York Times* best-seller list for one week.

Other categories: Classic, *New York Times* Best Seller

Also by the author: Brosnan published *The Pennant Race* in 1962, which focuses on life with his new team, the Cincinnati Reds, to whom he was traded in the middle of his 1961 season while he was writing *The Long Season*, giving him some extra material.

84. *The Lords of Baseball,* by Harold Parrott. New York: Praeger, 1976.

Parrott had the unique perspective of having served as both a newspaperman and, later, road secretary for the Brooklyn Dodgers. As such, he had a lot of stories to tell, not all of which were complimentary. And retirement—free from the fear of retribution—always offers a good opportunity to get issues off your chest.

The phrase *lords of baseball* refers to the owners and executives who make policy, and not necessarily in a flattering way. Of course, it's usually used tongue-in-cheek and Parrott treats them accordingly, saving special approbation for the likes of former commissioner "Happy" Chandler and Charlie Finley, Arnholdt Smith, and Dewey Soriano, the bubble-headed owners of the Oakland A's, San Diego Padres, and Seattle Pilots, respectively. (The Pilots barely made it through their inaugural—and only—season in 1969.)

One can almost picture Parrott, troubleshooting for the Dodgers, battling the injustices inherent in trying to find accommodations for Jackie Robinson and his black teammates, trying to downplay the latest Leo Durocher or Larry MacPhail set-to with the press, all the while knowing that just a few years prior, he was one of them—and he was anxious to report on the behind-the-scenes goodies that made a sportswriter's life interesting.

Parrott's memoir is not to be confused with John Heylar's excellent *Lords of the Realm*, which covers the history of Big League business.

Other categories: Behind the Scenes, Business, History

85. *Me and Hank: A Boy and His Hero, Twenty-Five Years Later,* by Sandy Tolan. New York: Free Press, 2000.

In this nostalgic tale, Tolan blends the sweet simplicity of childhood with the realism of adulthood.

As a young boy, Tolan chose to plight his hero trough with Hank Aaron simply because his sister gave him the Braves slugger's baseball card. What followed was the usual idol worship, via scrapbooks and letters written in the hopes of receiving a photo or autograph.

Eleven years later, as Aaron was approaching Babe Ruth's career home run record in the face of racist knuckleheads, Tolan sent a note of support to which the superstar personally responded, further cementing the young man's adoration.

Years later, Tolan had the opportunity to meet his hero. Would the experience live up to a fan's imagination, or would it fall disappointingly short? Fortunately, their meeting went so well that Tolan, by then a journalist, turned it into a story for National Public Radio. This event became the launching point for this book, for which he interviewed family, friends, and others who were involved with his own memories of the home run record-setting game.

Other categories: History, Pop Culture

86. *The Mind of Bill James: How a Complete Outsider Changed Baseball,* by Scott Gray. New York: Doubleday, 2006.

To paraphrase once again the too-often used Jacques Barzun quote, anyone who wants to know the hearts and minds of modern baseball fans had better know Bill James.

James turned many a casual fan into a more thoughtful purveyor of insider baseball thanks to his *Abstracts* and all the writings — and commentary from others — that followed. The so-called lords of baseball thought so much of him that they thought to make him one of their own; he is currently a consultant for the Boston Red Sox. And would we have the whole *Moneyball* phenomenon without James?

Gray presents his story as if James was Abraham Lincoln, learning his letters and numbers on slate board by candlelight on his way to becoming a great leader, from his nights as a humble security guard to one of the most influential people in pop culture, let alone merely the sports world.

The book features a helpful appendix explaining some of James's "essential ideas."

Other categories: Analysis, Pop Culture, Statistics

87. *Money Pitcher: Chief Bender and the Tragedy of Indian Assimilation*, by William Kashatus. University Park: Pennsylvania State University Press, 2006.

Kashatus, author of several titles about baseball in Philadelphia, published this watershed biography about the plight of Native American ballplayers in the early part of the last century. Albert Charles "Chief" Bender was one of the best pitchers of his era, winning more than two hundred games for Connie Mack's Athletics and helping the team to five World Series appearances and three world championships.

So where's the tragic part?

In the unenlightened days before African Americans were allowed to play in the Majors, players were often targeted because of their ethnicity. Bender and other Native Americans were the recipients of racial taunts from opponents, fans, and even their own teammates. They were also frequently the subjects of what would now be considered grotesque and politically incorrect cartoon depictions.

Most of the book follows a simple biographical format: highlights of the subject's career and descriptions of individual games. The sociological aspects of assimilation are reserved for the final chapters, in which Kashatus chides Bender and other Native Americans for succumbing to the lures of white America—a case of blaming the victim.

Despite its questionable premise and conclusions, *Money Pitcher*—which won SABR's Seymour Medal in 2009—is ultimately an interesting and sympathetic look at one of the underappreciated stars of the game.

Other categories: Award Winner, Ethnicity, History

Also by the author: *September Swoon: Richie Allen, the '64 Phillies, and Racial Integration* (2004)

88. *My 66 Years in the Big Leagues*, by Connie Mack. Philadelphia: Winston, 1950.

One record guaranteed to remain unbroken: Connie Mack's fifty years as manager of a Major League team. He served in that capacity for the Philadelphia Athletics following three years at the helm of the Pittsburgh Pirates and eleven seasons as a player in the late 1800s.

Cornelius Alexander McGillicuddy—nicknamed the Tall Tactician even though was just over six feet in height—had a run of a few great years followed by decades of mediocrity, for a career mark of 3,731-3,948. His Athletics won world championships in 1910–11 and 1913, thanks in no small part to his "$100,000 infield." But after the 1914 campaign, pressure from the rival Player's League forced Mack to have an early version of the baseball fire sale, and the A's finished last for *eight consecutive seasons.*

The team eventually enjoyed a resurgence, winning three straight pennants from 1928–30 and back-to-back World Series in 1928–29. Then it was back to second division for most of the remainder of his stewardship, which ended in 1953.

Mack's book consists mostly of brief anecdotes as he discusses favorite players, respected opponents, and his philosophies of the game and of life. An amusing chapter, "To The Ladies," allows him to answer questions he received over the years such as, "Should a mother allow her son to become a ballplayer" and "Do ballplayers make for good husbands?"

Ever the distinguished gentleman—he was one of the few managers who never wore the team's uniform—Mack stands as a symbol of how we like to remember early baseball in the good old days.

89. *My Turn at Bat: The Sad Saga of the Expos,* by Claude R. Brochu, Daniel Poulin, and Mario Bolduc; translated by Stephanie Myles. Toronto ON: ECW Press, 2002.

He may not be on a par with the O'Malleys or the Stonehams who stole the Brooklyn Dodgers and New York Giants, respectively, from their beloved fans, but Brochu did not want to be the fall guy for the fate of the Montreal Expos. *My Turn at Bat* is his attempt to describe the disarray among his fellow partners as they tried to figure out the best way to keep the flailing team viable.

Brochu served as president of the team from 1991 to 1998, when he sold his shares to Jeffrey Loria, the current owner of the Miami Marlins.

Much like the Dodgers of a generation before, the Expos ran into resistance when they sought to have a new stadium built in the more accessible downtown area. Instead of Robert Moses, New York City's master builder, Brochu had Quebec premier Lucien Bouchard. With no real interest on the part of the province and little money to spend on a team with sagging attendance, Loria and company eventually abandoned the team through a complicated deal with Major League Baseball, which eventually moved the franchise to Washington DC.

It is interesting that Brochu used two coauthors. One wonders what their roles were in shaping the account, as well as the editorial input of translator Myles, who covers sports for the *Montreal Gazette*, the city's only English-language newspaper.

Other categories: History/Team, International

90. *Now Pitching, Bob Feller,* by Bob Feller with Bill Gilbert. New York: Birch Lane Press, 1990.

The Hall of Fame pitcher was probably the most prolific of player-authors coming out of the greatest generation, with five titles to his credit.

Feller missed more than three full seasons to military service during World War II. And while he served with distinction, he made no bones later in life in discussing how much better his numbers could have been—and how much more money he could have made—had he taken advantage of his Selective Service status as the sole supporter of his family. The outspoken hurler also chided subsequent generations for their poor work ethic, comparing their time spent with video games or in front of the TV with his own long list of chores on the family farm.

Rapid Robert had speed to burn. He was once filmed throwing a ball through a small target before a police motorcycle could reach an adjacent mark as a way to measure his fastball (there were no radar guns in those days). And his debut as a teenager—small-town farm boy makes good—endeared him to a country that was finally coming out of the Great Depression. He also had some progressive ideas about integrated play (see Timothy Gay's *Dizzy, Satch, and Rapid Robert: The Wild Saga of Interracial Baseball Before Jackie Robinson,* entry number 288 in this volume).

Later in life, however, Feller showed something of a miserly nature as he tried to recoup some of the money he sacrificed by appearing at card and memorabilia shows and even continuing to pitch in exhibition old-timers games.

He picked a sympathetic collaborator in Gilbert, who wrote about baseball during World War II in *They Also Served: Baseball and the Home Front, 1941–45* (1992).

Other categories: History, Wartime Baseball

91. *Now Pitching for the Yankees: Spinning the News on Mickey, Billy, and George,* by Marty Appel. Kingston NY: Total Sports Illustrated, 2001.

On the one hand, you would think being the public relations director for one of the most popular franchises in all of pro sports would be a plum gig. Everybody wants to be your friend, you get to pal around with the Bronx Bombers, and you can pick and choose those whom *you* deign to deal with.

But as Appel points out, with great power comes great responsibility, and working for an owner like George Steinbrenner could indeed be challenging. Appel had to put out a number of virtual fires, sooth a lot of egos, and balance a demanding New York media during his tenure — no easy task when you're dealing with the likes of Billy Martin, Mickey Mantle, and Reggie Jackson, among others.

Appel's advancement within the Yankee organization is a testimony to persistence. The story begins when, as a teenager, he started asking for a job, any job, with the Yankees. After several requests, he got his wish and started by answering Mantle's fan mail. The rest is PR history.

Appel, who now runs his own public relations company that specializes in sports, is a prolific author, both of his own work and as a collaborator for numerous autobiographies and memoirs. He most recently published *Pinstripe Empire: The New York Yankees from Before the Babe to After the Boss.*

Other categories: Behind the Scenes, Business, History

92. *The Oldest Rookie: Big-League Dreams From a Small-Town Guy,* by Jim Morris with Joel Engel. Boston: Little, Brown, 2001.

Everyone loves an underdog and a comeback story. *The Oldest Rookie* gives you both in one volume.

Morris was drafted as a nineteen-year-old by the Milwaukee Brewers in 1983. After toiling in the minors for five seasons — missing the entire 1986 and 1988 campaigns due to injuries — he called it quits, taking a job as a teacher and baseball coach for a high school in Texas.

Almost a decade later, he improbably discovered he still had a 95 MPH fastball and accepted a challenge from his team: if they made the playoffs, he would have to try out for a Major League team. As fortune would have it, they did, and Morris followed through on his promise.

Not expecting much to come of it, and even embarrassed to show up at an open tryout where some of the other hopefuls were half his age, Morris, at the age of thirty-five, accomplished the incredible: he was signed to a contract by the Tampa Bay Devil Rays. He made his Major League debut late in that 1999 season, striking out the first batter he faced.

The story was recreated in the Walt Disney feature, *The Rookie*, starring Dennis Quaid, one of the more enjoyable baseball films in years.

93. *Out of My League*, by George Plimpton. Guilford CT: Lyons Press, 2003.

Plimpton was not the first journalist to embed himself in the sports world, but no writer elevated the genre to such lofty and entertaining heights as the Harvard and Cambridge–educated writer.

Out of My League, originally published in 1961 and reissued several times since, represents the first sport Plimpton tackled; football, hockey, golf, and boxing would follow. He participated in a fantasy camp situation before such a moneymaking venture was even conceived. While taking in a game at Yankee Stadium, Plimpton, like many fans, thought he could do just as well as the pitcher on the mound, who had just given up a soul-crushing home run to Mickey Mantle. The difference was that Plimpton had the connections to actually make it happen. So fueled by a fit of enthusiasm and some high school and college experience, the lanky amateur embarked on his mission—to pitch to Major League batters in a postseason All-Star exhibition at Yankee Stadium in 1958.

Not surprisingly, he was met with a good deal of skepticism, mostly from players like Ernie Banks, Richie Ashburn, and other stars of the day. It was decided that he would throw to both teams, and whoever got the most hits off him would earn one thousand dollars, paid by *Sports Illustrated*. Suffice it to say that Plimpton didn't awe any of the professionals; he was done before even getting through one team's lineup. Should the reader be happy with the blow to Plimpton's ego or sympathetic to his plight?

Other categories: Classic, History

Also by the author: In addition to his nonfiction first-person sports exploits, Plimpton published a novel, *The Curious Case of Sidd Finch*, an expansion of his faux-news story about a surreal pitcher that ran in the 1985 April Fools' Day issue of *Sports Illustrated*.

94. *Pitching in a Pinch*, by Christy Mathewson with John Wheeler. New York: Putnam, 1912.

One of the earliest player-written books, *Pitching in a Pinch* was originally a series of articles by Mathewson, the New York Giants' ace at the beginning of the twentieth century and one of the first class of inductees into the Baseball Hall of Fame in 1936. Published with the assistance of Wheeler, a newspaper syndicate operator, the chapters depict the rigors of pro baseball life through the eyes (pen?) of one of its all-time greats. It has been reprinted several times over the years.

In the vernacular of the day, a *pinch* was a tight spot when one was expected to suck it up and give it that extra 10 percent; Mathewson had to do that a time or two in an era when starting pitchers were expected to go the distance.

Everything old is new again, as Mathewson writes about the complexities of his craft; working under the leadership of the legendary manager John McGraw, who was a good friend despite his rough reputation; dealing with umpires; and stealing signs through acceptable and unacceptable methods. Of particular note is a chapter exonerating teammate Fred Merkle for his bonehead play against the Chicago Cubs in 1908, which ended up costing the Giants the pennant that year.

The language employed in Mathewson's narrative is at once quaint and onerous, as the edition maintains the spelling and typographical quirks of his era, which includes placing most of the players' nicknames within quotation marks. A bit clunky, but well worth the eyestrain.

Other categories: Classic, History, Instructional

95. *Playing the Game: My Early Years in Baseball,* by Babe Ruth. Mineola NY: Dover, 2011.

Ruth "wrote" this one the season after the Yankees bought him from the Boston Red Sox in 1920. According to the introduction to the Dover edition, *Playing the Game* is actually a collection of individual stories he may have written (at least a couple) with the help of newspaperman Westbrook Pegler. More likely, Pegler, tired of waiting for the unreliable ballplayer to get his act together, did the whole thing himself.

Ruth discusses his childhood only briefly, and mostly in context with his arrival at the Saint Mary Industrial School in Baltimore. (But just once, wouldn't you like to hear what he *really* thought about his dysfunctional family?)

Most of the narrative is about Ruth's baseball accomplishments, beginning with his first home run on the school playground as a seven-year-old and continuing through the middle of the 1920 campaign. There is a little bit about his first marriage, but I suspect that was just a way to make the series more palatable to female readers.

The Dover reissue offers an excellent lesson in the player-written newspaper article, which was almost always ghosted by a staff writer, and includes an additional series of columns under Ruth's ostensible byline describing the home runs he hit late in the season — he ended up with a then-record fifty-four — as well as his predictions on that year's World Series between the Brooklyn Robins (later known as the Dodgers) and the Cleveland Indians; he correctly picked the American League entry to win the championship.

Other categories: History, Sportswriting

96. *The Power and the Darkness: The Life of Josh Gibson in the Shadows of the Game,* by Mark Ribowsky. New York: Simon and Schuster, 1996.

How sad and frustrating must it be to have your identity linked to someone else? Josh Gibson was known as the Babe Ruth of the Negro Leagues. While some might see this as a compliment, it meant that the power hitter would forever remain something of an afterthought, tied to Ruth because he did not have the opportunity for his own Major League career.

The *power* in the book's title is evident: given the organization of the Negro Leagues, official statistics are unavailable, but Gibson was said to have hit almost eight hundred home runs. The *darkness,* however, could have a number of meanings, including the color of his skin or the mental illness that hung over him, manifesting itself through anger, depression, alcoholism, and suicidal thoughts, which were no doubt exacerbated by his inability to advance in his career. This made for a vicious cycle, since placing Gibson in the white leagues was considered a big risk because of his drinking and anger issues. Then, when he and contemporaries like Satchel Paige and Buck Leonard saw that Jackie Robinson was going to be the chosen one, it added to their resentment even more. Gibson—who was elected to the Baseball Hall of Fame in 1972—died just three months before Robinson's debut.

Other categories: Ethnicity, History, Negro Leagues

Also by the author: *Don't Look Back: Satchel Paige in the Shadow of Baseball* (1994); *A Complete History of the Negro Leagues, 1884–1955* (1995); *The Complete History of the Home Run* (2005)

97. *Praying for Gil Hodges: A Memoir of the 1955 World Series and One Family's Love of the Brooklyn Dodgers,* by Thomas Oliphant. New York: Thomas Dunne/St. Martin's Press, 2005.

Here's another example of a fine baseball book coming from an unexpected source: Oliphant is a political writer and Pulitzer Prize winner who would seemingly have more important things to write about.

But Oliphant shares a poignant and personal perspective about what the long-delayed success of the local team meant to him and his parents.

Since Jackie Robinson's debut in 1947, the Dodgers and Yankees faced off in the Fall Classic six times, with Brooklyn losing all but one. The author fondly recalls that day when their beloved Bums finally beat the Bronx Bombers for the first and only time, when his father let him cut school to stay home and watch the game on TV. The tears of joy shed between a nine-year-old Oliphant and his folks are touching, especially since his dad, a freelance writer, was often in poor health since returning from serving in World War II.

He recreates the pitch-by-pitch tension of that final game in which Johnny Podres shut down the mighty Yankee attack and outfielder Sandy Amoros made his remarkable catch that is still talked about more than sixty years later.

Oliphant also touches on the deeper meaning of the team to its Brooklyn rooters, a conglomeration of races often at odds with each other but brought together for a few moments of shared pride. Sadly, the Dodgers were on the verge of abandoning the city for the sunny shores of the West Coast, an event that *still* rankles some older fans.

Other categories: History, *New York Times* Best Seller

98. *Public Bonehead, Private Hero: The Real Legacy of Baseball's Fred Merkle,* by Mike Cameron. Crystal Lake IL: Sporting Chance Press, 2010.

When Fred Merkle, the New York Giants' nineteen-year-old rookie, failed to touch second base in what would have been a crucial win over the Chicago Cubs in 1908, it was the biggest blunder the game had ever seen. To this day "Merkle's Boner" remains the mark of a brain freeze moment, symbolic of one of the all-time great fails in sports.

Despite the support of his manager, the notoriously tough John McGraw, and his teammates, the young man would forever be branded a loser. He was ridiculed in the press and no doubt received a threat or two of physical violence or worse.

But not everyone believes Merkle should have had to live with a lifetime of ridicule. Cameron goes a long way in presenting him as a good athlete who enjoyed an otherwise solid sixteen-year career. More important, he was a fine human being, well-loved and respected long after his playing days were over.

Other category: History

99. *Recollections of a Baseball Junkie,* by Art Rust Jr. New York: William Morrow, 1985.

Rust was a popular sports reporter both in print and as a radio and TV broadcaster from the 1960s through the 1980s. *Recollections* begins with his youth in the 1930s, when society put limits on what he, an African American, could do, what he could say, and where he could go. Although he grew up in New York City, he was still stung by racist comments when he went to the ballpark. As he grew to adulthood, Rust became much more aware about the realities of life for blacks in the United States.

He divides his memories into chapters on owners, including several in the Negro Leagues; managers and coaches; umpires; and gambling and politics. He also pays special tribute to women involved in the game, from female journalists struggling for the right to have full access to the players, to owners like Effa Manley of the Newark Eagles and Helene Schuyler Britton, the first woman to serve as president of a Major League organization (the Saint Louis Cardinals in 1914).

In fact, he concentrates more on his preprofessional life, which gives the book a more personal flavor since it lacks the usual name-dropping conceit, which is a staple of celebrity memoirs. There's a certain innocence as he writes about following Stan Musial, his favorite player, into the subway and all the way to his Manhattan hotel. Despite the tension of the times, Rust writes with a sense of joy rather than bitterness.

Recollections marks the first time I can recall reading about steroids. Remember, this book was published in 1985, which means it could have been written even a couple of years prior, way before McGwire, Sosa, and company schooled the world on the issue.

Other categories: History, Negro Leagues

100. *Remembrance of Swings Past*, by Ron Luciano and David Fisher. New York: Bantam, 1988.

For the most part, the body that governs Major League Baseball's umpires does not take kindly to their employees drawing attention to themselves. Just make the calls, they instruct; just do your job. Don't cause a scene but don't take any guff, either. Just walk away at the end of the game.

I guess Ron Luciano didn't get the memo.

The late umpire—he committed suicide by carbon monoxide poisoning in 1995—was no shrinking violet. At six feet four and three hundred pounds, he figuratively went after base runners by pointing his finger at them in mock-shootout fashion when calling them out. He would also shake hands with players after good performances, which also did not put him in great standing with his superiors.

His confrontations with managers were also something to behold, particularly with Baltimore Orioles skipper Earl Weaver. Their feud began in the Minors, and Luciano once threw Weaver out of both ends of a doubleheader.

Luciano parlayed his extroverted personality into a stint as a color commenter for NBC's *Game of the Week* in the early 1980s and a series of late-night talk-show appearances.

Other category: Umpires

Also by the author: Luciano collaborated with Fisher on two other books, including *The Umpire Strikes Back* (1982), *Strike Two* (1984), that are more autobiographical, and another, *The Fall of The Roman Umpire* (1988), in which Luciano turns on his noted charm and conducts interviews with some of the popular players of the day.

101. *The Road to Cooperstown: A Father, Two Sons, and the Journey of a Lifetime,* by Tom Stanton. New York: Thomas Dunne, 2003.

What is this, a book or a Hallmark Channel movie?

Stanton writes about a decades-postponed trip he finally got to take to the Baseball Hall of Fame, which, as is often the case, had been interrupted by real life: Stanton's mother suffered a life-threatening illness, and his dad and brother had major differences over the Vietnam War that caused a long-standing riff.

But upon reconciliation, the Stanton men eventually made that trip from Michigan to upstate New York. Like many travel-based stories, this is also a tale about people met along the way, as well as the Stantons' recollections about happier times, sadder times, and modern times.

Living in relatively close proximity and having visited the Hall on a few occasions, I often forget that travelling to Cooperstown is, for many, an elusive dream, but it's one certainly worth the effort, as the author and his companions discovered to their—and their readers'—enjoyment.

The Road to Cooperstown—which won the 2001 *Spitball* magazine CASEY Award and the Dave Moore Award from the *Elysian Fields Quarterly*—is also one of the better attempts to capture the bond that baseball traditionally makes between fathers and their children.

Other categories: Award Winner, Classic, History

102. *The Rocket That Fell to Earth: Roger Clemens and the Rage for Baseball Immortality,* by Jeff Pearlman. New York: HarperCollins, 2009.

Interesting choice, to use *rage* in the title. Clemens, of course, was one of several Hall of Fame–bound players accused of using performance-enhancing drugs to prolong an already-legendary career.

Pearlman goes back to the pitcher's tough childhood to look for an explanation as to what drove Clemens to succeed. How much should a player go through to get to and stay at the top? Is it a question of money? Ambition? A combination of the two? Or is it more primal: the need to survive and even to cheat death through the immortality of the record books and Cooperstown?

As a young man Clemens did not give much indication of the player he would become. He was chubby and not exceptionally skilled as an athlete, but he blossomed in college and gained a reputation as a hard worker. That attitude would serve him well as he rose through the ranks and became one of the best in the history of the game. Nevertheless, the Red Sox decided not to sign him as a free agent in 1996 after his 10-13 season at the age of 33. That blow to his ego pushed him to show Boston they had made a mistake. Over the next eight years, he won four Cy Young Awards. But how much came as the result of intense training and how much from (alleged) drug use?

> Also by the author: Pearlman has a reputation for going against the grain. His previous baseball titles considered Barry Bonds (*Love Me, Hate Me,* 2004) and the 1986 New York Mets (*The Bad Guys Won,* 2006), who went from merely talented to obnoxiously braggadocio.

103. *Ruling Over Monarchs, Giants, and Stars: Umpiring in the Negro Leagues and Beyond,* by Bob Motley with Byron Motley. Champaign IL: Sports Publishing, 2007.

There have been several excellent accounts of the Negro Leagues, from oral histories to biographies, but almost all have considered the players' experiences exclusively.

Motley served as an umpire from the late 1940s to the early 1950s, calling balls and strikes on some of the greats, including Willie Mays, Hank Aaron, and Ernie Banks. He weaves his story with an entertaining and light touch, discussing his upbringing in the heart of Jim Crow America and serving in the military during World War II before getting his break in baseball.

When Jackie Robinson broke the color line, it marked the slow death of the Negro Leagues. Motley applied to and was accepted by the Al Somers Umpire School and passed his exams with flying colors. But that wasn't enough, and Motley faced an ugly truth: organized baseball still did not have a place for African American umpires. Undaunted, he found employment where he could: at schools, in amateur leagues, even in Cuba. To a degree, his perseverance paid off: While he was hired as one of the two African American umpires in the Pacific Coast League, he never did make it to the Majors.

Other categories: History, Negro Leagues

104. *Sadaharu Oh: A Zen Way of Baseball,* by Sadaharu Oh and David Falkner. New York: Times, 1984.

You can't find many English-language biographies about stars who earned their fame outside North America, which is why this publication became an object of particular interest when it came out in 1984.

Oh was considered the Japanese Babe Ruth — perhaps the greatest player in that nation's game. A first baseman for the Tokyo Yomiuri Giants from 1959–80, he led the league in home runs for thirteen consecutive seasons (and fifteen out of sixteen), and he holds the official professional record of 868 round-trippers. But it was only when Hank Aaron was approaching Ruth's career mark of 714 that the American media began to take notice of what Oh had been doing and he began to receive recognition outside Japan.

It was not an easy road for Oh. His circumstances in the early stages of his career were more like Aaron's than like Ruth's. The child of a Chinese father and Japanese mother, Oh faced discrimination in a society that shunned the children of mixed marriages. Nevertheless, as he explains, his desire and inner strength drove him to success, but only after he submitted himself to the concept of *wa*, the philosophy that the team comes before the interests of the individual.

An unusual feature in this volume is a series of photographs on consecutive pages of Oh batting that harkens back to the days of the flip book: riffle through them quickly and it becomes a moving image of his swing. The book also includes a brief glossary of Japanese terms, both for baseball and philosophical explanations.

Other categories: Classic, History, International

105. *Sandy Koufax: A Lefty's Legacy*, by Jane Leavy. New York: HarperCollins, 2002.

The fact that there are so few biographies about Koufax—authorized or otherwise—is a testament to what a private person he has been. Of the handful of books about him, most were written during his playing days and intended for a younger audience. A few of them highlight his religious heritage and his decision to sit out the first game of the 1965 World Series, which fell on Yom Kippur, the holiest day on the Jewish calendar.

Leavy uses that Fall Classic as her focal point, albeit the seventh and deciding game in which Koufax battled with the constant pain that would force him to retire after the following season at the age of thirty. She alternates chapters between the nine scoreless innings he threw that day and the rest of his rags-to-riches story, not in terms of economic status, but in evolving from a fast but wild pitcher into a Hall of Famer despite his abbreviated career.

Naturally, Judaism plays a key component in her book. A generation after Hank Greenberg took a similar position in a crucial game during the Detroit Tigers' drive for a pennant, Koufax helped refute the continuing stereotype of the unathletic Jew.

Koufax had it all, writes Leavy: movie-star looks, a nimble brain, and, of course, outstanding ability. But his shy personality—at least outside the confines of the ballpark—make him a mysterious and alluring figure to this day, and Leavy does an excellent job of portraying him as a complex person with many hues, not just in terms of black and white—or Dodger blue.

A Lefty's Legacy spent sixteen weeks on *The New York Times* bestseller list.

Other categories: Classic, Ethnicity, History, *New York Times* Best Seller

106. *Satchel: The Life and Times of an American Legend,* by Larry Tye. New York: Random House, 2009.

According to his contemporaries, Satchel Paige — not Jackie Robinson — should have been the first African American to break the color line.

Paige was a real crowd pleaser, known for his entertaining, if at times bizarre, antics on the field, such as calling in his fielders and proceeding to strike out the opposition or exhibiting — almost literally — pinpoint control. At the height of his career, Paige was the most recognizable African American athlete in the country, more so than even Joe Louis or Jesse Owens.

The problem with writing the biography of a legend like Paige is that the story can never be told with absolute accuracy. The mainstream media of the day took little note of the Negro Leagues. Most of the information available comes from haphazard reports in the African American press and the anecdotes of former players in biographies, memoirs, or other interviews.

When Paige finally made it to the Majors in 1948 at an advanced but not wholly reliable age, he was well past his prime, years beyond his storybook ability to snuff out a match with a perfectly thrown pitch.

Tye, a writer for the *Boston Globe,* won critical acclaim for his book, which won both the CASEY Award from *Spitball* magazine in 2009 and SABR's Seymour Medal the following year. It also spent a week on the *New York Times* best-seller list.

Other categories: Award Winner, History, Negro Leagues, *New York Times* Best Seller

107. *Sleeper Cars and Flannel Uniforms: A Lifetime of Memories from Striking Out The Babe to Teeing it up with the President,* by Elden Auker with Tom Keegan. Chicago: Triumph, 2001.

You can read any one of hundreds of books about Babe Ruth, Ted Williams, Joe DiMaggio, and Jackie Robinson. But to get a feel for the regular Joes, you have to read the stories of guys like Elden Auker, who pitched for the Detroit Tigers, Boston Red Sox, and Saint Louis Browns from 1933–42, averaging a 15-12 record over his career, bringing it from underneath with his unique submarine style.

Auker was an everyman who shared stories about the good fortune he had playing with and against some of the greats of the game. He paints a pretty idyllic picture. There was more team togetherness back in the day, as the teams travelled by train (the *Sleeper Car* of the title) and labored under the same conditions, sans the comforts of the modern era (the heavy *Flannel Uniforms*).

The reminiscences flow easily and, thankfully, Auker doesn't go into minute detail. He just touches on the highlights, which makes this a quick and easy way to learn about those good old days from someone who lived through them.

By the way, Ruth did not appreciate being struck out by Auker when the pitcher was a rookie. And the president with whom he enjoyed that game of golf was none other than Gerald Ford, who was known to send a ball or two into the gallery.

Other category: History

108. *Slugging It Out in Japan: An American Major Leaguer on the Tokyo Outfield,* by Warren Cromartie with Robert Whiting. New York: Signet, 1992.

Cromartie, a member of the Montreal Expos from 1975–83, left the Majors at the age of twenty-nine to take his talents to the Far East. He played for the Tokyo Giants for the next seven seasons, learning the intricacies of the Japanese game and adjusting to their culture. In fact, Cromartie did a much better job than a lot of his fellow *gai-*

jin (foreign-born players), who couldn't get used the philosophy of *wa*: putting the needs of the team ahead of that of the individual.

Cromartie—who, along with Tim Raines and future Hall of Famer Andre Dawson, formed one of the most exciting outfields in the Major Leagues during the late 1970s—had some struggles with umpires, managers, and teammates during his adjustment period. The separation from his family and friends added to the isolation that many non-Japanese players suffer. But he slowly began to adapt and accept his new opportunity to the point where he remains a popular figure to this day.

The choice of Whiting, perhaps *the* most knowledgeable American writer on Japanese baseball, goes a long way to lending *Slugging it Out* an extra degree of credibility.

Other category: International

109. *The Soul of Baseball: A Road Trip Through Buck O'Neil's America*, by Joe Posnanski. New York: William Morrow, 2007.

Buck O'Neil's second act began when he appeared as a recurring guest on Ken Burns's *Baseball* documentary in 1995. Despite the hardships normally associated with life in the Negro Leagues, the fact that O'Neil bore no animosity and had such an upbeat attitude made him a popular speaker, with numerous appearances and speaking engagements as a result.

Posnanski, a writer for *Sports Illustrated*, accompanied O'Neil on a one of his road trips in 2005, as the elder statesman spread his sunshine, pressed the flesh, and flirted good-naturedly with the ladies. Posnanski—who won the 2007 CASEY Award from *Spitball* magazine—found him as advertised, with no artifice about him. It's too bad for O'Neil and his fans that his fame came so late in life, but he certainly seemed to enjoy every minute of it.

Other categories: Award Winner, History, Negro Leagues

110. *Steinbrenner: The Last Lion of Baseball,* by Bill Madden. New York: Harper, 2010.

Love him or hate him, there's no denying that the Yankees volatile owner had a tremendous impact on the game. He set the tone for paying ridiculous amounts of money for free agents, only to berate them when they failed to live up to his high expectations. He also micromanaged the front office to a ridiculous degree. But you can't argue with success: he restored the New York Yankees to their once-proud glory as a team perennially in the hunt for a world championship.

Yankees fans and haters are well aware of Steinbrenner's mercurial nature. Prior to Joe Torre's lengthy stay as skipper, the Bronx Bombers went through twenty managerial changes between 1973 and 1995, including many repeat performers, most notably the late Billy Martin. Steinbrenner would fire, then rehire, anyone — managers, coaches, secretaries, concessionaires — at the drop of a hat, often excusing the hasty behavior by saying, "I didn't really mean it," or "I'll let it go this time."

Madden includes the praise as well as the lash, but the former is far between or generally underreported throughout the years; for all his desire to be the center of attention, Steinbrenner didn't like to publicize his good deeds.

Madden won the Baseball Hall of Fame's 2010 Spink Award for outstanding accomplishments as a writer, and he strives to be evenhanded. His role with the New York papers put him in a great position to write a firsthand account, but he uses that relationship with a light hand, relying on his skills as a journalist rather than employing his personal observations. The book spent five weeks on the *New York Times* best-seller list.

Other categories: History, *New York Times* Best Seller

111. *A Tiger in His Time: Hal Newhouser and the Burden of Wartime Baseball,* by David M. Jordan. South Bend IN: Diamond Communications, 1990.

Authors usually undertake biographical projects with admirable motives, such as bringing renewed attention to outstanding players who have slipped from the spotlight in order to give them perhaps their last chance of election to the Hall of Fame.

Newhouser, who spent most of his career with the Detroit Tigers, was by most accounts one of the most accomplished pitchers of the World War II era. He won back-to-back MVP awards in 1944 and 1945, finished with a career record of 207-150 and a 3.06 ERA, and led Detroit to the World Series in 1945, winning two games in the Fall Classic, including the finale. Some would argue that his statistics were inflated, facing teams full of 4Fs and others who might not have been in the big leagues under ordinary circumstances. While he led the American League in wins in 1944 and 1945, he did the same in 1946 and 1948, when the boys came back and the competition presumably·got stiffer.

Books like this run the risk of getting bogged down in the details of individual games, and while Jordan indeed digs into the news of World War II's effects on the players who chose (or had) to serve, where exactly is the burden he mentions in the title? I'm not quite sure. Newhouser was declared ineligible to serve because of a heart condition. Perhaps that was the burden: deemed unfit for duty, they felt they had to perform their best, giving enjoyment to fans in difficult times.

Other categories: History, Wartime Baseball

112. *Tony C: The Triumph and Tragedy of Tony Conigliaro,* by David Cataneo. Nashville: Rutledge Hill Press, 1997.

Cataneo's book is light on triumph and heavy on tragedy, and it serves as a testimony to the frailty of the athlete's career.

Tony Conigliaro was the poster boy for the ideal of "local kid makes good." The handsome, talented, and tremendously popular slugger amassed one hundred home runs before he was twenty-three and was touted by some as the next big thing.

But on August 18, 1967, a Jack Hamilton fastball brought everything to a crashing halt. Photos following the incident show the ugly aftereffects: Conigliaro carried off the field on a stretcher, his grotesque black eye swollen shut, effectively putting an end to his career.

Conigliaro made a valiant comeback attempt though. After sitting out the rest of 1967 and the entire 1968 season, he returned to the Red Sox, hitting 20 home runs and driving in 82 runs. The next year was even better: 36 HRS and 116 RBIS. But what most outsiders didn't know was that his eyesight was failing; Tony C. was out of the game after 1971, with a last-gasp attempt to reinvent himself as a pitcher in 1975.

Bad luck continued to dog him in his postathletic career. Several business opportunities, including a co-owning a health-food store and a stint as a TV sportscaster, failed to pan out. Conigliaro succumbed to increasingly serious health issues and died in 1990 at the age of forty-five.

113. *Ty Cobb: His Life and Tumultuous Times: An Illustrated History*, by Richard Bak. Dallas: Taylor, 1994.

Because baseball is such a visual endeavor, I believe the best books are the ones that combine thoughtful prose with eye-catching illustrations. This one is a good example, made even more so because of Cobb's cantankerous reputation.

It would be easy to produce such a book about Babe Ruth or Willie Mays or Mickey Mantle, because they were so genial, symbols of what's good about the game (at least on the field). For all his talents, Cobb was never held in the same esteem, not by the public or his teammates, and certainly not by his opponents.

Some loyalists have gone back and tried to shine up Cobb's image, claiming he did a lot of good, such as giving lots of money to charity later in life and setting up hospitals and foundations. But he could never escape the negative images put forth by writers like Al Stump (even though he worked *with* Cobb on one of his autobiographies).

Bak, who also wrote biographies on Casey Stengel, Lou Gehrig, and Turkey Stearnes (a star outfielder in the Negro Leagues), does an admirable job in assembling both words and pictures about Cobb from his childhood to his death.

One of the more interesting aspects of the Georgia Peach's storied life was the mysterious circumstances surrounding the death of his father, who was killed either accidentally or on purpose by his wife, who allegedly mistook him for a burglar. A book like this can't spend too much time on any single event, but it's certainly a poser and makes for a good starting point for further information available in more detailed bios.

Other categories: History, Pop Culture

114. *Veeck — as in Wreck: The Autobiography of Bill Veeck,* by Bill Veeck with Ed Linn. New York: Putnam, 1962.

If I were forced to pick just one baseball executive's autobiography, biography, or memoir to read, it would have to be Veeck's candid and entertaining story, which spent fifteen weeks on the *New York Times* best-seller list.

Veeck enjoyed great success with the Cleveland Indians, making Larry Doby the American League's first black player and bringing on Satchel Paige in 1948; the team won the World Series that season. A few years later, Veeck bought the bottom-of-the-barrel Saint Louis Browns, with whom he tried various stunts to bring fans to the ballpark. Perhaps his most famous — and the story that leads off the book — was signing Eddie Gaedel, a midget, as a player. The three-foot-seven-inch Gaedel walked on four pitches, was replaced by a pinch runner, and was banned from further play by Commissioner Landis. Veeck held other promotions, including one gimmick where fans voted on strategy with the use of placards distributed upon their entrance to the stadium.

He moved back to his native Chicago, where he bought the White Sox in 1958; they appeared in the Fall Classic the following year.

Veeck tells his saga with a mix of humility and bravado few others could have pulled off. He writes frankly about his relationships with contentious players and managers, fellow owners, and commissioners who would dare try to curtail his enthusiasm for putting out a product that was entertaining and attractive to consumers. The fans were his people, and he would frequently sit out in the bleachers among them, shirt off, smoking a cigar, and enjoying a frosty malt beverage.

Veeck's son, Mike, carried on the family tradition of innovative decision making at the ballpark, but unless Mark Cuban manages to acquire a team in the near future, the days of the maverick owner in baseball seem to be over.

Other categories: Business, Classic, History, *New York Times* Best Seller

Also by the authors: *The Hustler's Handbook* (1965)

115. *Wait Till Next Year: A Memoir*, by Doris Kearns Goodwin. New York: Simon and Schuster, 1997.

This sweet, nostalgic memoir isn't wholly about baseball, but there's enough there to merit inclusion.

Kearns Goodwin, a Pulitzer Prize–winning historian, recalls how she came to love the national pastime, thanks to her father, who was seemingly out of the Ozzie Nelson and Ward Cleaver school of dads from the 1950s whose love, strength, and gentleness made a lifelong impression on her.

Their shared interest in the Brooklyn Dodgers — at the time featuring such stars as Jackie Robinson, Roy Campanella, Duke Snider, Gil Hodges, and company — is the stuff of three-handkerchief movies. Amid all the other joys and disappointments of adolescence, Kearns Goodwin would find time to pore over the box scores and discuss the previous afternoon's contest with her dad.

Kearns Goodwin — better known for her presidential biographies — is a frequent talking head on baseball documentaries; the general public was introduced to her in Ken Burns's *Baseball*, where she proved that women, too, can have a strong affinity for the history and love of the game.

Wait Till Next Year spent ten weeks on the *New York Times* bestseller list.

Other categories: History, *New York Times* Best Seller

116. *Walter Johnson: Baseball's Big Train,* by Henry W. Thomas. Washington DC: Phenom Press, 1995.

Johnson was inducted into the same Hall of Fame class as Babe Ruth, but if you compare their records, Johnson, the pitcher who won 417 games in 21 seasons for a team that frequently found itself in the lower half of the standings, comes out looking like a bush leaguer. Can you imagine how idolized he would have been had he been a member of the Yankees or Giants?

Such is the unfair plight of the starting pitcher, who appears, at best, only once every four days.

Thankfully, Thomas—who won the 1995 CASEY Award for his book—presents a thorough examination of the quiet and gentle hurler who was adjudged as owning one of the great fastballs in baseball history, and whose name is always mentioned in the same breath as pitching descendants like Sandy Koufax, Bob Feller, and Nolan Ryan.

Johnson unfortunately toiled in an era before technology could measure his talents, and much of the evidence of his skills is anecdotal; for all his ability and potential to instill fear in the hearts of his opponents, Johnson refused to take the inside-pitch road.

In addition to being a wonderful tribute to the ballplayer, *Walter Johnson* is a fine account of baseball and American life in the early twentieth century.

Other categories: Award Winner, History, Pop Culture

117. *The Way It Is,* by Curt Flood with Richard Carter. New York: Trident Press, 1970.

Vince Coleman once embarrassed himself by saying he didn't know anything about Jackie Robinson. Although it wouldn't be on the same scale, I wonder how many active ballplayers might say the same about Flood? Yet where would they be without the sacrifices he made?

At the peak of his career, the three-time All-Star was earning $110,000, so it was hard for the average fan to build up much sympathy when he was traded to the Philadelphia Phillies in 1971 for Richie Allen.

Flood shocked his old bosses, his news bosses, and the baseball establishment by refusing to accept the deal. He was not, he said, a possession to be moved around on a whim by management against his own wishes and best interests; he and his family had built a nice life in Saint Louis and he did not wish to disrupt that. He sued Major League Baseball (*Flood v. Kuhn*), attempting to strike down the reserve clause that bound a player to his team in perpetuity for as long as that team wanted him.

Flood sat out the 1970 season and eventually lost his court battle, but the stage was set for future attempts and eventual freedom for his athletic successors. He made a comeback attempt in 1971, but his skill and desire had abandoned him and he retired by the end of April.

The first hundred or so pages tell a basic story of the black player of that era. Flood grew up in tough circumstances but relative social acceptance and he was stunned by the prejudice he encountered playing ball in the Deep South, and even later in the majors. There are also some fairly typical but titillating tales about the advantages of being a professional athlete.

Other categories: Business, Classic, History/Event

118. *A Well-Paid Slave: Curt Flood's Fight for Free Agency in Professional Sports,* by Brad Snyder. New York: Viking, 2006.

The fact that this book has no preface or introduction is an excellent indication that the author means business.

Picking up where Flood's own story—*The Way It Is*—left off, Snyder concentrates almost exclusively on the legal issues and courtroom presentations, and he does a marvelous job in recapturing the industry-altering tension of Flood's fight for emancipation from the metaphoric chains put upon him by his baseball "masters."

Former Supreme Court justice Arthur Goldberg, who served as counsel for Flood, takes the bulk of the blame for the negative outcome. Snyder reports how Goldberg bungled his closing arguments in amazing fashion, as if he expected to coast on his reputation.

This is not a book for the casual fan. It gets a bit too bogged down with legal technicalities to qualify as a popular title, but Snyder is the perfect author for such an undertaking. Not only is he well-versed in the baseball component (his previous book, *Beyond the Shadow of the Senators*, about black baseball in Washington DC earned nominations for awards from the Society for American Baseball Research, *Spitball* magazine, and *Elysian Fields Quarterly*), but as a lawyer he is also well-versed on both sides of the table.

A Well-Paid Slave, which won the *Elysian Fields Quarterly*'s Dave Moore Award in 2006, is a good start for anyone who wants to understand the genesis of the free-agency era and the role Flood played—and the price he paid—in making sure those who followed him did not have to suffer the same indignities.

Other categories: Award Winner, Business, History, Pop Culture

119. *Wherever I Wind Up: My Quest for Truth, Authenticity, and the Perfect Knuckleball,* by R. A. Dickey with Wayne Coffey. New York: Blue Rider Press, 2012.

When word came out several months before publication that Dickey, a journeyman pitcher most recently with the New York Mets, was writing a book, it got the usual buzz. But when, just prior to release, excerpts and previews mentioned incidents of the author's sexual abuse as a child, it took on a whole 'nother spin and I had qualms about another sensational memoir playing on personal tragedy to increase interest and sales. How wrong I was.

While Dickey's personal background and his faith play major roles in the story, there's also plenty of baseball as he writes about the psychological and emotional difficulties in going from prospect to suspect. The former came when he was named as the Texas Rangers' first-round draft pick in 1996; the latter a short time later following the discovery of a physical anomaly that greatly reduced his status and sent him through the desert of several ball clubs' Minor League systems until he found success with the Mets in 2010.

During interviews on various outlets following publication, Dickey — an English major at the University of Tennessee, Knoxville — admitted writing *Wherever* was a sort of catharsis and an avenue through which others in his situation might find some solace and hope. It is an amazingly thoughtful and introspective work, as Dickey discusses how the abuse shaped his life as a teenager and beyond. It is also especially unusual in the macho world of sports, where athletes have historically been loath to bring up such issues.

120. *Where Have You Gone, Joe DiMaggio: The Story of America's Last Hero,* by Maury Allen. New York: Dutton, 1975.

Several books published in the last thirty-five-plus years would refute that "the great DiMaggio," as Ernest Hemingway described him in *The Old Man and The Sea*, was America's last hero. But Allen's biography does seem to be one of the last of *its* kind, a volume that relies on the anecdotes and reminiscences about its subject rather than extensively cited research. Subsequent volumes on the Yankee Clipper paint him in a less heroic but more human light. And by more human I mean a man with a dark side, given to bouts of anger, paranoia, depression, and uncertainty about his place in the history of the game, despite all his accomplishments.

Allen, who had almost forty baseball titles to his credit, was also a throwback, a writer who had strong moral code of his own but recognized and forgave human frailty in others. The last book he published before his death in 2010 was about Dixie Walker, another of his heroes, who, as a member of the Brooklyn Dodgers in 1947, requested a trade rather than remain on the same team as Jackie Robinson. But Allen's research showed that it was more for practical reasons at the time — Walker had a hardware store in Alabama and was under pressure from his neighbors to uphold the southern traditions of strict segregation — and that the ballplayer later regretted his actions.

So Allen's book on DiMaggio is not so much a prime piece of biography as it is an example of a style of writing that has been slowly phased out, for better or worse, as more edgy (and perhaps cynical) approaches have become the norm.

Other categories: History, Pop Culture

121. *Where Have You Gone, Vince DiMaggio?* by Edward Kiersh. New York: Bantam, 1983.

Like Gummo Marx, the oldest of the ballplaying DiMaggios was the forgotten brother. But thanks to this nostalgic volume, Vince and fifty-five other ballplayers from the 1940s to the 1970s get a little love.

Some — Ernie Banks, Willie McCovey, Warren Spahn, Harmon Killebrew, Jim Bunning, and Orlando Cepeda, to name a few — don't really need the attention, having received plenty of ink for their exploits. Many of Kiersh's subjects might have been top tier for a brief time, while the majority were the spear carriers who made up the rest of their team's cast. What they all had in common was that they played prior to the age of free agency and multimillion dollar contracts, forcing them to actually go back to work after their first retirements.

The book is at once sad and funny as we discover some of these postbaseball careers. Elroy Face, who still holds the single-season record for winning percentage, became a carpenter at an insane asylum when he left baseball after the 1969 season. His story is typical of many of the players Kiersh profiles, most of whom did not have a college degree.

And Vince? Sadly, he had to scuffle quite a bit, working as a bartender, carpenter, milkman, and door-to-door salesman.

Other categories: History, Pop Culture

122. *A Whole Different Ball Game: The Sport and Business of Baseball,* by Marvin Miller. Seacaucus NJ: Carol Publishing, 1991.

Miller served as executive director of the Major League Baseball Players Association from 1966 to 1982. He oversaw the most revolutionary period in the history of the game, if not sports in general. His skills helped open the door, for better or worse, for all athletes to earn grotesquely large salaries. Safely distanced from his association with baseball by the late 1980s, Miller felt free to publish his book, which is part memoir, part labor history lesson, and part business primer.

One would be surprised to learn that the initial resistance he faced when he came on the scene came not from baseball executives but from the players themselves, who looked at this slight, Jewish wise guy from New York with suspicion. Many of them were not brought up to embrace the idea of unions, but enough were fed up with being treated like merchandise that they took a chance, backed Miller, and never looked back. Miller was there to support Curt Flood's challenge of the reserve clause and to battle against the collusive practices of the early 1980s when owners conspired to keep free agent salaries low.

His book is opinionated, as it should be coming from a person in his position. Considering the impact and effect Miller has had on the game, the lack of additional books about him is a travesty, as is the failure over the past several years to elect him to the Hall of Fame.

Other categories: Business, History

123. *Willie Mays: The Life, The Legend,* by James S. Hirsch. New York: Scribner, 2010.

While there have been many serious biographies about Mantle, Robinson, and Ruth, there have been practically none about the Say Hey Kid. Mays was notoriously reluctant to allow an authorized treatment of his life, but Hirsch, a former writer for the *New York Times* and the *Wall Street Journal*, was patient, and after repeated attempts over seven years he received the Hall of Famer's approval.

Willie Mays — which enjoyed four weeks on the *New York Times* best-seller list — may be a straightforward biography, but that's the kind of player and man Willie was, according to the author: brilliant at his craft, even if he wasn't always the friendly guy people expected him to be.

The crux of the book seems to be that despite his success and all the accolades and applause, Mays never received his full due and was never embraced as was Mantle, garnering only a fraction of the Mick's endorsements. Chalk that up to 1950s America, where blond and blue-eyed won almost every time. Things didn't improve much when the Giants moved to San Francisco; Mays and his teammates didn't find unconditional love from their new fans, who looked on them as mere transplants.

One of the most iconic images in sports history is "The Catch" in the 1954 World Series against the Cleveland Indians, to which Hirsch devotes an entire chapter. Had Vic Wertz's wallop taken place in a different, more hitter-friendly stadium, he probably would have had a home run. Instead, we have the grainy video of Mays running, running, running, making that over-the-shoulder catch, and completing his effort with an amazing throw back to the infield. Hirsch's interpretation of the play could easily stand on its own, and it's comparable to John Updike's essay *"Hub Fans Bid Kid Adieu."* What would Mays's career have been without that defining moment?

A book like this has implications beyond baseball. For that reason, I didn't begrudge Hirsch's exposition of people, places, and events that most fans already know. Rather, Mays should be considered not just within the narrow label of baseball biography but in the broader arena of America in boomer lit.

Other categories: History, *New York Times* Best Seller, Pop Culture

124. *A Woman's Work: Writing Baseball History with Harold Seymour,* by Dorothy Jane Mills. Jefferson NC: McFarland, 2004.

Anyone familiar with serious baseball literature will recognize the name Harold Seymour. He is credited as being the first to publish an academic history of the national pastime, and in 1995 the Society for American Baseball Research created an annual award in his honor for the best history or biography.

But according to his widow, Dorothy Jane Mills, he didn't do it alone. She wrote *A Woman's Work* in an attempt to set the record straight, arguing that her late husband never gave her proper credit for her substantial work as his researcher, editor, and, later, writer for substantial portions of the final book in his trilogy, *Baseball: The People's Game.*

She describes in great detail her contributions to his projects and her increasing resentment as Seymour steadfastly refused her appeals. Still, she remained silent, stewing at the injustice of the situation.

Mills was a talented writer in her own right, having published books on everything from cooking to children's stories to historical fiction. Contrary to the book's title, though, this woman's work in regards to clearing up a major misconception and shedding light on the collaborative process is indeed done and has gone a long way toward achieving her goal, as belated as it was.

Other categories: History, Women

125. *Yogi Berra: Eternal Yankee,* by Allen Barra. New York: W. W. Norton, 2009.

In some small way, you almost have to feel sorry for Yogi Berra. Hall of Famer, three-time Most Valuable Player, winner of more world championship rings than anyone else, and a member of fifteen consecutive All-Star teams—not to mention the fact that he helped win pennants for *two* New York franchises. But what will he be remembered for? Yogisms. In addition to all his other talents, Berra was adept in mangling language, but they still have some fortune-cookie-philosophy bits of truth. "No one goes there anymore, it's too crowded"; "It gets dark out there early"; and perhaps the most famous of all, "It ain't over 'til it's over."

Author Barra wants you to know that the popular Berra was not to be taken lightly. Okay, so he liked to read comic books. So what? He also came through in the clutch with frightening regularity, driving in one hundred or more runs five times and striking out just 414 strikeouts in 8,364 plate appearances. All this while holding down the fort behind the plate—don't forget Berra anchored some great Yankee pitching staffs—where he held the career record for home runs for a catcher until it was broken by Johnny Bench.

In one of four appendices, Barra uses a variety of metrics to suggest that Berra just might be the greatest backstop of all time, compared with the likes of Bench, Roy Campanella, Mickey Cochrane, and Bill Dickey. In another, he pits Berra's aphorisms against some of the greatest *thinkers* of all time, such as Churchill, Proust, and Einstein.

Also by the author: *Brushbacks and Knockdowns: The Greatest Baseball Debates of Two Centuries* (2005)

126. *The Yogi Book: I Really Didn't Say Everything I Said!*, by Yogi Berra. New York: Workman, 1998.

There have been many books by and about this beloved Yankee (and Met and Astro) figure. The ones *about* him are usually straightforward biographies. The ones ostensibly *by* him—many have either been co- or wholly written by his frequent collaborator, Dave Kaplan—deal mainly with his unique way of turning a phrase.

In *The Yogi Book*, the Hall of Famer wants to make one thing perfectly clear. Well, perhaps *perfectly* and *clear* might not be strictly accurate, but he does address misconceptions regarding many of the quotes attributed to him throughout his long and colorful career. Known as Yogisms, many of these aphorisms (see previous entry) have achieved folklore status.

Berra freely admits that some of these expressions were simple syntactical errors, but deeper parsing proves they make a lot of sense. Take his signature phrase, "It ain't over 'til it's over." Viewed in a strictly baseball context, it's absolutely true. How often has a team been behind late in a game, only to come back from the brink of defeat? From a technical standpoint, it's accurate as well: a thing is not over until it is. It's a comment worthy of Voltaire.

Other category: Pop Culture

3
Ballparks

Few components of the national pastime are as cliché-driven as ballparks. Authors frequently write about the vast expanse of verdant patches or the majestic columns or the way the sun sets over the left field wall, bidding farewell to the day.

Most of the books about baseball stadiums build on this nostalgia and fall into a few categories: photo-albums that consider all the ballparks in one volume; fact-packed books that inform the reader about the parks' dimensions, firsts, and other bits of trivia; and the popular ode when a beloved edifice shuts its doors, such as the glut of titles that appeared when the old Yankee Stadium turned off its lights in 2008. Similarly, Fenway Park, venerable home of the Boston Red Sox, was a boon for the genre when it celebrated its centennial in 2012.

Even a crumbling park, like Shea Stadium, Wrigley Field, and Tiger Stadium, has a degree of charm. But ballparks are like families. No matter how much a fan might agree with the assessments, any outsider better take care when it comes offering insults. "This is my house," you say: "It may not be perfect, but it's my baseball home. So watch it!"

127. *Ballpark: Camden Yards and the Building of an American Dream*, by Peter Richmond. New York: Simon and Schuster, 1993.

Camden Yards was the first of the most recent generation of retro ballparks, moving away from the cookie-cutter fields of the mid-1970s (Veteran's Stadium and Three Rivers Stadium, to name two), to open the door to imagination, quirkiness, and just plain fun. At the same time, one of the detriments to a philosophy of trying to serve so many differing definitions of a ballpark experience is that it detracts from actually watching the game, as people shop, eat, swim, and partake in other amusements.

Ballparks do not just grow like Topsy. Unless you're a real student of architecture and don't live in the city where a new stadium is being constructed, you're not privy to the day-by-day evolution of the structure or the impact it has on the local residents.

In any new stadium project there are politics going on behind the scenes, as well as battles between the designers and the client as to whose vision will win. In this case, it was also a matter of community, as an old warehouse was saved and incorporated into the overall charm of the new facility.

Richmond, a veteran newspaper journalist and magazine writer, is an astute and nuanced reporter in presenting the long, slow process in a manner that doesn't seem either long or slow.

Other categories: Analysis, Business, History

128. *Ballparks: Yesterday and Today,* by John Pastier, Michael Heatley, Jim Sutton, Ian Westwell, and Marc Sandalow. Edison NJ: Chartwell, 2007

Another hefty coffee-table entry that takes an overall view of stadiums through the modern era, this volume is actually a revised and combined version of *Ballparks* (2007) and *Historic Ballparks* (2006). It covers the evolution from nineteenth-century fields unfettered by walls or fences, to primitive wooden constructions, to steel and concrete (a major safety improvement), and it considers design changes over the years, such as fully enclosed circular ballparks, domes, and retractable roofs. One can only wonder how history might have changed had Branch Rickey gotten his way when he asked for an early version of an enclosed facility in the heart of downtown Brooklyn in the late 1950s.

The bulk of *Ballparks* takes an alphabetic city-by-city tour of the homes of each major league franchise, as well as several Minor League teams. A nice nod is the credit given to the architects and engineers who brought those plans from the drawing board to reality. One interesting fact is that over half of all ballparks more than twenty years old were designed by the same firm. Such acknowledgment accounts for just two out of four-hundred-plus pages, but that's two more than usual.

Other categories: Coffee Table/Gift, History

129. *Blue Skies, Green Fields: A Celebration of 50 Major League Baseball Stadiums*, by Ira Rosen. New York: Clarkson Potter, 2001.

Many books replete with dimensions, facts, and photos discuss the beauty and lore of the ballfield. Rosen's colorful contribution stands apart because he supplements the standard stuff with memories and anecdotes from people who had firsthand experiences with the facilities: the players, broadcasters, and team employees who called these places their office, and the fans who came by just to visit.

Of course, some ballparks have a greater tradition than others. How can you compare a Yankee Stadium to a Network Associates Coliseum? Do you even know who plays there? It's the Oakland A's. Wrigley Field and Fenway Park are also baseball meccas, almost sacred for their place in the game's history.

This volume includes fifty locations, which obviously means some are no longer in use, such as Ebbets Field, the Polo Grounds, and Candlestick Park, among others. Regardless of whether general consensus deemed it a palace (Tiger Stadium in its heyday) or an outhouse (Candlestick Park was frequently too windy), they were all settings for special moments for players and fans alike.

Other categories: Coffee Table/Gift, History, Minor Leagues, Pop Culture

130. *Remembering Yankee Stadium: An Oral and Narrative History of the House That Ruth Built,* by Harvey Frommer. New York: Stewart, Tabori and Chang, 2008.

131. *Remembering Fenway: An Oral and Narrative History of the Home of the Boston Red Sox,* by Harvey Frommer. New York: Stewart, Tabori and Chang, 2011.

Few structures evoke the as much nostalgia and emotion as these proud old ballparks, one still active, the other, sadly, out of business.

Frommer, who specializes in books filled with photographs and memories, from the Hall of Fame player to the peanut vendor to the fans in the stands, composed these two volumes about the ballparks of the longtime rival organizations. *Yankee Stadium* provided a fond farewell to the home of the Bronx Bombers in 2008, while the Boston landmark marked its centennial in 2012.

Both books follow the same format: a chronology, with scores of black-and-white and color photos that mark not just the high notes, but the ordinary, the day-to-day experiences of coming out to see the home team play. Frommer supplements the illustrations with comments from an array of fans and players who enjoyed the experiences and emotions of the settings.

Rounding out the book is a roster of broadcasters, key moments in ballpark history, and various statistical factoids about Fenway and Yankee Stadiums.

Other categories: Coffee Table/Gift, History/Oral, Pop Culture

132. *Take Me Out to the Ballpark: An Illustrated Tour of Baseball Parks, Past and Present,* by Josh Leventhal. New York: Black Dog and Leventhal, 2000.

Good luck trying to find space on your bookshelf for this one. The book has one right angle and rounded corners, something like a large misshapen vinyl record jacket, which makes it as interesting in format as content.

Leventhal considers some of the landmark ballfields as well as memorable moments, such as the introduction of lights, ballpark food, Minor and Negro Leagues stadiums, advertising, scoreboards, and groundskeeping.

Other categories: Pop Culture, Reference

133. *Target Field: The New Home of the Minnesota Twins,* by Steve Berg. Minneapolis: MVP, 2010.

Ever since Baltimore opened Oriole Park at Camden Yards in 1992, teams have been clamoring for a redo. Now they all want retro stadiums, reminiscent of the classic ballparks, but with twenty-first-century personalities and amenities. Some have done it better than others.

What's unique about *Target Field* is how the author blends the narrative about the nuts and bolts of the Twins' new facility with the effects it would have on the community. Berg, a former reporter and editorial writer for the Minneapolis *Star Tribune* and an urban design consultant, combines his love for baseball with his expertise in architecture in this colorful coffee-table edition, which follows the massive undertaking from initial conception and planning through blueprinting and implementation. There's so much more that goes into bringing such a project to fruition than the average fan realizes, and it frequently goes unreported on a daily basis by most of the local media. That's why a book like *Target Field* is so welcome, as it puts all these components together.

Other categories: Coffee Table/Gift, Photography, Pop Culture

134. *Why Fenway? Exploring the Red Sox Mystique,* by John W. Ferguson. Chicago: Triumph, 2011.

Fenway Park celebrated its one hundredth anniversary in 2012. More than just a place to play baseball, it is a Boston landmark, a part of the neighborhood, both locally and throughout Red Sox Nation.

Ferguson, an editorial photographer, uses both black-and-white and color shots to evoke the sense of tradition that has become the hallmark of the oldest Major League stadium still in use.

There must be some reason the team couldn't pull the trigger and build a new home. Sure, there have been renovations to a relatively small degree, but can you imagine the team playing its home games without the Monstah?

Other categories: Coffee Table/Gift, History, Photography, Pop Culture

4
Behind the Scenes

Sure, the players get all the money and glory, but you have to give props to the people behind the scenes, from the ticket taker to the public-address announcer to the guys on the grounds crew to the team's webmaster. Without these men and women, fans wouldn't be able to enjoy the game nearly as much. This is even truer today, as the new ballclubs are almost as interested (if not more so) in what goes on in the gift shops, restaurants, and in-house museums as on the field.

A lot of it is thankless work, performed by people who labor in anonymity, so it's nice to find several books that pay tribute to these unsung folks — in greater or lesser detail, their stories told either in the first or third person, with or without illustrations, for adults and for younger readers.

135. *The Ballpark: One Day Behind the Scenes at a Major League Game,* by William Jaspherson. Boston: Little, Brown, 1979.

Even though this is definitely dated (just look at those clothes, haircuts, and computers in the press box), *The Ballpark* is a great introduction for everyone, not just younger readers, to all the collaborative efforts that go into producing a ball game.

The book opens with an almost empty Fenway Park, as the grounds crew begins their work of getting the field in shape for the day's event. Slowly, the stadium fills with players, trainers, public address announcers, ushers, media members, concessionaires, and numerous others, all of whom have the shared goal of making the ballpark experience as memorable and enjoyable for the fans as possible. In this case, the Red Sox sent them home happy, thanks to their 1–0 win over the Kansas City Royals.

The book lends credence to the old theater adage: there are no small roles when it comes to putting on a production.

Other categories: Ballparks, Behind the Scenes, History, Pop Culture

136. *Banana Bats and Ding-Dong Balls: A Century of Unique Baseball Inventions,* by Dan Gutman. New York: Macmillan, 1995.

Part Sears-Roebuck catalog, part back-of-the-book advertising in baseball periodicals, *Banana Bats* takes an amusing yet respectful look at the hundreds of inventions designed to improve training techniques, increase efficiency and strategy, and make life generally better and more enjoyable for players and fans alike.

Gutman, author of a popular series of young-adult baseball fiction, opens up the vault as he recalls such items as the Amazing Bat-O-Matic, which claimed to help hitters see the ball better on the bat because the sweet spot was transparent! (And doesn't is seem like a lot of products created in the 1950s and 60s had "o-matic" in their names?)

Some items were actually legitimate and are still in use, such as batting donuts and other weighted-bat devices, batting tees, and protective equipment; others were either just plain silly or downright fraudulent.

Gutman also writes up an ancillary product one might not associate specifically with the game, despite its obviousness: television, which was used as a teaching tool for both fans and players.

Since the book was produced some fifteen years ago, there are a lot of items—primarily the batter's personal body armor of shin guards and elbow pads worn, as popularized by Barry Bonds—that are missing. Perhaps in the revised edition.

Other categories: Pop Culture, Reference

137. *Innocence and Wonder: Baseball Through the Lives of Batboys,* by Neil D. Isaacs. Indianapolis IN: Masters Press, 1994.

A lot of kids I know think it would be the coolest thing ever to work for a Major League team. After all, you get to wear a uniform and hang out with your favorite players.

But as the dozens of interviewees attest in *Innocence and Wonder,* it's not all fun and games. The hours are long, expectations and competition are high, pay is low, and not everyone is as nice as they used to be portrayed in the movies, like Roy Hobbs and batboy Bobby Savoy in the film version of *The Natural.*

Still, as the subjects in this oral history describe their duties and offer their impressions of some of the game's biggest stars, we get the sense that they wouldn't trade their experiences for anything. This seems especially true in the rosy glow of nostalgia, as the former batboys age and take on more grown-up responsibilities. Each entry concludes with a brief "where are they now" update.

There have been a few full-length autobiographies, biographies, and memoirs by former nonplaying pros, most notably *Searching for Heroes: The Quest of a Yankee Batboy,* by Joe R. Carrieri (1996); *Bat Boy: Coming of Age with the New York Yankees,* by Matthew McGough (2007); and *Clubhouse Confidential: A Yankee Bat Boy's Insider Tale of Wild Nights, Gambling, and Good Times with Modern Baseball's Greatest Team,* by Luis Castillo and William Cane (2011) (don't any other teams use batboys?). It's interesting to see how the tone changes across the generations: Carrieri was with the team in the 1950s, so his recollections are more in line with that sense of innocence and wonder. More recent books in this tabloid-driven world tend to be edgier, with the increased desire to dish the dirt.

Other category: History/Oral

138. *In the Ballpark: The Working Lives of Baseball People,* by George Gmelch and J. J. Weiner. Washington DC: Smithsonian Institution Press, 1998.

Fans interested as much in the process as the product will enjoy this collection of first-person baseball job descriptions that give a new meaning to concept of teamwork.

It's like the proverbial link in a chain: if something is missing or broken, the whole thing falls apart. Without the managers, trainers, and groundskeepers, the athletes couldn't play. Without the media-relations director, the press couldn't do their jobs, which in turn means fans couldn't follow the game as easily. Without the concessionaires and mascots, the fans in the stands wouldn't enjoy a full experience.

Gmelch divides the workers by geography: in the stands, on the field (including the players and managers), in the press box and in the front office. There's something almost mystical about being employed within the world of baseball, and the twenty-one men and women profiled — from the minimum-wage usher to the owner and general manager of a Minor League team — take great pride in what they do, even under difficult situations. One woman who worked as an assistant director of media relations for a Major League team recalls the time when she wasn't allowed to eat in the press lounge. The lounge fell under the control of the Baseball Writers Association, which, as a membership organization, felt it was their right to exclude her.

It might seem like fun, working for a professional sports team, but there's a lot of sacrifice involved. The pay is often not commensurate with what the employee might make in the real world; the job often takes place on nights and weekends, taking away from family time; and, as mentioned before, when it comes to certain positions, there's still an old-boy network that forms something of a glass ceiling when it comes to women in the world of baseball.

The title might also allude to the fact that a lot of these people are *close* to the game, but they are not actually *in* the game, a designation reserved for the players and their on-field leaders.

Other categories: Auto/Bio/Mem, Business

139. *No Cheering in the Press Box*, recorded and edited by Jerome Holtzman. New York: Holt, Rinehart and Winston, 1974.

Holtzman, a veteran sportswriter who received the J. G. Taylor Spink Award from the Baseball Hall of Fame in 1989, turns the tables in this tribute to an esteemed group of fellow scribes.

Most of these names may not be familiar, but in their day they represented the highest quality in sportswriting, including Dan Daniel, John Kieran, Fred Lieb, Paul Gallico, Richards Vidmer, Shirley Povich, Ford Frick (who would later serve as commissioner of baseball), John Drebinger, Red Smith, John R. Tunis, Jimmy Cannon, and Wendell Smith, who was perhaps the premier African American sports journalist in the era immediately before and after Jackie Robinson broke the color line.

Each profile is preceded by a brief introduction, and then Holtzman channels Lawrence Ritter as he probes his subjects about the highlights and difficult moments of their careers.

No Cheering was revised and expanded in 1995, with the restoration of eight writers who were dropped from the first edition.

Other category: History/Oral

140. *Prophet of the Sandlots: Journeys with a Major League Scout*, by Mark Winegardner. New York: Prentice Hall, 1990.

For want of a nail, the horseshoe was lost . . .

For want of a scout, a potential Hall of Famer was lost. That's the idea behind books like Winegardner's classic on the profession.

The prophet of this story is Tony Lucadello, a failed ballplayer who couldn't give up on the game. In a scouting career that spanned almost fifty years, he signed fifty ballplayers who eventually made it to the Majors with the Cubs and Phillies, including future Hall of Famers Ferguson Jenkins and Mike Schmidt.

But in Lucadello's profession, you can't rest on your laurels. It's a constant road trip; you're always looking for that next great player, the one with the physical and mental fortitude to work his way up the ladder.

Winegardner isn't your usual journalist who needs to separate himself from his subject. He befriends Lucadello, empathizing with the veteran scout, who was in his midseventies at the time of their meeting and still carrying on, as he accompanies him on his last year on the job.

Not every prospect Lucadello meets is bound for a pro career, but he treats all the young men, as well as their coaches and families, with respect while trying to serve his bosses and come up with the next big star. The term used to describe a scout's job (and the name of a 1982 book by Frank Dolson) is "beating the bushes," and one can envision Lucadello and his peers whacking the shrubbery with sticks, hopeful that a five-tool player will emerge.

The book has a bittersweet feel throughout that's made all the more realistic by its surprise ending.

Other category: Business

Also by the author: *The Veracruz Blues* (1996)

141. *Scouting Reports: The Original Review of Some of Baseball's Greatest Stars*, by Stan Hart. New York: Macmillan, 1995.

Before any player is signed as a pro, he is examined by several front-office people to see if he's even worth a contract.

Baseball scouts stake their reputations and livelihoods on the ability to find that diamond in the rough, the one who will beat the long odds.

The difference maker between this book and others about the profession is the reproduction of original player evaluations, which vary from complex forms in more recent years to a much simpler narrative format, such as the one submitted on behalf of Willie Mays. It's hard to believe that some less-enlightened gentlemen didn't even think him worthy of being offered a tryout.

Hart also includes informal comments from scouts on a handful of players such as Ken Griffey Jr., Pete Rose, Mike Schmidt, Frank Thomas, and others. The book concludes with brief profiles of a few of scouts the author felt deserved special recognition for this mostly anonymous job.

Other categories: Analysis, Auto/Bio/Mem, Business

142. *Sweet Spot: 125 Years of Baseball and the Louisville Slugger,* by Dave Magee and Philip Shirley. Chicago: Triumph, 2009.

There are thousands of books about the players, but without the bats the game would be little more than a painful version of punchball.

This large-format edition highlights the legendary company that has provided the most essential piece of equipment, other than the ball itself, for more than one hundred years. As such, Hillerich and Bradsby, the company that turns out thousands of Sluggers a year, has a right to crow a bit.

Sweet Spot traces the evolution of the company and the relationship it has enjoyed with professional baseball and some of the best hitters in the game. Like a family album, they proudly show off, with photos of Ted Williams, one of the most astute judges of lumber, visiting the factory. Other All-Star and Hall of Famer clients include Ken Griffey Jr., Steve Garvey, Tony Gwynn, and Pee Wee Reese. In fact, until relatively recently, Louisville Slugger was the only game in town before companies like Mizuno, Easton, Adirondack, and a handful of others came on the scene.

For those interested in back stories, *Sweet Spot* is an excellent selection to learn more about what goes into producing the instruments that make a quality hitter perform like a concert musician.

Other category: History

5
Business

I would venture to say that many fans don't really want to know too much about the business aspects of sports. Taxes, bond structures to build a stadium, antitrust issues — the eyes glaze over. We just want to be left alone to enjoy the game, without considering the nuts and bolts of what it takes to bring the product to the field.

Well, it may not be the most exciting stuff, but the well-read fan should probably know a few of the basics, if only to appreciate how the modern game got to this point. Several books explain the business of baseball without being mind-numbingly dull, and, in fact, a little knowledge goes a long way in bringing about a new appreciation for how complicated it all is.

143. *Baseball and Billions: A Probing Look into the Big Business of Our National Pastime,* by Andrew Zimbalist. New York: Basic, 1994.

Zimbalist, one of the preeminent writers on sports and economics, produced one of the more cogent books on the business of baseball. He covers multiple topics, all of which pertain to the transformation of the sport from an amateur pastime to a multibillion-dollar enterprise.

Beginning with a concise history of labor and management since the late 1870s, Zimbalist takes the reader on a journey where no item is too small for consideration or too large that it can't be explained in basic terms that you don't have to be an economics major to comprehend.

In addition to issues one would expect to find in a book like this — player compensation, free agency, the reserve clause, the owners' collusion in the early 1980s — Zimbalist adds a brief chapter on the Minor Leagues, which he maintains is an inefficient way to develop players, both in terms of the money spent on affiliates and how poorly the players are compensated and trained.

Zimbalist also discusses how the host city influences and in turn is influenced by having a team. How much does New York benefit from the Yankees, and what do the Bronx Bombers get from playing in the largest market in the United States? This segues nicely into a chapter on the role of the media in adding to the teams' coffers through broadcasting rights.

The 1994 reissue adds a postscript covering events of the 1992–93 seasons. I'm a bit surprised he hasn't come out with a new book covering the aftermath of the 1994–95 strike and the effect it had on the business of baseball.

Other category: Classic

Also by the author: *May the Best Team Win: Baseball Economics and Public Policy* (2004); *In the Best Interests of the Game: The Remarkable Reign of Bud Selig* (2007).

144. *The Baseball Player: An Economic Study*, by Paul M. Gregory. Washington DC: Public Affairs Press, 1956.

A famous what-if scenario has Joe DiMaggio in his prime visiting Yankees owner George Steinbrenner to discuss a new contract in the age of free agency and atmospheric salaries. When Steinbrenner asks what amount DiMaggio had in mind, he merely answers, "Hello, partner."

Gregory, an economist and social philosopher, published *The Baseball Player* at a time when the average salary was about $13,000, with the highest amounts going to superstars like Ted Williams and Stan Musial at just over $100,000.

The prescient author discusses issues that weren't big concerns in the mid-1950s, such as player representation. One chapter that would be practically a non sequitur today considers off-season activities. Now a team worries about a player being injured in a pick-up basketball game; fifty years ago, owners feared for some sort of industrial accident, since it was commonplace for even the elite athletes to have off-season jobs.

When it comes to facts, figures, and issues, the book has a na-ïveté that registers high on the nostalgia factor. At the same time, it reminds us that baseball has always been a business, even in an era when a ballclub was more often owned by a family than a corporation.

145. *Big League, Big Times: The Birth of the Arizona Diamondbacks, the Billion-Dollar Business of Sports, and the Power of the Media in Baseball,* by Len Sherman. New York: Pocket, 1998.

146. *Playing Hardball: The High-Stakes Battle for Baseball's New Franchises,* by David Whitford. New York: Doubleday, 1993.

Lovers of baseball, politics, and business will find these two titles of great interest. Whitford and Sherman go behind the scenes to re-port on the scores of tiny details that go into transforming a Major League franchise from pipe dream to reality.

For politicians, getting a team to play in your city is like a dog chasing a car. You think you want it and you make a lot of noise about it, but what do you do when you actually get it? It's a tremen-dous expense even before you sign your first player. The Rockies and Marlins had to pony up ninety-five million dollars in franchise fees just to get into the National League.

In *Playing Hardball,* Whitford divides his narrative between the politicians and the competing groups of prospective owners for the Miami-based Florida Marlins and the Colorado Rockies (Denver), scheduled to open for business in 1993. Both cities had hosted suc-cessful Minor League franchises; now the stakes were substantially greater.

Big League, Big Times focuses on the Diamondbacks from the day the franchise was awarded through the end of their first spring training two years later. Sherman covers all aspects of putting a team together from the bottom up, beginning with the hiring of Buck Showalter as manager as the first official act, almost three years before the Dbacks' first Opening Day.

One concept that's often lost in the euphoria of getting a team is the value of civic pride versus economic cost for the host city. Obviously, not every local resident is a baseball or sports fan who's 100 percent behind the project, especially when it means additional tax burdens since owners practically never pay for their own stadiums anymore.

Showalter has a reputation as a manager with a short leash, so it's most interesting to read about the numerous rules imposed on the new team, including their appearance, deportment, and play on the field. Something obviously worked—the team won the NL West title in just their second year. Unfortunately, he was fired after a third-place finish in 2000.

Other category: History/Team

147. *Coming Apart at the Seams: How Baseball Owners, Players, and Television Executives Have Led Our National Pastime to the Brink of Disaster,* by John Sands and Peter Gammons. New York: Macmillan, 1993.

This amazingly prophetic book came out the year before the most devastating strike in Major League history. Not even World War II had been able to cancel the postseason, but this catastrophe, which most fans hoped and expected would be resolved quickly, had the concurrent effect of killing a lot of goodwill, as many fans turned their backs on the national pastime, if not forever then for a long time.

The writing team of Sands, a sports attorney, and Gammons, a noted baseball broadcaster and journalist, brings an interesting perspective as they engagingly report on the labor difficulties, which started at the beginning 1990s and they effects they could, and did, have on the game.

The issues involved—mismanagement of resources, a thinning talent pool, disregard for the fans in deference to the demands of television—are still relevant and even more dire today, given the current economic situation.

This is not an examination of the aftermath; this was a warning of things to come, which everyone ignored. It's a pity; if *Coming Apart* had been published a year or two earlier and the right people had read it, maybe a lot of the tsuris could have been avoided.

Other categories: Analysis, History

148. *The Diamond Revolution: The Prospects for Baseball After the Collapse of Its Ruling Class,* by Neil J. Sullivan. New York: St. Martin's Press, 1992.

According to Sullivan, an associate professor of public administration at Baruch College in New York, those prospects mentioned in the book's title were a bit shaky. After citing several historical problems with the game—from the exclusions of African-American players, to the detriment of several teams' fortunes; to the folly of expansion which puts an inferior product on the field and earns the indifference of its fans; to the hypocrisy of letting alcohol companies sponsor teams while at the same time paying lip service for the need to drink responsibly—Sullivan decries the disharmony among the owners, who, unlike the players standing solidly together under the umbrella of their union, have little in the way of common interests other than in the aggregate. In an industry where they control everything, the owners have no inclination to stick together.

To whom do we refer when we talk about protecting the game for the sake of self-interest? asks Sullivan. And who is the *self*? The commissioner's office has traditionally made decisions based on the best interests of the game, but to whom does that apply?

The author wraps up with a weak hope that future generations will continue to celebrate the great game of baseball, but based on the rest of the book, it's clear he's not too optimistic.

Also by the author: *The Minors: The Struggles and the Triumph of Baseball's Poor Relation from 1876 to The Present* (1990); *Diamond in the Bronx: Yankee Stadium and the Politics of New York* (2001)

149. *Dollar Sign on the Muscle: The World of Baseball Scouting,* by Kevin Kerrane. New York: Beaufort, 1984.

Written in the pre-*Moneyball* days, Kerrane sheds a lot of light on scouting, an underrepresented side of the baseball world.

More than a few of these grizzled veteran scouts were players themselves, and failed players for the most part. But they had an eye for talent and a bit of a psychologist's mind. They could tell if a kid wanted to go to the pros rather than college and would therefore be more amenable to signing for less money.

They also know you can't tell how good a player is on paper; charts and statistics go only so far and can even change from one report to the next. (Sorry, Michael Lewis.) Everyone's circumstance is different. Smith might be a .400 batter, but what kind of pitching did he face, in what kind of ballpark, in what kind of climate? What's his home life like? Some things you can see with your eyes, the saying goes, and others you can't. All these factors come into play, especially these days with such big money at stake.

One of the more interesting chapters divulges the secret language employed by scouts, using a Harvard pitcher named Ron Darling as the subject for the vocabulary lesson. Part oral history, part business management, *Dollar Sign* — included in a 2002 *Sports Illustrated* list of the best sports books — is a classic that could make for an interesting revised edition.

Other categories: Behind the Scenes, Classic, History

150. *The Extra 2%: How Wall Street Strategies Took a Major League Baseball Team from Worst to First,* by Jonah Keri. New York: Ballantine, 2011.

According to business primers, the extra 2 percent refers to the one-step-further philosophy a company has to be willing to implement in order to win over the customer. That was the attitude for a couple of Wall Streeters who became majority partners in the Tampa Bay Devil Rays, one of the worst in a history of bad expansion teams.

The Devil Rays joined the American League in 1998. The original owner was a penny-pinching, shortsighted curmudgeon who was always looking to cut corners at the expense of the fans while ill-advisedly overpaying for high-profile but low-performing players.

The new ownership, which took control in 2005, envisioned a kinder, gentler regime. By employing a combination of common-sense policies and bold business models, the Rays (they went so far as to drop the "Devil") were able to reinvent and rebrand themselves, winning back fans by making the ballpark a more user-friendly environment. That was business smarts; the field smarts led to the acquisition of the low-cost, high-quality players that would catapult them from the cellar to the pennant—in fact, all the way to the World Series—by 2008. And that's with a budget substantially smaller than those of their division rivals, the New York Yankees and Boston Red Sox.

Keri does a nice job of mixing the baseball with the business so that those more interested in one topic will not be put off by the other.

151. *Getting in the Game: Inside Baseball's Winter Meetings,* by Josh Lewin. Washington DC: Brassey's, 2004.

Fans are always anxious to hear the latest news from baseball's winter meetings, but there's always more than just wheeling and dealing going on. Like any convention, there are entrepreneurs hawking their newest inventions, established companies showing off their latest wares, and people looking for front-office jobs in the national pastime at a job fair held over three days in Nashville in 2002.

Lewin, a regional announcer for FOX Sports and the TV voice for the Texas Rangers (he now does radio for the New York Mets), follows three such hopefuls as they hunt down that elusive opportunity. Do they realize what they're in for? Long hours, low pay, agita . . . If they do know, do they care? Not really. All they want is a chance.

There's certainly more to *Getting in the Game,* however. Lewin presents a good deal of background into the never-ending demands that are staples of Minor League ball, the best opportunity for dewy-eyed newcomers to break into the field.

The book is presented in a journal format. The various time stamps give a slight indication of the 24-7 lunacy involved. But this is the type of schedule all of the applicants — and there are lots of them vying for a handful of positions — are willing to deal with.

Nervous humor is the best way to describe the action. Lewin tries to keep things light, but there's almost a do-or-die feeling for this trio. Will they achieve their goals, or, like game-show contestants, head home without the prize? The answers might surprise, which makes this behind-the-scenes story worth the time.

Other category: Behind the Scenes

152. *Going, Going, Gone!: The Art of the Trade in Major League Baseball,* by Fran Zimniuch. Dallas: Taylor Trade, 2008.

Strictly speaking, Zimniuch is not talking just about trades here. He's addressing all the types of transactions that make following baseball so interesting. As spring training progresses, rumors abound as fans wonder if their favorite team will make any moves. The same excitement builds around the July 31 interleague trading deadline. Will a struggling team part with a high-salaried player? Will a veteran All-Star in his declining years be transferred to a new employer?

Going differs from other books on the topic in that rather than offering a list or assessment of transactions, it concentrates on behind-the-scenes issues. For example, the reserve clause bound the player to his respective team in perpetuity, taking all control — save for retirement — out of his hands. The author then goes into discourse on the evolution of free agency, beginning with Curt Flood but reminding us that there were other pioneers involved, including pitchers Andy Messersmith and Dave McNally. The answer to a great trivia question: All-Star Dick Allen was the player for whom Flood was traded.

But it's not all heavy emotion and history here. Zimniuch keeps his book entertaining with tales of wacky trades, like this: one player was swapped for ten pounds of catfish as part of the deal.

Other category: History

153. *License to Deal: A Season on the Run with a Maverick Baseball Agent,* by Jerry Crasnick. Emmaus PA: Rodale, 2005.

Crasnick, a writer for ESPN.com, produced one of the best books that peers inside the inner world of this often-vilified profession.

It's amazing how Jerry McGuire–like these stories are. The agents undercut each other as they attempt to lure potential clients or employ hardball negotiating tactics with the teams or companies who wish to engage the player for anything from product endorsements to bar mitzvah appearances.

Crasnick devotes the main focus of *License* to Matt Scosnick, who gave up a steady position as the CEO of a California high-tech company in the late 1990s for the erratic life of an agent. We follow him as he swims through the proverbial shark-infested waters, trying to find money and opportunity for his marquee client, Dontrelle Willis, at the time an up-and-coming pitcher for the Florida Marlins.

The narrative features some of the highest-profile names in the business, like Scott Boras and Jeff Morad, and exposes the ups and downs of the job: trying to be all things to all people, scrambling to find new clients on their way up the ladder, and keeping them once they attain a certain level of success.

The author also takes time to pay his respects to the pioneers of the players' movement, like Marvin Miller and Jerry Kapstein, whom many players and agents seem to have forgotten.

Other categories: Analysis, Behind the Scenes

154. *Moneyball: The Art of Winning an Unfair Game,* by Michael Lewis. New York: W. W. Norton, 2003.

Lewis, whose previous books focused primarily on financial matters, turned his attention to the machinations of baseball's front offices in this classic.

When Billy Beane, general manager of the Oakland Athletics, decided to incorporate sabermetrics — esoteric statistics designed to predict trends of draft-eligible players — into the team's decisions, he was ridiculed by old-school veterans who went by "the book" (which actually isn't a book at all but a consensus held by baseball veterans developed over years of experience). Beane and his assistants concluded after tireless research that it was more advantageous to build their team around batters who were patient at the plate and could work out a walk and get on base often, instead of relying on sluggers to hit a three-run homer. Beane's process also favored control pitchers rather than those who could throw a ball through a brick wall. And best of all, since these players were often overlooked by other teams, they could be signed on the cheap.

Since the A's had some initial success in the early aughts, other teams began to emulate Beane's philosophy, with varying results.

Moneyball, which was released as a feature film starring Brad Pitt and Jonah Hill in 2011, spent twenty weeks on the *New York Times* best-seller list and was the recipient of the 2003 CASEY Award from *Spitball* magazine.

> Other categories: Analysis, Award Winner, Classic, History/Team, *New York Times* Best Seller, Pop Culture

155. *Never Just a Game: Players, Owners, and American Baseball to 1920*, by Robert F. Burk. Chapel Hill: University of North Carolina Press, 1994.

156. *Much More Than Just a Game: Players, Owners, and American Baseball Since 1921*, by Robert F. Burk. Chapel Hill: University of North Carolina Press, 2001.

How sad it is that what was devised as a pleasant day's friendly competition among men had to evolve into such a business, with animosity building between those who played and those who owned from the get-go.

Burk, a professor and chair of the history department at Muskingum University, published these two authoritative volumes that focus primarily on the game behind the game, in which owners for the most part sought to exert the most control possible, whether it was via minimum or maximum salaries, the reserve clause, or monopolistic practices protected by tacit congressional approval.

The second volume tilts the bottom line in favor of the athletes, as Marvin Miller strengthened the players' union to an almost obscene level, which detracted from the sympathy fans might have had for them generations ago.

Burk tells this history with an almost biblical foreboding (the final chapter in *Much More* carries the title "Armageddon"), as events fall into line, which may well prove to bring the national pastime crashing to ruin. Unlike many books of this type, the author does not offer suggestions on how to fix the problems, which makes his work all the more depressing.

Other category: History

157. *Traded: The Most Lopsided Trades in Baseball History*, by Doug Decatur. Skokie IL: ACTA Sports, 2009.

Prior to Decatur's book, most publications on this topic were mostly anecdotal with a few rudimentary statistics thrown in as a means of comparing the players involved in the deal. You would always hear about steals like Lou Brock for Ernie Broglio or Nolan Ryan for Jim Fregosi. But until now there was no definitive book analyzing the true injustice of the transactions through arithmetic.

Traded employs the simple sabermetric "win shares" to determine the best and worst deals, which considers how much the principals involved contributed to their new employers with "net future win shares" used as the determining factor. Don't worry—it's actually not as complex as most new-generation stats.

The most lopsided trade, according to the Decatur's research, was the 1991 deal in which the Houston Astros received outfielder Steve Finley and pitchers Pete Harnish and Curt Schilling in exchange for first baseman Glenn Davis from the Baltimore Orioles. Even given that it was a three-for-one swap, Davis came up woefully short in Baltimore, with a future value (FV) of just 12, compared with 621 for the Astros' additions. The next worst? The Red Sox's sale of Babe Ruth to the Yankees, which netted them nothing but the cash, while the Sultan of Swat had an FV of 576.

After a list of more than three hundred deals, Decatur analyzes each team's success in the trade business. The Indians come out on top, with the Athletics on the bottom. He also provides some anecdotal material about some of the strangest transactions of all time, including the Fritz Peterson–Mike Kekich "family trade" in 1973.

Other categories: Analysis, Statistics

6

Fiction

I find fiction the hardest category for which to offer suggestions. It's such a subjective area. You say toe-may-toe, I say toe-mah-toe. Some readers love W. P. Kinsella (author of Shoeless Joe, among others), while others find him too sentimental and overrated. The same could be said for Mark Harris, author of the Southpaw Trilogy that includes Bang the Drum Slowly, as well as Bernard Malamud, author of The Natural. I've tried to pay homage to those classics while at the same time bringing to light a variety of authors and subgenres that the casual baseball reader might have missed.

158. *The Annotated Baseball Stories of Ring W. Lardner, 1914–1919*, edited by George W. Hilton. Stanford: Stanford University Press, 1995.

Lardner, one of the legendary sportswriters of the early twentieth century, had a unique way with language, especially in his fiction. His Jack Keefe character (featured in *You Know Me, Al* and "Alibi Ike") was a naïf, a good-natured doofus who was not so much an egomaniac as just very self-assured. Ten short stories featuring Keefe are included in this six-hundred-plus page collection, along with another dozen tales.

The annotations in this volume go a long way in parsing Lardner's elaborate prose and dialogue, incorporating real-life events and characters the author throws in for authenticity, as well as the lingo of the era.

Lardner adapted some of these stories for a couple of Joe E. Brown movies in the mid-1930s, including *Elmer the Great* and *Alibi Ike*. Brown, a staunch baseball fan, does an excellent job of translating the character to the big screen.

Other category: Classic

159. *The Art of Fielding: A Novel,* by Chad Harbach. New York: Little, Brown, 2011.

The favorable reviews, which compared this debut novel to the works of Malamud, Harris, and Kinsella, started coming in before it even hit the stores. The fact that Harbach received a $650,000 advance for the manuscript only added to the buzz.

The Art of Fielding focuses on a college shortstop who just may be the best player of his generation. That is, until the inevitable turn of events causes a crisis of faith not just for him, but for the book's supporting cast: his teammate mentor, who has a few secrets of his own; the gay roommate (likewise); the college president, ditto. Come to think of it, secrets are a big part of the novel.

Does it live up to the hype? Should it indeed be mentioned in the same breath as the other classics of baseball fiction? Is it even a book about baseball? (Are *any* of them really about baseball, since the game is the archetypal metaphor?) Opinions may differ, but *The Art of Fielding* is a must-read, if only to lay these questions to rest.

160. *Baseball Fantastic,* edited by W. P. Kinsella. Kingston ON: Quarry Press, 2000.

The author of *Shoeless Joe* returns to baseball short fiction here, editing and contributing two pieces to this collection of ambitiously bizarre ideas. The stories at times take on a *Twilight Zone* atmosphere; you almost expect to hear Rod Serling rendering his trademark stentorian introductions.

Among the topics: the dangers of time travel, the unlikely combination of the undead and little league, communications with legendary baseball spirits, and a player's ability to control the game's physical environment, which wreaks havoc on the notion of a level playing field.

Kinsella's contributions are "The Franchise," a yarn about an alternative universe in which George H. W. Bush and Cuban leader Fidel Castro face off as antagonistic opponents in the 1959 World Series, and "The Indestructible Hadrian Wilks," which offers a not-unreasonable explanation for Cal Ripken Jr.'s longevity.

As with many assemblages like this one, the stories in *Fantastic* are hit or miss, but the wildly eccentric eccentricity of Kinsella's selections is part of what endears him to his fans.

161. *Brittle Innings*, by Michael Bishop. New York: Bantam, 1994.

Part *Moby Dick*, part *Biloxi Blues*, part *Of Mice and Men*, but mostly *Frankenstein*, *Brittle Innings* features a ragtag collection of athletes who bond in the common raison d'etre of baseball.

Set during World War Two, shortstop Danny Boles (call him Ishmael?) joins the Minor League Highbridge Hellbenders. There he meets some oddball teammates, as was the norm since most able-bodied men were in the service, including "Jumbo" Hank Cerval (Queequeg?), who is as erudite and mannered as he is frightening in appearance: a giant with multiple scars, who "seems to have put together in a meat-packing plant" (62). His violence at the plate, however, mirrors the favored metaphor of the dark side.

Boles—who spends most of the novel voiceless as the result of a beating sustained on his way to camp—and Cerval come to respect each other, but situations conspire to make sure that Jumbo continues to find no peace.

This quirky novel has not received nearly enough attention. Bishop received the Locus Award for Best Science Fiction Novel in 1995, and was nominated for several other honors that year. An obvious choice for a feature film, *Brittle Innings* was, in fact, purchased by 20th Century Fox in 1995 but remains unmade.

Other categories: Award Winner, Classic, Underrated

162. *The Celebrant,* by Eric Rolfe Greenberg. New York: Everest House, 1983.

Greenberg's novel has been a favorite of literature professors for years for its elegant stylings and of baseball fans for its attention to detail.

The Celebrant revolves around the unlikely relationship between Jake Kapp (née Yakov Kapinski), a Jewish jewelry designer, and his idol, Christy Mathewson, the pitching ace of the New York, who was considered the epitome of a Christian gentleman. Each time the Giants win the pennant and/or World Series, Kapp is the man to see to design rings worthy of champions.

The narrative follows both men over several years as they prosper in their respective fields. Kapp works with his brother, Eli, who's much more extroverted and a bit of an operator, and Mathewson is on his way to the Hall of Fame—and, sadly, an early grave as the result of a World War I training exercise gone awry.

Opinions differ as to the main theme of the story: Is it hero worship? Homoerotic fascination? Assimilation? Like many Jews of the early twentieth century, the Kapp brothers reject the ways of their parents and the old country. Whatever it is, *The Celebrant* is a classic that many reviewers have placed at or near the top of the list as the best baseball novel.

The Celebrant won *Spitball* magazine's first CASEY Award in 1983.

Other categories: Award Winner, Classic

163. *The End of Baseball,* by Peter Schilling Jr. Chicago: Ivan R. Dee, 2008.

What if the rumors were true? What if Bill Veeck, baseball's über-maverick, had been secretly planning to break the color line not to just with one African American, but an entire team of them? How would *that* sit with the lords of baseball?

How do you think, in those lily-white days? Schilling realistically creates such a scenario in 1944 America, with Judge Landis still toeing the line by keeping the door closed without instituting an official prohibition, with J. Edgar Hoover trying to figure out Veeck's Communist angle, and with newsman and social commentator Walter Winchell whispering in President Roosevelt's ear as his "good conscience."

Even the black players who would be Major Leaguers have their doubts. Some think things are fine as they are and are almost contemptuous of organized baseball as antithetical to their style of competition, while others are chomping at the bit to show what they can do.

And poor Veeck, master showman that he is, stands on the precipice. What will it be: personal ruin and disgrace, or success that has much broader implications on American society? Schilling keeps readers guessing with some unexpected twists that make *The End of Baseball*—the novel's doomsayers warning if an all-black major League team came to pass—a classic.

164. *Extra Innings: A Story for the Aged,* by Lane Strauss. Raleigh NC: Lulu, 2011.

If you think contemporary ballgames—with their constant pitching changes and hitters stepping out of the box to adjust their batting gloves—seem to go on forever, get a load of this: a contest between the Cleveland Indians and Detroit Tigers that began in 1947 and was still going strong in 2011.

The affair has gone on so long that it's distracted to the point where the rest of pro baseball has shut down. These players—now deep into their AARP benefits—are still as feisty and competitive as ever, even if they need canes and walkers to chase (if that term is appropriate) after the ball.

Strauss takes into consideration today's shorter attention span by limiting his chapters to a page or two at most, telling this raucous tale from several first-person viewpoints. Warning: the language is definitely not PG-13.

165. *The Great American Novel,* by Philip Roth. New York: Holt, Rinehart and Winston, 1973.

With his typical tongue-in-cheek style, Roth employs the trope of the old sportswriter looking back over his long career to tell the story of the pitiful Port Ruppert Mundys, a team so downtrodden that they have to vacate their home stadium in New Jersey for the war effort in the 1940s. Luke Gofannon, Mike Mazda, and Smokey Woden are the Patriot League equivalent of Ruth, Gehrig, and Cobb. But the modern world will never know their names, because all records of the existence of this third Major League have been expunged, Communist Russia–style, as the result of a major scandal.

This gem is often overlooked in discussions of the best baseball novels, due to the constant praise heaped on the works of Malamud, Harris, and Kinsella. Roth received mixed reviews for TGAN. Those who looked at it strictly from a literary standpoint were a bit harsh, opining the author tried too hard to combine his usual biting insight with the world of baseball, while others with a more relaxed view enjoyed it as a good, if somewhat lengthy, yarn for grownups, something that remains a rare animal when it comes to great American novels about the national pastime.

Other category: Classic

166. *If I Never Get Back: A Novel,* by Darryl Brock. New York: Crown, 1990.

There was an episode in the original *Twilight Zone* in which a man, harried by the burdens of his life, finds himself transported to a simpler era when his commuter train somehow goes back in time.

Darryl Brock turns that theme into a baseball novel with his story of Sam Fowler, who is unhappy about his job, his failed marriage, and the recent death of his father. His journey takes him back to the Cincinnati Reds of 1869, baseball's first professional team.

Putting aside the incredulity of the situation and the ensuing culture shock, Fowler summons up his baseball skills to become a member of the team. How will he be able to adjust to his new circumstances, and can he find a way to return to his former (future) life? After he's lived there awhile, a bigger question emerges: Does he even want to?

Brock uses his background as a history and English teacher to weave this fantasy, with great attention to the particulars of nineteenth-century language and mores, as he puts Fowler in this fish-out-of-water situation.

Also by the author: *Havana Heat* (2000)

167. *Japanese Baseball and Other Stories*, by W. P. Kinsella. Saskatoon SK: Thistledown Press, 2000.

This collection of short stories marked Kinsella's return to the baseball quick read after an absence of several years.

The entries range from wry to melancholy. Many are full of disappointment over lost opportunities, in the game of life as well as the sport. In some instances, baseball seems merely to serve as an arbitrary setting for the theme. In both "Tulips" and "Understanding Lynn Johannsen," for example, the protagonists could just as easily have been football players or wrestlers.

In this collection, Kinsella's voice has matured somewhat from the comparatively youthful exuberance of his earlier work, which in many ways could be compared with that of Garrison Keillor: folksy, anecdotal, and gently humorous. Several of his new stories take on darker, more weary and resigned tones. Is this a sign of the Kinsella's advancing age and outlook?

The author whisks his readers from America's heartland to the impoverished streets of Latin America to the spectacular mountains of the Far East. In the title story, "Japanese Baseball," the hero is anything but an ugly American, as he wins the heart of a Japanese maid who also happens to be the daughter of his team's general manager. Rather than the usual anti-*gaijin* sentiments, his overtures are most welcome — and therein lies a disturbing family secret.

Two other noteworthy pieces are "The Kowloon Cafe," which is probably the first time the term *feng shui* appears in a story about baseball, and "The Indestructible Hadrian Wilks," a Cal Ripken–esque tale with a *Dorian Gray* twist; this piece also appears in *Baseball Fantastic,* for which Kinsella served as editor and contributor.

Stories of resignation can be found in "The Arbiter," about an umpire who must decide between his profession and his family; "The Lime Tree," in which two elderly friends confront memories of lost loved ones; and "Wavelengths," another buddy piece, which follows two Minor League teammates headed in different directions.

168. *Man on Spikes,* by Eliot Asinof. Carbondale: Southern Illinois University Press, 1998.

First published in 1955 by McGraw-Hill, *Man on Spikes* tells the jarring and spot-on story of Mike Kutner, a career Minor Leaguer who just can't seem to catch a break. His ascendancy to the Majors is blocked by military service during World War II, playing at a time when it was beneficial for clubs to promote African American players, injury, and even laboring under the stereotype that good athletes don't wear glasses.

The sad story unfolds over fourteen chapters, each of which focuses on a single person who played an integral role in Kutner's development or a acted as a roadblock to his success.

Kutner was based on Asinof's friend and real-life Major Leaguer Mickey Rutner, who at least had the good fortune to appear in twelve games for the Philadelphia Athletics in 1947. Asinof himself was a Minor Leaguer but his manager's anti-Semitism made him reconsider his career options.

Man on Spikes was reprinted with a new foreword by Marvin Miller as part of the Southern Illinois University Press's Writing Baseball series.

Other category: Classic

169. *Murder at Fenway Park,* by Troy Soos. New York: Kensington, 1994.

Meet Mickey Rawlings, an early-twentieth-century utility man who has just joined the Boston Red Sox. While he may not be a star on the field, he is a whiz at detecting, which is immediately put to the test when he discovers a corpse in the bowels of the then brand-new ballpark.

Murder at Fenway Park was the first in a series. Other volumes had Rawlings as a member of the Chicago Cubs, Cincinnati Reds, and the Detroit Tigers. As a journeyman, he was able to move about with a more realistic anonymity than if Babe Ruth had been the featured sleuth.

Soos, a high school teacher, seamlessly blends in real players of the day, including Ty Cobb and Casey Stengel, who serves as an unlikely Watson to Rawlings's Holmes, among others. The author's attention to detail—for example, studying old city maps and weather reports—goes a long way in adding authenticity to the stories, which also address some of the important topics of the day, such as anti-German sentiment during World War I and the Ku Klux Klan and race relations in Detroit.

Soos had planned to publish a Rawlings novel for each of the original sixteen Major League teams, but that ambition fell through because each book required so much research.

170. *Murderers' Row: Baseball Mysteries,* edited by Otto Penzler. Beverly Hills: New Millennium Press, 2002.

Thirteen writers contributed to this unusual collection, teaming up baseball with mysteries to make for a unique doubleheader in this anthology of original works.

Among the highlights: Troy Soos and Max Allen Collins serve up their specialties: historical fiction. Soos does this via his signature character, Mickey Rawlings, and Collins writes about the "murder" of Eddie Gaedel, the midget hired by Bill Veeck as a publicity stunt in 1951.

Elmore Leonard offers another odd-ball yarn in his story of an ex-ballplayer with a gift for gab (if not the talent to back it up) looking for a job. Veteran sports columnist/young adult novelist Mike Lupica takes a decidedly more adult turn with a latter-day Ralph Branca/Bobby Thomson showdown with the proverbial twist.

What makes for a good mystery? Well-developed scenarios and a surprise ending, mostly, and in that, *Murders' Row* is a bit uneven. But then, it's not easy trying to squeeze it all the requisite components into a baseball theme in a short-story format.

Other category: Anthology

171. *The Natural,* by Bernard Malamud, New York: Harcourt, 1952.

The granddaddy of adult baseball fiction, *The Natural* is one of the most written-about works in modern literature, both in general examinations and in baseball anthologies that discuss fiction. Yet it only enjoyed a single week on the *New York Times* best-seller list.

Roy Hobbs got his first taste of glory in an exhibition of skill against a Ruthian batter known as the Whammer. Hobbs was Ted Williams, in that he wanted to be regarded as the best who ever played. He was also Eddie Waitkus, who was shot by a crazed female fan. And he was Shoeless Joe Jackson as well, for his conduct that undermined all the values of fair play. As you can see, there are many parallels with the actual game.

Space does not permit an extended deconstruction here. Suffice it to say that it is much darker than the Robert Redford feature film of 1984. *The Natural* has been described as a book about mythology, daddy issues, mommy issues, abandonment, religion (Hobbs's wise and caring manager, Pop Fisher can be read as the fisher king), and death and resurrection. Hobbs plays for the Knights and is on a quest for glory as well as the pennant. But he is not the gallant sort as portrayed in the film version. He's meaner, more selfish, and does not enjoy a happy Hollywood ending.

However you care to interpret it, *The Natural* is a staple when talking about the best baseball fiction. It appeared on the *New York*

Times best-seller list in 1984 — the year the movie came out — and was ranked twenty-fourth out of the one hundred best sports books in a 2002 poll by *Sports Illustrated* editors. What's most amazing is that this was Malamud's first novel.

Other categories: *New York Times* Best Seller, Classic

172. *Play for a Kingdom*, by Thomas Dyja. New York: Harcourt Brace, 1997.

Baseball was just taking its first wobbly steps on the way to becoming the national game when the Civil War broke out, and Dyja seeks to convey the sport's importance as a respite in troubling times.

When a company of Union troops from Brooklyn chances upon a clear patch of green in Spotsylvania, as yet unsullied by the bodies of the dead and wounded, they see it as the perfect way to blow off some steam amid the carnage. Unfortunately, a band of soldiers from Alabama has the same idea. Everyone is tired from the fighting and they wearily and warily broach the idea of taking time out for paradise, as Bart Giamatti would say more than one hundred years later, and play a little baseball. A solitary contest turns into a series of games, with both teams trying to hold on to a fragile peace, knowing that fraternizing with the enemy was punishable by death but still willing to take the chance.

Play for a Kingdom is no simple story of the magical curative powers of baseball; it is also a spy thriller, with the twists and turns endemic to the genre. Dyja's eye for detail is praiseworthy as he conveys the brutality of war, the old-time game, and the various ethnic groups that may have had their differences back in Brooklyn, but found themselves serving together, not unlike the bands of brothers portrayed in movies about World War II.

Play for a Kingdom is one of only two novels to win *Spitball* magazine's CASEY Award.

Other category: Award Winner

173. *The Redheaded Outfield and Other Baseball Stories*, by Zane Grey.
Avenel NJ: Gramercy, 1996.

Although better known for his tales of the old west, Grey was actually a Minor League player for a couple of seasons at the end of the nineteenth century. His keen eye prepared him well, and his experiences as a player brought credibility to his writings about the rough-and-tumble days on the ball field.

These early pieces depict the purity of the game at a time when there were few distractions from outside sources to get in the way, aside from the occasional gambler or — gasp — woman.

Four of the eleven stories employ the often-used device of the player who excels in his small-town surroundings, is scouted and signed to the big team, has trouble adjusting to his new situation (especially if it's in the big city), and takes a lot of abuse from teammates, opponents, and fans before coming through in the clutch, much to the relief of the manager, scout, or little tyke supporter who "knew it all along." As for the title piece, ballplayers were notorious for their superstitions, and a redheaded player, as an oddity, was perceived as a flake. So to have three of them patrolling the pasture surely gave their managers fits.

Because the copyright for *The Redheaded Outfield* has expired, it is readily available for free online reading.

Other category: Classic

174. *Safe at Home*, by Richard Doster. Colorado Springs: David C. Cook, 2008.

As amazing as it seems, some people still have the mistaken notion that when Jackie Robinson broke the color line in 1947, the road was cleared for subsequent African Americans players. But the first generation of black players assigned to minor league teams in small southern towns had it just as bad, if not worse, than Robinson.

Safe at Home looks at one such situation in the early 1950s, as one ball club, faced with dwindling attendance and in dire financial straits, must decide whether to take a substantial social risk and add a black player to its roster. On the one hand, it would show them to be forward thinking, and it would provide a curiosity factor that could bring more fans to the ballpark. On the other hand, such a bold move would set the young man up as a target — literally and figuratively — of outraged fans, opponents, and even members of his own team. Needless to say, it's a slow process as the newcomer struggles to make inroads and win acceptance.

As is often the case in such tales of morality, Doster uses an enterprising and upright journalist as the voice of reason, urging others to reconsider their long-held beliefs about race and station and to do the right thing against overwhelming prejudice and odds. That the reporter is white adds a patronizing quality that may rankle some readers.

One can easily picture this as a feature film aimed at teaching the virtues of tolerance to a younger audience.

175. *The Southpaw*, by Mark Harris. Indianapolis IN: Bobbs-Merrill, 1953.

176. *Bang the Drum Slowly*, by Mark Harris. New York, Knopf, 1956.

177. *A Ticket for a Seamstitch*, by Mark Harris. New York, Knopf, 1957.

Like Bernard Malamud, Harris's grown-up baseball novels were a radical departure from the Frank Merriwell stories for young readers. The players were often unheroic, petty, selfish, oafish, and mean, and they created a difficult environment for a pitcher like Henry "Author" Wiggen to conduct business.

The first novel, *The Southpaw*, introduces us to Wiggen, a cross between a pitching ace (like Tom Seaver) and a smart-ass aspiring writer (like Jim Bouton), who will soon become the savior of the lowly New York Mammoths. Author (because sports nicknames are so clever) writes in the first person, somewhat like Ring Lardner's characters, and he tells his story in language that could come straight off Lardner's typewriter. In the unenlightened days of the 1950s, anyone who showed a bit of intellect was looked on with suspicion, but Wiggen's ability on the mound gives him a pass among his teammates, who view him as merely eccentric.

Bang the Drum Slowly is no doubt the most popular of the three books because of the classic television and feature films that brought the story to a wider audience. Wiggen's final line — "From here on, I rag nobody" — is almost as famous to baseball lit fans as "Frankly, my dear, I don't give a damn" is to movie buffs.

Ticket for a Seamstitch, perhaps the weakest of the lot, considers an infatuated fan — a seamstress — who travels across the country to see Wiggen play, but the novel did make for a nice coda. That is, until Harris decided, some twenty years later, to publish *It Looked Like Forever*, a seriocomic look at Wiggen's final days in the game after a long and successful career.

Harris' books are perennially included on lists of best sports fiction — a 2002 *Sports Illustrated* poll listed *Bang the Drum Slowly* at number fourteen — and have been reprinted several times. A single-volume paperback of the trilogy was published by Bard Books in 1977.

Other category: Classic

178. *Tales of the Diamond: Selected Gems of Baseball Fiction*, edited by Laurence J. Hyman and Laura Thorpe. San Francisco: Woodford Press, 1991.

An old-fashioned sensibility runs through most of the short stories in *Tales of the Diamond*, with the writers representing a broad range of styles and topics. You expect to see a piece by W. P. Kinsella ("The Thrill of the Grass"), and even James Thurber ("You Can Look It Up"), but P. G. Woodhouse, the British author of the Jeeves and Wooster series? Damon Runyon and Paul Gallico got their starts at the sports-desk of daily newspapers before turning their attention to fiction. Roger Angell, on the other hand, is not usually associated with projects outside his *New Yorker* columns.

Other contributors include Garrison Keillor, with a yarn about the first woman to play in the pro men's league ("What Did We Do Wrong?"), Zane Grey on the game's most famous fan ("Old Well-Well"), and T. Coraghessan Boyle telling the bittersweet story of the fading career of a legendary Latin hero ("The Hector Quesadilla Story").

Kudos must also go to Miles Hyman, who did the illustrations; that must have been some challenging assignment.

Other category: Anthology

179. *Universal Baseball Association, Inc., J. Henry Waugh, Prop.*, by Robert Coover. New York: Random House, 1968.

If *UBA* had been written circa 1990, the protagonist, J. Henry Waugh, would probably be playing Dungeons and Dragons or Myst or some other video- or role-playing game. As it is, he's the poster boy for the fantasy baseball crowd, a savant representing everything that is right and wrong with that pastime — and quite prescient, considering how long ago the book came out.

Talk about your god complexes. The name of the association's commissioner can be phonetically reduced to Yahweh (JHWH) as he creates his little baseball world, which increasingly leads to the exclusion of work, family, and friends. The make-believe players become his family in an almost *Twilight Zone* fantasy world, as Waugh gradually extends his powers beyond the games to life and death over his creations. I would say a movie could be made from *UBA*, but the story of the obsessed loner fan has already been done.

UBA is right up there with *The Natural* and *The Celebrant* for most-analyzed works of baseball fiction, as it discusses religion, the blur between fantasy and reality, obsession, and, of course, madness. Madness!

The latest edition of *UBA* was published by Penguin in 2011.

180. *The Year the Yankees Lost the Pennant*, by Douglass Wallop. New York: W. W. Norton, 1954.

Faust meets fastball in this tale of Joe Boyd, a middle-aged fan of the Washington Senators who, tired of seeing his beloved team eternally finishing in last place, makes a pact with the devil: In exchange for the chance to be young again and a hero who will lead the 'Nats to a pennant over the hated New York Yankees, he will forfeit his eternal soul.

What will win out in the end: brief stardom as Joe Hardy, aka Shoeless Joe from Hannibal, Mo., or the love for Mrs. Boyd and the recognition of what really matters in life?

Wallop cowrote the book for the musical version, *Damn Yankees*, one of the classics of the Broadway stage. The play opened on Broadway in 1955 and won eight Tony Awards, including best musical, best leading actor (Ray Walston as the devil, Mr. Applegate) and actress (Gwen Verdon as the seductive Lola), and best choreography. Walston and Verdon would reprise their roles in the 1958 movie version, which was nominated for several honors as well.

Giving the original novel an extra kick is the dust jacket drawn by Willard Mullin, renown for his Dodger Bum caricatures for the New York tabloids.

Other category: Classic

7
History

*Like biographies, histories can be divided into scholarly and general categories.
This division ultimately boils down to notes and citations versus no notes or citations. Some focus on specific events—anniversaries of major events are particularly popular—while others look at a single team or era, such as the game as it
was played in the nineteenth century or during wartime.*

GENERAL

181. *The 10 Best Years of Baseball: An Informal History of the Fifties,* by
Harold Rosenthal. Chicago: Contemporary, 1979.

There are several titles that refer to baseball's golden years, but how
exactly is that defined? Such an assertion is open to interpretation
and means different things to different people. For Rosenthal, a
sportswriter for the *New York Herald Tribune* from 1946–66, it was
the period covering the Truman and Eisenhower administrations,
before television began to dictate how and when the game would
be played, before lawyers and agents would put their stamp on the
game and drive a wedge between the players and the fans.

Rosenthal's book does not follow a strict timeline, nor does it ad-
here to a standard reporting of facts and figures. Instead, the author
writes anecdotally, recalling some of the characters from his years
on the beat.

In the chapter "We Got You in Bronze," he reports, perhaps not so tongue-in-cheek, about the of Hall of Fame election process. It seems that he had a problem with some of the old players coming up for consideration who suddenly wanted to be his best friend after years of benign neglect (or outright orneriness) during their careers.

Perhaps the most interesting observation is one that rarely gets much attention: the shift in travel from rail to air. Rosenthal fondly recalls the charm of trains and how the dynamic changed when plane use became the norm; it cut down on the time spent with teammates to discuss the nuances of the game, among other things

Rosenthal also addresses issues that have gotten short shrift over the years: plans for a third league, primarily as the result of the Dodgers and Giants leaving New York without a National League presence in the late 1950s; the rise of television throughout the decade; and the decline of print journalism, as the extraneous newspapers in Major League cities began to shut down, a trend that, unfortunately, is happening once again.

182. *30 Years of Baseball's Greatest Moments*, by Joseph Reichler. New York: Crown, 1974.

If highlight reels were available in the midseventies, most of the events in Reichler's book would be included.

But what, exactly, constitutes a great moment? As an Associated Press baseball editor for twenty-two years, Reichler had a few pretty good ideas. Some are truly outstanding and have stood the test of time, such as the catch made by Willie Mays in the 1954 World Series—or similarly impressive ones by Al Gionfriddo and Sandy Amoros for the Brooklyn Dodgers in the 1947 and 1955 Fall Classics, respectively. Or take your pick of dramatic home runs stroked by Roger Maris, Bobby Thomson, or Bill Mazeroski; or no-hitters by Sandy Koufax, Bobo Newsom, and Warren Spahn, not to mention Harvey Haddix's twelve-inning perfect game. Too bad it went another frame, which gave the Milwaukee Braves a chance to win.

Other events in his book, on the other hand, might no longer cut the muster, eclipsed by exploits since its publication forty years ago. At the time, however, they were something special, like Hoyt Wilhelm's thousandth appearance, or the batting title won on the last day of the season, or a seventeen-inning marathon.

Other categories: Analysis, Pop Culture

183. *American Baseball, Volume 1: From Gentlemen's Sport to the Commissioner System,* by David Quentin Voigt. Norman: University of Oklahoma Press, 1966.

184. *American Baseball, Volume 2: From the Commissioners to Continental Expansion,* by David Quentin Voigt. Norman: University of Oklahoma Press, 1970.

185. *American Baseball, Volume 3: From Postwar Expansion to the Electronic Age,* by David Quentin Voigt. University Park: Pennsylvania State University Press, 1983.

186. *Baseball: An Illustrated History,* by David Quentin Voigt. University Park: Pennsylvania State University Press, 1987.

Some people like vanilla; others, chocolate. Some fans like the Yankees; others, the Mets. Designated hitter? Extra wild-card spot? There are probably more opinions than fans, if you consider those thoughtful people who can see more than one side of an argument.

That's pretty much the way it is with Harold Seymour and Voigt, a professor emeritus of sociology and anthropology at Albright College in Harrisburg PA.

Unlike Seymour, whose multivolume project written with his wife, Dorothy Jane Mills, halts abruptly in the second volume with the ascendancy of Babe Ruth's star, Voigt presents an entire history of the game through the early 1980s.

Seymour may have gotten a head start, but Voigt's trilogy is perhaps more focused and readable, as he touches on the main events and issues of the various eras. If there's a detriment to Voigt's work, it may be that in his zeal to include so much information he might be too economical with his thoughts. (Then again, some might consider that a point in his favor.)

For a one-volume lite edition, pick up a copy of Voigt's *Baseball: An Illustrated History*.

Other category: Academic

187. *At Home and Away: 33 Years of Baseball Essays,* by John Kuenster. Jefferson NC: McFarland, Publishers, 2003.

These ninety-two pieces were published separately as Warm Up Tosses, Kuenster's column when he served as editor of *Baseball Digest*.

He used the space to write about his personal heroes or opine about the important issues of the day, such as strike-zone measurements or Pete Rose's gambling problems. More often than not, the veteran reporter, who began his career in 1957 with the *Chicago Daily News*, simply loved to reminisce and pay tribute to some of the old-timers, even years after they left the sporting (or earthly) scene. The variety and tone are interesting as well, since Kuenster includes a bit of the offbeat along with the serious.

Each essay includes the original date of publication, so it's almost jarring to see that a column about a World Series would not appear until the following February, but that's how monthly magazines rolled in the pre-Internet era.

Other categories: Anthology, Auto/Bio/Mem, Essays

188. *Baseball: 100 Classic Moments in the History of the Game,* edited by Joseph Wallace. New York: Dorling Kindersley, 2000.

Another handsome volume produced to mark the millennia, *Classic Moments* is part of a subgenre attempting to cash in on the twentieth-century-themed mania.

To be accurate, some of the items included are not individual moments but cumulative accomplishments, such as Cy Young's 511 wins or Babe Ruth's preslugger career as a pitcher.

Actual *moments* include exploits such as the Cardinals' Sunny Jim Bottomley's twelve RBIs against the Brooklyn Dodgers (matched by the Cards' Mark Whitten almost seventy years later); Grover Cleveland Alexander's World Series–saving relief appearance in 1926; the Dodgers' first and only World Championship in Brooklyn, and the signing of Jackie Robinson to break the color line.

The last entry features the 1998 home run race between Mark McGwire and Sammy Sosa. I wonder if an updated edition might replace this with something less controversial or keep it with an explanation of the whole sordid steroids situation.

Other categories: Coffee Table/Gift, Photography

189. *Baseball: 100 Years of The Modern Era: 1901–2000*, edited by Joe Hoppel. Saint Louis: Sporting News, 2001.

190. *Sports Illustrated: The Baseball Book*, New York: Times, 2006.

At the turn of the twenty-first century, publishers were tripping over themselves to produce books about the greatest players, events, bloopers, you name it, from the previous one hundred years. Outfits like the *Sporting News* had a leg up in that they could just dip into their vaults for tons of material.

In honor of the occasion, *TSN* published this family-album-style edition that was long on photos, fillers, and factoids, but short on narrative. Many of the items included have been forgotten by all but the most ardent historians and fans, and because they are not so famous, this volume provides a welcome, fresh recap.

Sports Illustrated, on the other hand, has only been around since 1954, so it does not share the same place as *TSN* when it comes to serving as the publication of record. (The two magazines' editorial directions were also quite different.) Nevertheless, *SI* did a great job with its own baseball book.

What differentiates this oversized volume is its use of statistics and nonsports pop culture landmarks. What an arduous job it must have been to choose just one player who made his debut or retired from the game to represent each year. What must the discussions have been like in the editorial process when it came to the selecting members of their all-decade teams? Perhaps it was not all that different from what went into selecting books for the volume you are reading right now.

Although the book follows a generally chronological format, there's a lot of jumping around. One of my favorite items is a double-spread photo featuring pitchers Warren Spahn and Randy Johnson in near-identical poses, each peering over the top of his glove, some thirty years apart.

The original articles in *The Baseball Book* were contributed by current and former *si* writers, including Frank Deford, Tom Verducci, Roy Blount Jr., and Steve Rushin, and are just enough to fill the bill, especially since the title on the magazine's cover prominently features the word *Illustrated*.

Other categories: Classic, Coffee Table/Gift, Photography

191. *Baseball: A History of America's Game,* by Benjamin G. Rader. Urbana: University of Illinois Press, 1992.

Rader, a professor emeritus of history at the University of Nebraska, is considered part of a troika of authors (with Seymour and Voigt) who published scholarly treatises on the national pastime. Unlike his colleagues who put out multivolume works, Rader manages to cover the game from its pastoral beginnings up through the early 1990s in a single book. His condensed version might even be more palatable to readers who want the salient points without the minutiae some writers love to include. I wonder if it might improve sales if his book, now in its third edition, was retitled *Baseball: A Concise History of America's Game.* Just a thought—feel free to use it, Professor Rader.

History is a no-frills study, light on fawning over players except where those players impacted the course of the game as a whole, such as Babe Ruth or Jackie Robinson. It is, taken as a whole, something of a depressing story, full of the problems that have come and gone, such as low attendance, population shifts and consequent team relocations, the Black Sox scandal, and a diluted talent pool brought on by expansion. This is by no means a criticism; not every baseball story has to sign off with a smiley face. In fact, *History* is a welcome alternative to the dewy-eyed pontificators who feel the game has the unmitigated capacity to cure all of society's ills.

Other category: Academic

192. *Baseball: An Illustrated History,* by Ken Burns and Geoffrey C. Ward. New York: Knopf, 1994.

This elegant, lushly illustrated volume was published as a companion to Burns's PBS miniseries, with a major assist from Ward, a historian and former editor of *American Heritage* magazine.

Baseball follows the televised format, dividing the decades into "innings" and mixing text and narrative with an epic blend of vintage and modern photos. The interviewee comments, a major component of the documentary, carry over well to the book as excerpts, including snippets of baseball literature by Thomas Boswell, Roger Angell, Doris Kearns Goodwin, Bill James, and others.

The only thing that's missing is the television version's terrific soundtrack.

Other categories: Coffee Table/Gift, Photography

193. *Baseball: The Early Years,* by Harold Seymour. New York: Oxford University Press, 1960.

194. *Baseball: The Golden Age,* by Harold Seymour. New York: Oxford University Press, 1971.

195. *Baseball: The People's Game,* by Harold Seymour. New York: Oxford University Press, 1980.

Seymour is the patriarch of the scholarly baseball history genre. He published the first volume of his trilogy, which considered the national pastime from its pastoral origins through the early years of the present Major League structure, in 1960.

It took eleven years to follow up with *Golden Age,* which covered a much smaller time period, ending with the 1930 season and with an emphasis on the wars with outlaw leagues, the 1919 Black Sox scandal and the establishment of the commissioner system, and baseball's subsequent redemption thanks to Babe Ruth's introduction of the power game.

The final book—*The People's Game*—does not pick up from that point. Instead it examines several nonprofessional aspects of the game. Seymour uses the curious likening of baseball to a house, with each room representing a different aspect. The foundation begins on the playground, whether it's a pickup game or little league. The ground floor is pretty much for the ages of twelve and older, including college and semipro. It's interesting to note that "prison baseball" is in the "basement," but the women's game is consigned to "the annex." It could have been worse; at least it wasn't the outhouse.

Each volume can be a bit arduous to get through; the font size in the Oxford paperback editions is small (at least to these eyes), and the dearth of illustrations does little to break up the text—practically a mortal sin these days in baseball histories.

In addition, Seymour's work has comes under a cloud of scrutiny in recent years: his lack of documentation has led to allegations that he might have misappropriated the research of other writers and scholars. Years after his death in 1992, Seymour's widow, Dorothy Jane Mills, made a pitch to be listed as coauthor, claiming she had done the lion's share of the research and a fair portion of the writing in later years, and that her husband had never given her proper credit. (See *A Women's Work*. Subsequent editions do indeed grant her coauthor status).

The Society for American Baseball Research named its most prestigious award, given annually to the best biography or history book, in honor of Seymour and Mills. But it was *Spitball* magazine that actually honored one of their books, giving its CASEY Award to *The People's Game* in 1990.

196. *Baseball: The President's Game,* by William Mead and Paul Dickson. New York: Walker, 1997.

It all began with William Howard Taft, who threw out the first pitch at the 1909 season opener between the Washington Senators and the Red Sox. Ever since, the so-called First Fan has been expected to participate in the Opening Day ritual.

Each commander in chief had his own style, although some certainly had better form than others. Some presidents reared back and let fly from the stands. In more recent years, though, it has become customary to make the toss from the pitcher's mound; few moments in the game—perhaps even American history—have been more emotional than George W. Bush's first-pitch strike to open the Yankees-Diamondbacks World Series in 2001.

We learn that Richard Nixon was a true baseball scholar. He even created his own all-time All-Star team in 1969 to mark the game's centennial. And who knows how history might have changed if a couple of chief execs had decided to go pro. George H. W. Bush was captain of his team at Yale and Dwight D. Eisenhower actually played semipro ball while in college under an assumed name. Not every president embraced the national game, however; Teddy Roosevelt considered the game a "mollycoddle sport."

Regardless of party affiliation, Opening Day is a time to put aside petty differences and pay attention to what's really important. And *The President's Game,* with its historical illustrations and sidebars full of interesting trivia, wins by a landslide.

Other category: Pop Culture

197. *The Baseball Chronicle: Year-by-Year History of Major League Baseball,* by David Nemec, Stuart Shea, and Stephen Hanks. Lincolnwood IL: Publications International, 2002.

Give credit to the corps of editors and contributing writers who distilled each campaign from 1901–2001 into a few pages. In the words of Spencer Tracy in the film *Pat and Mike,* "What's there is cherce" (Brooklyn-speak for *choice*).

Each season has a general recap accompanied by a headline and brief paragraph wrapping up the major stories, people, and events. Less important issues, as well as statistical leaders, run along the bottom of each page.

The *Chronicle* is a good choice for those who want a light overview of the game in a convenient and aesthetically pleasing format.

Other categories: Coffee Table/Gift, Pop Culture, Reference

198. *Baseball Days: Reflections of America's Favorite Pastime*, by Garret Mathews. Chicago: Contemporary, 2000.

Whichever network broadcasts the World Series or other prominent sporting events invariably uses the opportunity to promote its own shows. They will often focus on a new or popular program's stars sitting in the stands, or even interview them to get their opinions as stalwart fans of one team or the other — even if, in actuality, they have no interest whatever in baseball and are just shilling.

So I get a kick out of books like this, in which celebrities who really *are* fans share their memories. In *Baseball Days*, more than sixty notable personalities from various disciplines recall their own time on the diamond, whether they only played in pickup games on the local sandlot or in little league, or, in a few cases, they were lucky enough to make their affection a career.

The eclectic group includes *Peanuts* creator Charles Schulz; politicians Michael Dukakis and Julian Bond; entertainers Robert Goulet, Eli Wallach, Julius La Rosa, and the Amazing Kreskin; writers Dave Barry, Clive Cussler, and Mickey Spillane; and media pundits Edwin Newman and Patrick Buchanan, just to name a few. Their anecdotes might not all be earth shattering, but at least they are genuine and serve as a link from the writers to their readers, making us all equals when it comes to the community of baseball.

Other categories: Anthology, Auto/Bio/Mem, Pop Culture

199. *Baseball Extra: A Newspaper History of the Glorious Game from Its Beginnings to the Present,* from the Eric C. Caren Collection. Edison NJ: Castle, 2000.

This is a marvelous collection of full-page reproductions from broadsheets and tabloids that gives the reader a sense of how baseball news has been presented throughout the years.

The oversized volume begins with an illustration of a ballgame on the cover of the September 12, 1857 issue of *Porter's Spirit*, a New York City publication which carried a tag line of "A Chronicle of the Turf, Field Sports, Literature and the Stage." It ends with the *New York Daily News* proudly proclaiming the Yankees the "Team of the Century" following their 1999 World Championship.

In between are hundreds of important events that took place on and around ballfields across the United States.

Not every baseball story is revelatory, but that's the charm of this book: it's a fair representation of the editorial policies and attitudes of the times. For example, the Kingston *Daily Freeman* published a photo of Peter Gray, the one-armed outfielder who became a symbol of World War II baseball, with his parents prior to a game in Yankee Stadium. Similar off-the-field items appeared on the pages of newspapers across the country.

Perhaps more interesting is the juxtaposition of the stories within the layout of the page. The June 3, 1941 issue of the *Baltimore News-Post* notes the death of Lou Gehrig above news of the war in Europe. Then there are the advertisements, such as a brand new Federal Knight delivery truck on sale for $1,095 in 1924, or men's dress shoes for $6.25 in 1933.

Baseball Extra is like a museum in your lap, designed to be examined in a leisurely manner to get the most out of it.

Other categories: Coffee Table/Gift, Media

200. *Baseball Fathers, Baseball Sons,* by Dick Wimmer. New York: William Morrow, 1988.

Among the many traditions of the national pastime is the handing down of the love for the game from father to child.

In the mid-1980s, Wimmer took his two adolescent sons on a road trip to meet some of the most famous players — current and former — in the game to discuss this symbiotic relationship.

It's a side of the players fans rarely get to see, as Wimmer, a creative writing teacher who wrote the screenplay for the 1982 made-for-TV movie *The Million-Dollar Infield,* queries the athletes on their familial relationships, expectations, disappointments, and a range of other topics. Yogi Berra's son Dale had his own career as a member of the Pirates, Yankees, and Astros. Cal Ripken Jr. succeeded on the Major League diamond where his brother Billy did not; their dad, Cal Sr., never even made it to the big leagues as a player. Other family affairs are included, as are conversations with players about what their dads' support meant to them growing up and traveling the long, hard road to the Show.

These players and managers also took an interest in Wimmer's boys, peppering the author and his kids with questions about *their* experiences. In all, it's a sweet book that could easily be rereleased or updated even now, thirty years after its original publication.

Other categories: Auto/Bio/Mem, Pop Culture

201. *Baseball in America,* by Robert Smith. New York: Holt, Reinhart and Winston, 1961.

This is basically an album of photos from the first quarter of the twentieth century. The material, provided by the Museum of the City of New York, concentrates on the game as played on the fields of the Big Apple (which seems to run counter the use of *America* in the book's title).

The slim volume waxes nostalgic about the early game, its antecedents, and its star players. The last few chapters attempt to bring the book up to date, but they seem more of an afterthought as they focus, as one might expect, on the Giants, Yankees, and Dodgers, pre-1957.

Other categories: Pop Culture, Photography

Also by the author: *Babe Ruth's America* (1974); *Baseball: A Historical Narrative of the Game, The Men Who Have Played It, and Its Place in American Life* (1947)

202. *Baseball in the Garden of Eden: The Secret History of the Early Game*, by John Thorn. New York: Simon and Schuster, 2011.

Abner Doubleday did not invent baseball on a cow pasture in Cooperstown NY? Say it ain't so, John! Next you'll be telling us that George Washington didn't cut down the cherry tree.

Old legends die hard, admits Thorn, but the truth is really not a secret. Baseball didn't just grow out of the head of a single individual, regardless of how nice and American that story might seem or how long we've heard it.

And, as we pretty much all know now, Doubleday had little, if anything, to do with making the game a national phenomenon. Those honors go to a quartet of gentlemen whom I would daresay had received little, if any, credit until this publication. In fact, writes Thorn, the game as we know it was more of a smorgasbord, combining the best parts of several regional variations.

The result is an authoritative treatise on the origins of the game, which is a topic near and dear to Thorn's heart, and it is an eye-opener not just for its revelations about baseball, but also about the culture of middle-to-late nineteenth-century America.

Thorn is a bit of a polyglot when it comes to the national pastime. While many prolific writers stick to a specific area—statistics, biography, or history, for example—he excels in just about everything, from *Garden of Eden* to his reference books (such as *Total Baseball*), statistical analysis (*The Hidden Game of Baseball*), and even children's books (one of which is *First Pitch*, an introduction to the game's origins).

Other category: Nineteenth Century

203. *Baseball's Best 1,000: Rankings of the Skills, the Achievements, and the Performances of the Greatest Players of All Time,* by Derek Gentile. New York: Black Dog and Leventhal, 2008.

As of this writing, about 17,500 men have played in the Majors, to which Gentile has added another 2,500 from the Negro Leagues.

His rules for inclusion are fairly straightforward and generally reasonable for such a weeding-out process: a minimum of ten years in the game (for Major Leaguers), good stats, and recognition in the form of awards, adjusted for the different eras and conditions.

His top one hundred consists of the usual suspects: Babe Ruth leads the group, followed by Willie Mays, Honus Wagner, Ty Cobb, and Walter Johnson. You can argue that Joe DiMaggio should be number 37 rather than Mickey Mantle, but that's not even interesting at this point. It's the guys at the middle to bottom that you wonder about. Toby Harrah at 408? Mo Vaughn, 526? Mike McFarlane — a catcher for the Royals and Red Sox from 1987–99; I had to look him up — at 773? And should you feel sorry for Orioles infielder Rich Dauer? On the one hand, he makes the list; on the other, he's number 1,000.

Originally published in 2004, the book was revised and took into account the performance-enhancing drug period. And Gentile hints that there might be more updates on the way. (Note: Another updated version was released in 2012, basically just moving around some of the players' order.)

Other categories: Auto/Bio/Mem, Reference, Statistics

204. *Baseball's Forgotten Heroes: One Fan's Search for the Game's Most Interesting Overlooked Players,* by Tony Salin. New York: McGraw-Hill. 1999.

Salin recalls a handful of ballplayers who meant something special to him, as well as a host of others, although he offers no introduction or explanation as to exactly what it is that earns them his adulation.

He intersperses his narrative with first-person interviews with players and others who wish to weigh in on a particular subject, beginning with Pete Gray, the one-armed outfielder for the Saint Louis Browns who became a symbol of the national pastime during World War II. Other heroes include Chuck Connors, who had a single at bat with the Brooklyn Dodgers and appeared in sixty-six games for the Chicago Cubs before moving to greener pastures on the big and small screens, and Joe Bauman, a Minor League slugger who clubbed seventy-two home runs in a single season for the Roswell Rockets in 1954 but never made it to the Majors.

Although most of the names might not be familiar to even the most zealous fans, Salin's work proves that we love who we love, and that we identify our favorites by our own set of standards.

Other category: Pop Culture

205. *Breaking the Slump: Baseball in the Depression Era*, by Charles C. Alexander. New York: Columbia University Press, 2002.

Alexander, one of the foremost historians and biographers of the national pastime, recounts the difficulties faced by owners in putting their product on the field at a time when people had trouble buying groceries or paying the rent. One result was the advent of night baseball, which allowed fans to blow off some steam following a hard day at the factory or office, if they were still lucky enough to have jobs.

Just like the rest of America, baseball had to make major adjustments during the Depression, and, according to the author, some of the greatest innovations came out of the desperation.

For one thing, baseball offered an employment opportunity for many young men with a talent for sports who could find no other means of work. Having secured a spot on a team, they fought like hell to keep it, which meant performing through injury and pain that would sideline one of today's players or even put him on the disabled list. The intrateam competition was also strong; new players, rarely welcomed in the best of circumstances, were the targets of jealously and anger from veterans fearful of losing employment.

Even though salaries were kept low by a combination of the reserve clause and the diminished attendance caused by the economy, the players were still doing relatively better than many of their fellow Americans. They were grateful to have such an easy job, albeit often only for a few years, that they were more or less unconcerned about workers' rights or the injustice of keeping African Americans out of organized ball.

Life in baseball in those years may not have been as glamorous or financially rewarding as those that came before and after, but it sure beat the alternative of having no baseball at all.

Other categories: Academic, Business, Pop Culture

206. *Carrying Jackie's Torch: The Players Who Integrated Baseball — and America*, by Steve Jacobson. Chicago: Lawrence Hill, 2007.

The cover of this underrated book features Hank Aaron and Ernie Banks, two African American players who made their debuts in the early 1950s, just a few years after Robinson had broken the color line. But for every African American Hall of Famer like Aaron and Banks, there were dozens who had the drive but not necessarily the talent to ease their way into professional baseball.

Jacobson, a veteran New York sports reporter, reminds us about the Ed Charleses and Tommy Davises, the Mudcat Grants and Al Jacksons, not to mention Emmett Ashford, the first black umpire in the Major Leagues, and former player Bob Watson, who served as general manager for the Houston Astros and New York Yankees and was later the Major League vice president of rules and on-field operations.

In spite of the readers rooting for the individuals for all the pain and suffering they had to endure to try to reach their goals, not all the stories have happy endings. But Jacobson has the right touch — neither preachy nor maudlin, but not totally objective as his profession demands, either.

Other categories: Ethnic, Negro Leagues, Underrated

207. *Catcher: How the Man Behind the Plate Became an American Folk Hero*, by Peter Morris. Chicago: Ivan R. Dee, 2009.

Morris, who has published several excellent baseball books of a more general nature, focuses on one position in this overview of the evolution of the position, with its rewards and punishments.

In the early days, the man behind the plate wore virtually nothing in the way of protection. He stood alone, a last line of defense, protecting his team from those who would rob their home. And when changes inevitably came — gloves, masks, chest protectors, and shin guards — those who chose to take advantage were the laughingstock of their peers, as is frequently the case when new ideas are embraced by some. Many would rather continue to sustain broken bones, spikings, and other life-altering injuries than have someone question their manhood.

Morris provides plenty of examples of these brave but foolhardy fellows and the physical — and mental — toll the position exacted. The catcher's gear has become known as "the tools of ignorance," but the ignorance was in *not* using these innovations. However, old habits die hard, and Morris recounts the stories of some of the pioneers of that rough-and-tumble era (*Catcher* leaves off in the early 1920s).

While the technology has obviously improved — catchers now wear hockey-style masks and have more impervious and flexible materials — they're still the same basic tools created more than one hundred years ago. So did the game change to take the equipment into account, or was it the other way around? Hurlers began experimenting new deliveries and pitches, such as the spitball and the knuckleball, among numerous others, which made for concurrent changes in the catchers' chores.

Other category: Analysis

208. *The Complete Book of Baseball: A* New York Times *Scrapbook History,* edited by Gene Brown. New York: Arno Press, 1980.

This slim volume is just like the kind of scrapbooks I used to keep when I was a kid, cutting out articles about my favorite teams and players.

This "complete" book (when will they stop using that word in the title?) primarily covers the major events from the 1920s through the late 1970s as produced from the typewriters of some of the "Paper of Record's" best sportswriters, including John Drebinger, Joseph Durso, Murray Chass, and Leonard Koppett.

No space goes unfilled in *The Complete Book of Baseball.* In addition to the feature stories and columns, smaller wire-service items report such earth-shattering news as the 1921 announcement that fans in Pittsburgh were allowed to keep foul balls.

The presentation is a bit rough; some of the reproductions are scaled down to fit the book's page trim, and some of the photocopies aren't especially clear. In addition, as might be expected given the source, the book has a regional slant. It's especially engaged with the Brooklyn Dodgers, New York Giants, Yankees, and Mets, none of which really seems out of place since these teams were legitimate newsmakers.

Other categories: Anthology, Coffee Table/Gift, Pop Culture

209. *The Crooked Pitch: The Curveball in American Baseball History,* by Martin Quigley. Chapel Hill NC: Algonquin, 1988.

The title of this unassuming little book is something of a misnomer. It's not just the curve, the deuce, the Lord Charles (or Uncle Charley), or the old number two that the author considers; it's any ball that doesn't travel straight and fast from the pitcher to the catcher. So it's also the slider, screwball, knuckler, forkball, palm ball, and even the spitter, among numerous others.

As the saying goes, hitting is all about timing and pitching is about disrupting that timing. If pitchers threw only fastballs, baseball might be a pretty long, boring game. But as Quigley notes, the beauty lies in that strategy of deciding what to throw in which situations.

Quigley tracks the use — and abuse — of the off-speed chuck, paying homage to those who excelled in each variety, even going so far as to attribute several no-hitters specifically to those "trick" pitches.

Other categories: Analysis, Auto/Bio/Mem

210. *Did Babe Ruth Call His Shot? And Other Unsolved Mysteries of Baseball*, by Paul Aron. Hoboken NJ: John Wiley and Sons, 2005.

Conspiracy theorists will love this modest paperback. Although several of the its twenty-eight questions are in reality *not* unsolved, this one will certainly open the door for lively discussion, which is really what the literary baseball fan is all about.

Many questions can't be answered with a simple yes or no, such as "Were yesterday's players better?" or "Does it pay to steal bases?" It depends on the situation. In addition, others don't quite qualify as true mysteries: "Can small market teams compete?" Sure. Just ask the Tampa Bay Rays, who went all the way to the World Series in 2008.

211. *Early Innings: A Documentary History of Baseball, 1825–1908*, by Dean Sullivan. Lincoln: University of Nebraska Press, 1995

212. *Middle Innings: A Documentary History of Baseball, 1900–1948*, by Dean Sullivan. Lincoln: University of Nebraska Press, 1998.

213. *Late Innings: A Documentary History of Baseball, 1945–1972*, by Dean Sullivan. Lincoln: University of Nebraska Press, 2002.

214. *Final Innings: A Documentary History of Baseball, 1972–2008*, by Dean Sullivan. Lincoln: University of Nebraska Press, 2010.

This quartet of literary time capsules features items culled from newspaper and magazine articles, personal correspondences, congressional hearings, official league documents, and other materials that cover the national pastime at all levels, from amateur to professional.

Each volume contains more than one hundred events selected to represent the individual time periods. Sullivan introduces each excerpted piece to offer perspective before turning to the entry itself, with its original language and writing style, from the likes of Grantland Rice on the death of Babe Ruth, to landmark events such as an article in the *New York Amsterdam News*, an African American newspaper, on the Hall of Fame's decision to establish a committee to find candidates from the Negro Leagues for induction consideration, to spot reporting ("Aluminum bats planned in Spokane," declares a 1944 Associated Press story).

Not all of the documents share the same gravitas, but like a good gumbo, it's the diversity of ingredients that gives this series its unique flavor.

Other category: Anthology

215. *From Cobb to "Catfish": 128 Illustrated Stories from* Baseball Digest, edited by John Kuenster. Chicago: Rand McNally, 1975.

Kuenster, who passed away in 2012, had been connected with the popular publication for more than forty years. He did a nice job of picking the best articles from its archives for inclusion in this volume.

True to the nature of a book like this, there's a lot of appreciation for history and key players, including a lot of "as told bys" from legends like Mickey Mantle, Bill Veeck, Tom Seaver, and Lou Boudreau, among others. There's also spot reporting on the important events, as well as profiles of other noteworthy athletes.

There are a few eyebrow raisers that merit special mention. In a 1973 article Emil Rothe recalled the final home run in Ted Williams's storied career, immortalized by John Updike in his essay "Hub Fans Bid Kid Adieu." Rothe, a master of understatement, referred to the blast as having to have been one of Williams's most dramatic. Gee, ya think?

Veteran scribe George Vass wrote about "Baseball's Unbeatable

Records," in which he opined that Lou Gehrig's consecutive games-played streak was safe but that single-season records for home runs, strikeouts, and stolen bases were "vulnerable."

Although a fascinating collection, it relies perhaps too much on articles written close to its 1975 publication. It also loses some sense of nostalgia as printed in this large-scale format rather than the more familiar digest trim size.

Other categories: Anthology, Sportswriting

216. *A Game of Inches: The Stories Behind the Innovations That Shaped Baseball; The Game On The Field,* by Peter Morris. Chicago: Ivan R. Dee, 2006.

217. *A Game of Inches: The Stories Behind the Innovations That Shaped Baseball; The Game Behind the Scenes,* by Peter Morris. Chicago: Ivan R. Dee, 2006.

As a kid, I used to love to read about the origins of my comic-book heroes. Morris supplies almost one thousand such stories vis-à-vis baseball, from the invention of the batter's box to the umpires' hand signals. Like the proverbial 110 percent that athletes are always implored to give, *On the Field* covers *more* than everything you would expect.

The organization is quite well thought out, like a biological classification system, beginning with "The Things We Take for Granted" before moving on to sections on batting, pitching, fielding, base running, managers, coaches, equipment, uniforms, "Skullduggery," and even time-outs. You want to know when turnstiles made their debut? You got it. The cultural history of beards and moustaches? Done.

The second volume is somewhat more cerebral and business oriented. Among the topics are media, behind-the-scenes workers, statistics, money, travel, and inclusion for African Americans, women, and various ethnic groups.

For this work Morris received the Seymour Medal from the Society for American Baseball Research and *Spitball* magazine's CASEY Award, the only writer beside Larry Tye (author of *Satchel:*

The Life and Times of an American Legend) to win both honors.

Game of Inches was rereleased by Dee in a revised one-volume paperback in 2010.

Other categories: Analysis, Award Winner, Behind the Scenes, Business, Reference

218. *Ghosts in the Gallery at Cooperstown: Sixteen Little-Known Members of the Hall of Fame,* by David L. Fleitz. Jefferson NC: McFarland, 2004

Some authors love the challenge of finding an obscure topic. That was Fleitz's motivation when he realized that just because a player has a plaque in Cooperstown, that doesn't make him a household name.

Fleitz believes these fellows — most of whom were involved in the game in the late nineteenth century — deserve their due and therefore offers these brief profiles in appreciation of their contributions.

Not *all* of the names will be unfamiliar to even the moderate student of baseball history. His lineup includes Candy Cummings, credited as inventor of the curve ball; Jack Chesbro, who holds the modern single-season record for victories with forty-one; John Clarkson, who won thirty or more games five times; Willie Wells, who excelled in the relative anonymity of the Negro Leagues; and manager Frank Selee, who lead the Boston Beaneaters (later known as the Braves) to five pennants in twelve years and finished his career with a .607 winning percentage

Even now, some of these gentlemen invoke controversy as some revisionist thinkers wonder whether it's feasible to remove some of the enshrined to make the Hall truly elite. A couple of names jump immediately to mind: Bobby Wallace, a solid but seemingly unspectacular player for twenty-five years who once led the American League in games played in 1905, and Eppa Rixey, who averaged 15-14 over a 21-year career. Did they benefit from the longevity factor?

Fleitz does a nice job of summing up these careers. He reminds readers of the differences in the game from the 1890s to the 1990s and why a different set of standards needs to be in place when considering those worthy of baseball's highest honor.

Others categories: Auto/Bio/Mem

Also by the author: *More Ghosts in the Gallery: Another Sixteen Little-Known Greats at Cooperstown* (2007)

219. *Glove Affairs: The Romance, History, and Tradition of the Baseball Glove,* by Noah Liberman. Chicago: Triumph, 2003.

The slightly romantic connotation of the title is no accident. Bats come and go, but a player's glove is an extremely personal possession. While he might lend his favorite bat to a teammate, it's doubtful he would do the same with his glove, which in most cases has been tended to, oiled, or otherwise treated, and kept lovingly for as long as possible. Buying a kid his or her first glove is almost a rite of passage in American—and, increasingly, international—life.

It's hard to believe that gloves were disdained by most position players as unmanly in the early years of the game, including the catcher—but those guys are a bit nuts to begin with.

Liberman takes a loving look at all things leather, at least as it pertains to the national pastime. From cutting up a piece of cowhide to keeping it in tiptop shape, he acts as a museum guide, taking the reader through the various evolutionary stages (early mitts were little more than oversized dress gloves). He details how to pick out an appropriate model and break it in, maintenance and repair, trivia, even collecting. The author makes his cases with a good use of photos—the old catalog advertisements are especially cool—and thoughtful narrative.

Other category: Reference

220. *Great Baseball Writing:* Sports Illustrated, *1954–2004,* edited by Rob Fleder. New York: Sports Illustrated, 2007.

Anthologies like this are great for pack rats like me. I used to either keep the whole magazines or just tear out the articles of interest. Either way, it made for a great deal of clutter.

Instead, here you have collected in one handy 557-page volume some of *SI*'s best work. These are truly classic stories, features, and profiles that are as informative and entertaining today as they were when they first appeared.

You'll find a 1962 piece by Jimmy Breslin on how the New York Mets were "The Worst Baseball Team Ever," and that was with six weeks left to go in the season. Robert Creamer, who would go on to publish the watershed baseball biography with *The Babe: The Legend Comes to Life*, revisits Johnny Podres a few months after he led the Dodgers to their only world championship. Other *Sports Illustrated* regulars include Roger Kahn, Frank Deford, Tom Verducci, Ron Fimrite, Steve Rushin, Steve Wulf, and Rick Reilly on a variety of serious, humorous, or tragic matters.

If there's any complaint, it's that the book is too short. Maybe they should consider a second volume. It would be shame to have to wait for *SI*'s seventy-fifth anniversary.

Other categories: Anthology, Sportswriting

221. *The Great Book of Baseball Knowledge: The Ultimate Test for the Ultimate Fan*, by David Nemec. Lincolnwood IL: Masters Press, 1999.

Nemec, who specializes in books on baseball trivia, has come up with a challenging edition for fans who seek to further their baseball education.

The questions are divided among some fifty categories under eight broad themes: pitching, batting, fielding, postseason and All-Stars, teams, honors and awards, historian's corner, and miscellaneous. They are quite thought provoking and fairly difficult for the low- to midlevel fan; hardcore students of the game should have a slightly easier time.

Nemec generously offers five clues for each question, along with tables, lists, and other helpful hints. One could easily imagine a group of baseball friends getting together and quizzing each other from this book during the off-season or rain delays.

Even the title is designed to make the reader think a bit, since it could be interpreted in at least two ways: Does he mean *great* as in large in scale, or, perhaps with a bit of hubris, as in *terrific*. It works either way, since the book consists of more than six hundred pages *and* is a fun read.

Other categories: Pop Culture, Statistics, Trivia

222. *High Heat: The Secret History of the Fastball and the Improbable Search for the Fastest Pitcher of All Time,* by Tim Wendell. Cambridge MA: Da Capo, 2010.

Much of what we have to go on when it comes to assessing the speed of the early fireballers is anecdotal. Who could say for sure how fast Walter Johnson or Amos Rusie or pre–twentieth-century hurler Pud Galvin were?

It wasn't until Bob "Rapid Robert" Feller staged his now-famous exhibition, racing a fastball against a speeding police motorcycle, that there were actual means to measure the velocity of a pitched ball.

Wendell begins his search by learning about the Johnsons, Rusies, and Galvins at the Hall of Fame. As he gets closer to more contemporary pitchers like Nolan Ryan, Randy Johnson, and David Price, he has the benefit of radar measurements to give more definitive answers (although those devices aren't foolproof either).

So what are the elements that would give that final answer to the question, Where does the speed come from? Is it the legs? The follow-through? Is it strength? Size? Randy Johnson was six feet ten; Steve Dalkowski, who never got out of the Minors, was almost a foot shorter, but anyone who saw him could tell you that if he could have just harnessed his wildness, he'd be in the Hall of Fame, all things being equal.

Wendell concludes with his top-twelve list from which he picks his ultimate choice, which I will not divulge here; suffice it to say it will not come as a stunning surprise.

The only cavil with the book is that it does not follow a logical progression. Even though the chapters are named for separate components of the pitch—windup, pivot, stride, arm acceleration, release, and so on — the information within each section has little to do with the heading, jumping back and forth to consider multiple issues. But *High Heat* does have that homespun, let-me-tell-you-a-story feeling.

223. *The Image of Their Greatness: An Illustrated History of Baseball from 1900 to the Present,* by Lawrence Ritter and Donald Honig. New York: Crown, 1979.

For some reason I have always considered this as a companion to Ritter's *The Glory of Their Times.* How wonderful that it was the product of two such veteran and esteemed baseball historians. It's almost as if Honig was the apprentice to Ritter and took over the family business after his mentor passed down the mantle.

The narrative is straightforward and is basically a brief history. The black-and-white photographs are the selling point here. Many of the hundreds of shots are posed rather than action shots, and they serve as almost a family album, with some interesting off-the-field and personal photos.

The book was updated in 1984 to include a look ahead into the new decade. This was Ritter and Honig's second collaboration; they published *The 100 Greatest Baseball Players of All Time* in 1981.

Other categories: Auto/Bio/Mem, Photography

224. *I Managed Good, But Boy Did They Play Bad,* by Jim Bouton with Neil Offen. New York: Dell, 1973.

With his playing career just about done, and perhaps still looking to capitalize on *Ball Four*'s notoriety, Bouton picked up the pen again in this amusing indictment of the narrow-minded but colorful guys who manned the helm.

Bouton selected fifteen managers — some for whom he had played — in this anthology, which contains profiles written by top-notch sportswriters. The roster includes several skippers who were voted into the Hall, such as Walter Alston, Leo Durocher, Joe McCarthy, Connie Mack, Casey Stengel, John McGraw, and Dick

Williams. Then you have the head-scratchers, like Rocky Bridges, credited with contributing the line used in the book's title; Yogi Berra (who was *not* voted into Cooperstown for his leadership skills), Johnny Keane, and Ralph Houk, who all share a chapter; Charlie Dressen; George Stallings, Joe Schultz, and Squawk McGraw, an ersatz manager created by James Thurber.

Bouton served as editor of this volume, writing the chapters for his own bosses Houk, Berra, and Keane, and Schultz, the field leader for the Seattle Pilots in 1969. He was ably assisted by the research skills of Offen, one of the generation of iconoclastic sportswriters in the seventies.

The preface is worth the cover price alone — $1.50 when it was first published — as Bouton explains the genesis of the book and how some publishers go about deciding which projects they pursue.

Other categories: Auto/Bio/Mem, Anthology

225. *Induction Day at Cooperstown: A History of the Baseball Hall of Fame Ceremony*, by Dennis Corcoran. Jefferson NC: McFarland, 2011.

There are plenty of books about the legend and lore of the National Baseball Hall of Fame, its treasures and inductees, and the arguments about who deserves to be enshrined and who has been overlooked. Corcoran prefers to focus on the celebratory aspects.

After a couple of standard chapters on the origins of the Hall, Corcoran provides a brief recap of each year's ceremony, including an analysis of the balloting, or lack thereof in the few instances where no one met the requirements, followed by brief profiles of the honorees.

A lot of the biographical and voting information is widely available elsewhere. What sets *Induction Day* apart is the summary of the actual event, including the speeches and other news of interest. This is where Corcoran gets a bit more personal, as he describes the joy for those on hand and, in the case of those elected posthumously, the bittersweet emotions of getting the call to the Hall but not being there to enjoy the festivities.

The book would have been greatly enhanced by additional—and color—pictures, but otherwise it's a fine look at a surprisingly overlooked topic.

Other category: Hall of Fame

226. *Ladies and Gentlemen, The Bronx is Burning: 1977, Baseball, Politics, and the Battle for the Soul of a City,* by Jonathan Mahler. New York: Farrar, Straus and Giroux, 2005.

So much was going on in New York during the summer of 1977. A psychotic David Berkowitz was shooting young couples all over parts of New York City. The city also suffered through a heat wave that contributed to a major blackout and subsequent looting while politicians argued over who was to blame, a chain of events symbolic of the decline of the once proud metropolis.

The Yankees were battling the American League and each other on the way to another pennant. Billy Martin fought to maintain control while dealing with the huge egos belonging to Reggie Jackson, Thurman Munson, and megalomaniacal owner George Steinbrenner. The author uses Jackson as a symbol for the struggles of the African American community, angry at what they perceived as being kept underfoot by "the man." It was a situation just waiting for the chance to explode.

Mahler, a contributing writer for the *New York Times Magazine*, mixes multiple beats in this urban study, though baseball is obviously front and center. He keeps the tensions sweltering on all fronts, combining sports history with political history and true crime, giving *Ladies and Gentleman* an extra sense of gravitas. I'm just grateful I was working at a summer camp in the Laurentian Mountains of Quebec and missed the whole mess.

The title was taken from a line apocryphally attributed to ABC sportscaster Howard Cosell during the telecast of Game Two of the World Series between the Yankees and the Los Angeles Dodgers. The book was turned into an ESPN miniseries in 2007, starring John Turturro as Martin and Oliver Platt as Steinbrenner.

Other categories: History/Team, Pop Culture

227. *Major League Careers Cut Short: Leading Players Gone by 30*, by Charles F. Faber. Jefferson NC: McFarland, 2011.

John Greenleaf Whittier wrote, "Of all the words of man and pen, the saddest are these: it might have been." Who knew he was a sportswriter?

Opinions vary depending on the source, but the average Major League career lasts about five years. So to have a longer career — especially in the preexpansion era — means you must have been doing something right. It is all the more shocking, therefore, to see young athletes on the verge of stardom who are basically here today, gone tomorrow.

If you're like me, you'll be surprised as to who qualifies for inclusion in this unusual and ultimately sad book. It's shocking how many quality players failed to enjoy lengthier careers, either due to injury or simply because of poor personal choices; some, such as Addie Joss and Ray Chapman, were felled by premature death. A handful — such as "Super Joe" Charboneau, who won the 1980 AL Rookie of the Year award and was out of the majors two years later — just seemed to drop off the map.

Faber begins with lengthy profiles of several of the best players at each position in this unfortunate demographic. For example, everyone knows that Sandy Koufax retired following the 1966 World Series because of injury, but I'll bet most fans believed him to be in his midthirties, given that he'd been around for a dozen years. Similarly, pitcher Amos Rusie won twenty or more games for eight consecutive seasons before he succumbed. On the other hand, you have twenty-eight-year-old Oscar Emil "Happy" Felsch, who was banned for his alleged complicity in the Black Sox scandal.

Faber follows with chapters for each position, offering more succinct profiles. He also ranks each player with a system of his own devising — which he does not explain — and includes the player's from the *Total Baseball* series.

Since so many of these fellows were around decades ago, you have to wonder how much longer they could have played and better they could have been had they had access to modern medical technology.

Other category: Auto/Bio/Mem

228. *Major Leagues: The Formation, Sometimes Absorption, and Mostly Inevitable Demise of 18 Professional Baseball Organizations, 1871 to Present,* by David Pietrusza. Jefferson NC: McFarland, 1991.

Most people who aren't students of the game don't realize there were actually several Major Leagues prior to and in competition with the present setup. In fact, the American League got its own start in 1901 as a competitor to the National League.

Pietrusza does a consistently good job at filling in the gaps, briefly touching on those organizations that had such high ideals and hopes but that always ended in failure.

Some came as the result of entrepreneurial plans, while other were merely the dreams of players' collectives for a more equitable situation devoid of the heavy-handed management and low salaries they were forced to endure by the reserve clause. This clause bound them to their teams in perpetuity, making players little more than "chattel," which was the popular term of the day to describe their status.

The biggest threat to organized baseball was the Federal League, which managed to stick around from 1913–15 and attracted some of the Majors' most talented players.

The last serious challenge to upstart leagues came following the Dodgers' and Giants' relocation to the West Coast. But rather than admit the Continental League as an entirely new and separate Major League, a compromise was reached to allow a round of expansion in 1961–62 that brought baseball back to the Big Apple, among three other locations.

Space here does not permit a recapitulation of all the proceedings of the Continental League contained in *Major Leagues*, which is worth the price of the book by itself.

Other category: Business

229. *The Man in the Dugout: Baseball's Top Managers and How They Got That Way,* by Leonard Koppett. New York: Crown, 1993.

Veteran sportswriter Koppett turns his attention from the game in general in his book *The Thinking Man's/Fan's Guide to Baseball* to concentrate on the men who lead it.

There have been more than 110 world championships, 220 pennants, and even more first-place finishes when you take divisional play into account. What does it take to get to the top? The knock on Casey Stengel when he led the New York Yankees from 1949–60 was that anyone could have succeeded with such powerhouse rosters. But is that really true?

Koppett puts Stengel and eighteen other managers under the microscope, including fellow Hall of Famers Joe McCarthy, John McGraw, Leo Durocher, Sparky Anderson, Tommy Lasorda, Walter Alston, and Earl Weaver, plus several others who get briefer examinations. One cool feature is a variation on the family tree that offers degrees of separation for every manager who finished in first place from 1961–91.

The book was updated in 2000 by Temple University Press to include the 1999 season, which closed the book on Lasorda and Anderson, who had retired by this point; supplemented material on others like Tony La Russa and Bobby Cox, who were briefly mentioned in the first edition; and provided an updated genealogy chart of the managers.

Other categories: Analysis, Auto/Bio/Mem

Also by the author: *The Thinking Fan's Guide to Baseball* (last updated in 2004); *Koppett's Concise History of Major League Baseball* (1998)

230. *The National Game,* second edition, by Alfred H. Spink. Carbondale: Southern Illinois University Press, 2000.

Considered one of the first baseball encyclopedias, *The National Game* was originally published in 1910. The second edition was expanded and contained updated profiles and photographs of hundreds of players, owners, executives, and other baseball personnel between 1871 and 1910. It also featured early versions of box scores and other rudimentary statistics.

The book is arranged to provide the maximum reader convenience, beginning with a brief history of the game, with sections for each team and defensive position; there's even a tutorial from the stars of the day on how to play the game "correctly." Considering the technology available, this was a massive undertaking and was well ahead of its time when it came to offering the most up-to-date information, or *dope*, available.

Spink, an early baseball writer, went on to found the *Sporting News*, which for many years was touted as "the bible of baseball." Perhaps that's why there's a section in *The National Game* listing many of the prominent sports journalists of the day.

The book was reprinted often, including this 2000 version, which was part of SIUP's Writing Baseball series, for which the editors were determined to reproduce the original formatting as faithfully as possible.

Other categories: Auto/Bio/Mem, Reference, Statistics

231. *The National Game: Baseball and American Culture*, by John P. Rossi. Chicago: Ivan R. Dee, 2000.

Despite the title, Rossi's book is not so much about American culture as it is a straightforward, albeit brief, history of the sport.

Rossi, a university history teacher, provides a good service, touching on the major points without going into the lugubrious detail that might turn off the casual reader.

It's always interesting to go back and read predictions from years-old books — as the saying goes, where's my flying car? That is, most prognostications are wrong in either their dire warnings or their rosy outlooks, although there are often much more of the former than the latter. It's safer to say, as Rossi does, that a crisis might be coming if players and owners can't work out any future difficulties.

Or not.

Also by the author: *A Whole New Game: Off the Field Changes in Baseball, 1946–1960* (1999); *The 1964 Phillies: The Story of Baseball's Most Memorable Collapse* (2005)

232. *The National Pastime*, edited by John Thorn. New York: Warner, 1987.

I've been a proud member of the Society for American Baseball Research for more than twenty-five years. Some folks perceive the organization as a meeting place for eggheads and stats geeks. While that may be true to some extent, it also provides wonderful services to all its members and is considered a major go-to source for the media when it comes to arcane questions about the national pastime, which happens to be the title of one of the organization's two annual publications.

Thorn, now the MLB's official historian, developed *The National Pastime* in 1982, and this unassuming little paperback contains thirty-four essays that highlight SABR's diverse nature. The publication is normally written by and produced for members, but for this specific anthology, they hauled out some of their more prominent constituents, including Fred Lieb, Bill James, G. H. Fleming, David Voigt, and Seymour Siwoff of the Elias Sports Bureau.

Topics range from opinion pieces about which players deserve Hall of Fame consideration, to politicking for wider use of new-age statistics, to an appreciation piece for Zane Grey's *The Redheaded Outfield*. Most of the essays are timeless, but even the few that might seem dated to a twenty-first-century audience are valuable for their historic significance.

Over the years SABR's signature publications—the other being the more academically driven *Baseball Research Journal*—have covered imaginative and influential issues that have opened the door to correcting misconceptions and even changing the record books, further proof of the organization's high standing in the baseball community.

Other categories: Analytics, Anthology, Statistics

233. *October 1964*, by David Halberstam. New York: Villard, 1994.

Published to mark the thirtieth anniversary of the 1964 World Series, it acknowledges the decline of the Yankee dynasty and the beginning of real inroads toward the end of racism in baseball.

The Bronx Bombers were the old guard, representing the pre–civil rights era. They were one of the last teams to bring an African American player onto the roster, and even *that* was done begrudgingly. On the other hand, the Saint Louis Cardinals were just getting started, with future Hall of Famer Bob Gibson and perennial All-Stars Curt Flood and Bill White heralding a new generation and moving baseball into the swinging sixties, with its restive antiestablishment sentiments. Faced with prospect of having to make separate living accommodations for its minority players during spring training, the Cardinals management bought a motel so the ballclub could stay together, which went a long way toward building team spirit.

Halberstam notes that the period marked the introduction of a new type of reporter into sports. These "chipmunks," as they were derisively called by old-school pressmen, represented a generation that was no longer content to accept the company line as handed down by the team's media-relations department; they often dug uncomfortably deep to get the real story, much to the annoyance of players and management.

The author does his usual excellent job in going behind the scenes to bring more than just a superficial retelling to the table.

234. *One Shining Season*, by Michael Fedo. New York: Pharos, 1991.

One of the hardest things to do in sports is maintain a level of consistency. In *One Shining Season*, Fedo interviews eleven players from the 1940s to the 1970s who enjoyed just one truly special year, even though they may have had lengthy careers. Wes Parker, for example, ably manned first base for the Dodgers for several seasons, but in 1971 he led the league in doubles, drove in 111 runs, won his second Gold Glove Award, and finished fifth in National League MVP voting.

The premise of the book is somewhat curious. With the exception of Bob Hazle, a much-heralded rookie who played for only three seasons, the rest of the subjects enjoyed careers of more than nine years. Why the author focused on *these* guys is a matter of conjecture. One thing they had in common was that one blip that stood out from the rest. Ned Garver won 20 games for the last-place Saint Louis Browns in 1951. Lee Thomas had 26 home runs and 104 RBIS for the 1962 Angels and was named to the All-Star team. Walt Dropo was the AL Rookie of the Year in 1950 on the strength of 34 home runs, a league-leading 144 RBIS, and a .322 batting average—all career highs.

Each of these men discusses what it felt like to hit the heights, and also what it felt like to experience the frustration of never being able to duplicate those feats.

235. *Opening Day: The Story of Jackie Robinson's First Season,* by Jonathan Eig. New York: Simon and Schuster, 2007.

As he did with his Lou Gehrig biography, *Luckiest Man,* Eig does a workmanlike job in presenting the unvarnished facts of Robinson's eventful debut year, which, as the author says in his notes section, speak for themselves and are in need of no amelioration.

What the author *does* include is the impact Robinson's presence had on slowly overcoming some of his teammates' prejudices. Even some of them who weren't southerners had never considered what it meant to live with and work in proximity to people they saw as not like themselves; it proved to be a revelation.

Some other long-held beliefs about Robinson's first season are supported while others are dispelled, but I won't spoil the discovery for you readers.

Other categories: Auto/Bio/Mem, Ethnicity

236. *Past Time: Baseball as History,* by Jules Tygiel. New York: Oxford University Press, 2000.

Tygiel took a break from his cottage industry of works on Jackie Robinson to produce this excellent general volume. But rather than look at the impact of the national pastime on America, he flipped it, observing how America put its stamp on the game.

Much of Tygiel's inquiry revolves around the idea of movement. What effects did the country's westward expansion in the mid- to late nineteenth century have on the evolution of rules and techniques? How did the growth of radio and, later, television change the fans' experience with baseball from their homes and the manner in which the individual teams presented their products?

Among the other variations on the movement theme was the impact on inner-city teams that occurred during the post-World War II exodus to the suburbs (also known as white flight), as well as improvements and innovations in travel on the geographic nature and economics of the national pastime.

Other categories: Academic, Pop Culture

237. *The Perfect Game,* edited by Mark Alvarez, with a foreword by Bill James. Dallas: Taylor, 1993.

Here's another anthology produced under the SABR's auspices. The topics, which are as far-reaching and eclectic as one would expect from the organization, are divided into three general categories: numbers (as in statistics and records), brief biographical profiles, and historical issues. Among the subjects included are the untold story of Jackie Robinson's signing, written by John Thorn and Jules Tygiel, one of the most respected Robinson scholars; the sad life of Eddie Gaedel, Bill Veeck's midget pinch-hitter.

Literary-minded fans will find Paul Adomites's entry on "The Essential Baseball Library" of particular interest, as he offers suggestions for classic titles in the areas of statistics, autobiography and biography, fiction, the Minor Leagues, anthologies and collections, the Negro Leagues, and ballparks. And since the key word is *essential*, we're only talking about the cream of the crop, the top two to five titles in each category.

Other categories: Analysis, Anthology, Classic, Statistics

238. *Play It Again: Baseball Experts on What Might Have Been*, edited by Jim Bresnahan. Jefferson NC: McFarland, Publishers, 2006.

What if . . . ?

A classic *Peanuts* cartoon shows the hard-luck Charlie Brown sitting silently on a curb with his best friend, Linus. Suddenly he cries out: "Why couldn't McCovey have hit the ball two feet higher?" It's a reference to the San Francisco Giants slugger lining out to the New York Yankees' second baseman, Bobby Richardson, with the tying and winning runs in scoring position in the last game of the 1962 World Series.

Thirty-eight experts plus an additional dozen contributors offer their thoughts on similar what-if situations and the possible outcomes had the planets been aligned differently.

The book is divided into time periods and asks questions such as, "What if the Black Sox didn't throw the 1919 World Series?" "What if integration had come prior to 1947?" "What if some of the game's stars had not lost time to [World War II]?"

My favorite ponders the plight of the Montreal Expos, who had the misfortune to play some of their best baseball in years that experienced major work stoppages: 1981, when they lost a heartbreaker in the final game of the NLCS, and 1994, when they had the best record in the Majors, only to have the rug pulled out from under them when the strike caused cancellation of the postseason. Who knows? If they had won it all in either of those seasons, perhaps their fan base would have been stronger, the team's success might have encouraged team officials to keep the good players on the roster and go after others—and perhaps they'd still be in Montreal! Perhaps, in an alternate universe, they are.

Contributors who provide their expertise to *Play It Again* include

Maury Allen, Darryl Brock, Jerry Eskenazi, Sean Foreman, Gary Gillette, Bill James, Rob Neyer, Alan Schwartz, and Dean Sullivan.

Other category: Analysis

239. *The Politics of Glory: How Baseball's Hall of Fame Really Works*, by Bill James. New York: Macmillan, 1994.

Just about every January, when the new inductees to the Hall of Fame are announced, the arguments begin anew. "Well, if Player X is in, then Player Y should be too" is a familiar refrain. Questions are also raised about whether it's possible to kick out some of those already enshrined, who, in light of new research, no longer seem up to snuff.

James mixes these arguments with the history of the creation and maintenance of the Hall. It will be an educational experience for most readers, who will no doubt be surprised or dismayed about the internal politics, both in the establishment of the institution back in the 1930s and the campaigns by those on the ballot for the honor of including "HoF" in their signatures (and increasing the value of their memorabilia).

Of course, having been written more than fifteen years ago, some of James's information is outdated and several players discussed in his book have been inducted in the interim. Maybe a revised edition would consider what to do about those who played during the steroids era of the 1990s and early 2000s. Nevertheless, *The Politics of Glory* still stands on its own as an indispensable resource for those interested in the Hall's backstory.

Other categories: Business, Hall of Fame

240. *The Rise and Fall of Dodgertown: 60 Years of Baseball in Vero Beach*, by Rody Johnson. Gainesville: University Press of Florida, 2008.

Aside from the fiercely loyal fan base that loved the team for their colorful and heroic players, the Brooklyn Dodgers were known for their innovation and creativity, thanks in no small part to their president and general manager, Branch Rickey.

Rickey and the Dodgers needed a place in the Deep South to hold spring training where Jackie Robinson and the other African American players on the team would be able to live and work in relative peace and safety. So they created Dodgertown, a state-of-the-art, self-contained facility where the outside world would not intrude—where the team would live, work, find entertainment, and bond during those early and tense days of baseball desegregation.

Through the decades, as Johnson chronicles, Dodgertown took on a deeper economic and social meaning within the Vero Beach community from its first planning stages to its closing after the 2007 season.

Other categories: Business, History, Spring Training

241. *Rob Neyer's Big Book of Baseball Legends: The Truth, the Lies, and Everything Else,* by Rob Neyer. New York: Fireside, 2008.

No book has influenced me as much in the past few years as much Neyer's most recent release.

Have you ever wondered how ballplayers have the amazing ability to recall dates, pitchers, weather conditions, opponents' alignments? Easy. *They make it up.* Well, perhaps not totally or consciously, but playing in hundreds, if not thousands of games, facing all those pitchers, with all those pitches—how can they really be expected to remember every little thing that went on? Neyer, head of sb Nation website, finally calls those guys out.

Baseball Legends does a lot of myth busting, including a somewhat disturbing story of Lawrence Ritter's methodology in compiling his well-received oral history, *The Glory of Their Times,* in which he admits making some editorial adjustments, enhancing the comments of several of the old ballplayers he interviewed, filling in the missing pieces, as it were, or just prettying up the story ever so slightly.

I received the largest number of visitors to my *Bookshelf* blog thanks to *Baseball Legends.* I had heard an anecdote from Moose Skowron, a player during the 1950s and 1960s, on the NPR quiz program *Wait Wait . . . Don't Tell Me!* that seemed too detailed to believe. Using some of the modern day tools available on the Internet, including Baseball-Reference.com and Retrosheet.org, I was able to ascertain that Mr. Skowron was, shall we say, erroneous.

Since then, I've used Neyer's book to debunk other claims. There are those who would kill the messenger: "Let us keep our cherished memories, even if they're wrong," say both the players and the fans, who dote on such stories. But if there's one service Neyer has provided, it's that contemporary players will be a bit more cautious when embellishing their tales in the glow of retirement.

Other categories: Pop Culture, Reference

Also by the author: *The Neyer/James Guide to Pitchers: An Historical Compendium of Pitching, Pitchers, and Pitches* (2004); *Rob Neyer's Big Book of Baseball Lineups: A Complete Guide to the Best, Worst, and Most Memorable Players to Ever Grace the Major Leagues* (2003); *Baseball Dynasties: The Greatest Teams of All Time* (2000); *Rob Neyer's Big Book of Baseball Blunders: A Complete Guide to the Worst Decisions and Stupidest Moments in Baseball History* (2006)

242. *Rookies of the Year,* by Bob Bloss. Philadelphia: Temple University Press, 2005.

Since the inception of the award honoring first-year players, scores of ballplayers have made their debuts each year. How many of them will perform at the elite level; how many will enjoy average, lengthy careers; and how many will fold after a season or two?

Following an initial introduction to the history of the award—which was renamed in honor of Jackie Robinson, the first player to be thus recognized, in 1987—Bloss separates the freshmen into just such categories, profiling each with the highlights, and in some cases the lowlights, of their career.

Of the 116 award winners up through the book's publication in 2004, an even dozen were eventually enshrined in the Hall of Fame. Seventeen have won both the RoY (as it is known in shorthand) and his league's MVP award, with Fred Lynn and Ichiro Suzuki each accomplishing the rare feat in their debut season. Eleven proved to be astute scholars of the game: they eventually became managers.

While the average career of a RoY was about twelve seasons, twelve players lasted seven years or fewer. The final chapter for several athletes had not yet been written, as they were still active as of the publication of the book.

Other category: Reference

243. *The* Sporting News *Salutes Baseball's 100 Greatest Players,* second edition, by Ron Smith. Saint Louis: Sporting News, 2005.

Originally published in 1998, this revised edition differs slightly by reranking a handful of players. Barry Bonds, for example moved from number thirty-four to number six, while others, like Kirby Puckett, Goose Goslin, Rollie Fingers, and Early Wynn were dropped in favor of Alex Rodriguez, Sammy Sosa, Derek Jeter, and Randy Johnson.

The book is divided into four twenty-five-man sections separated by snappy charts and graphics, including a timeline so the reader can see who played in relationship to whom and who was on the all-decade teams. Each athlete gets a two-page spread with a brief bio, a couple of photos, and a factoid box.

Smith holds out the possibility for future candidates that might force their way onto the elite list in the years following the book's publication, perhaps prepping fans for a third edition: Albert Pujols and Mariana Rivera seem like locks. Pedro Martinez, perhaps. But Manny Ramirez? Tough call considering how he left the game. It's also hard to believe Smith's assessment that Vlad Guerrero and Miguel Tejada could nudge their way into the upper echelon.

Other features include a breakdown of the top one hundred players by position and primary team, and a line of statistics for each athlete. The 1998 version also has a quiz and a section on top-ten selections as chosen by players and managers.

Other categories: Coffee Table/Gift, Reference

244. *SPORT Magazine's All-Time All Stars*, edited by Tom Murray. New York: Atheneum, 1997.

One of the premier publications in the genre, *SPORT* Magazine made its debut in 1946 and printed its last issue in 2000. Some of the best wordsmiths over the decades, such as Al Stump, who wrote with and about Ty Cobb; Ed Linn, who covered Bill Veeck and Leo Durocher, among others; Shirley Povich; Arnold Hano; and Jack Sher have published long-form essays in the magazine, several examples of which have been assembled and edited for *All-Time All Stars* as testaments to the writers' expertise to select this All-Star group.

Some of the featured athletes, such as Honus Wagner and Christy Mathewson, came along before the official midsummer classic was launched in 1933, so this is a nice way of giving them some extra recognition alongside official All-Stars like DiMaggio, Williams, Mantle, Musial, Campanella, Mays, and Aaron (serving here as DH for the National League).

As with any opinion-driven lineup, controversy ensues from the omissions: Where's Jackie Robinson, for example, or Yogi Berra? And having only two pitchers per each team leaves lots of room for second-guessing.

Works like this were especially common in 1969, the centennial of professional baseball; 1976, the United States' bicentennial, which served as an invitation to celebrate all things Americana; and the period surrounding the millennia, when books about the century's greatest were published fast and furiously.

Other categories: Anthology, Sportswriting

245. *This Great Game*, edited by Doris Townsend. Englewood Cliffs NJ: Rutledge, 1971.

This one is quite personal for me. It was the first expensive gift book I ever received, a present from my late sister when I was a kid.

At the time, I was entranced by the beautiful photos and artwork by LeRoy Neiman, but in retrospect there were some pretty good writers who contributed to the project as well.

Following several pages of sepia-toned photos on rough-grade paper, the book transitions into glossy images, both in color and black and white, with an essay by Roger Angell, who, then as now, was considered one of the top men at his craft. More photos follow, beginning with articles from manager Earl Weaver, who was in the middle of leading the Baltimore Orioles through several excellent seasons, on the leadership process. Other essays include "The Salaried Elite," a piece on a dozen greats of the late 1960s, by Douglas Wallop, author of *The Year the Yankees Lost the Pennant*, and illustrated by Neiman's stylish renderings on double-spread pages; umpire Al Barlick on "The Man in Blue"; Joseph Reichler on some of "The Great Plays" in MLB history, always a topic of debate and obviously revised numerous times over the years; Charles Maher on "The Glove Men"; Frank Slocum on "Battery," which considers pitchers and catchers; Milton Gross on "More Than Just Speed" (baserunning); William Leggett on "The Incomprehensible Art" of hitting; and Roy Blount Jr.'s humor essay, "Beware of Moe," which urges readers not to take any of this too seriously. Dick Young wraps things up with "They Call That a Hit in Detroit," about the thankless job of the official scorer.

Other categories: Coffee Table/Gift, Pop Culture, Sportswriting

246. *Touching Base: Professional Baseball and American Culture in the Progressive Era*, by Steven A. Reiss. Urbana: University of Illinois Press, 1999.

Neither baseball nor America was static throughout the late nineteenth and early twentieth centuries, as Reiss, a professor of history at Northeastern Illinois University, explains in this thoughtful exposition that focuses on how changes in the latter impacted on the former.

With the country expanding, due in no small part to a surfeit of immigration, the population shifted from the rural farmlands to the cities; Reiss concentrates on port cities of New York, Chicago, and Atlanta, all of which were enjoying a boom in the early 1900s.

With little competition from other sports or forms of entertainments, baseball enjoyed its greatest popularity. Coupled with an economic upturn, club owners began to replace rickety and unsafe wooden ballparks with steel and concrete edifices, and politicians were quick to jump on the bandwagon, making a great show of their support for the locals. Gone were the days of the gentlemen's sporting clubs; baseball was a business now, with larger-than-life heroes bursting on to the national stage.

Cultural sensibilities and economic realities—especially among the newcomers who wanted to embrace baseball but were still hamstrung by the necessity of working six days a week—began to erode the strictures against playing pro ball on Sundays. And for the sons of some of these immigrant families, baseball even offered the possibility of employment. What better way to become an American than playing the national pastime?

Not that it was without its problems. For as much as social integration was a key element of the Progressive Era, Reiss points out that African Americans were still not invited to participate in the American Dream with their fellow white citizens.

247. *Triumph and Tragedy in Mudville: A Lifelong Passion for Baseball*, by Stephen Jay Gould. New York: W. W. Norton, 2003.

Gould, primarily known as an paleontologist, educator, and writer on much more substantial matters than baseball, nevertheless was a devout fan who loved nothing more than finding ways to link the game with his areas of academic expertise, such as biology and history.

I doubt anyone but Gould could have drawn a connection, when discussing the foibles of history and perception, between the defeat of Jim Bowie and his fellow Texicans, who died at the Alamo in 1836, and the defeat of Bill Buckner and the Red Sox 150 years later.

Triumph and Tragedy contains the author's reminiscences—which he admits might be somewhat faulty given the nature of memory—of growing up in New York and discovering a lifelong passion for baseball, the New York Yankees in particular. Other sections include appreciations for long-cherished heroes like Mickey Mantle and Joe DiMaggio, and others who made their mark for a single moment, like the New York Giants' Dusty Rhodes in the 1954 World Series, as if to show the fickle and contradictory nature of fame.

This collection of essays and book reviews written for other publications over the years is a tribute to the late Gould, who rushed to complete the project while suffering from terminal cancer.

Other categories: Analysis, Anthology, Auto/Bio/Mem, Classic, Essays

248. *The Ultimate Baseball Book,* edited by Daniel Okrent and Harris Lewine. New York: Houghton Mifflin, 2000.

This is another fine example of a multipurpose title. It's a coffee-table book, a history book, a photography book, and an anthology. It combines archival pictures of the earliest annals of the game supplemented by excellent essays by some of the best writers around: Robert Creamer on the Baltimore Orioles of Ned Hanlon and John McGraw; Roy Blount Jr. on Joe DiMaggio; Mordecai Richler on pro ball in Montreal; and George F. Will on the Chicago style of play.

It's amazing how much information you can pack into less than 450 pages, especially when you consider how well the illustrations present the key players and events in the national pastime. Each decade gets is own inning, with an extra inning and postgame to accommodate the timeline through the end of the twentieth century; the 2000 edition was the third printing of the book. Students of the game will especially appreciate the pre-1950s chapters.

Other categories: Anthology, Coffee Table/Gift, Pop Culture
Also by the author: *Nine Innings: The Anatomy of a Baseball Game* (1985); *Baseball Anecdotes* (1989)

249. *The American Game: Baseball and Ethnicity*, edited by Lawrence Baldassaro and Richard A. Johnson. Carbondale: Southern Illinois University Press, 2002.

Many sons of immigrants wishing to assimilate into society and be considered "true Americans" found that route through the national pastime.

The nine essays in *The American Game* consider the stories of success, generally speaking, that these groups achieved over the years, although not at the same rate or at the same time.

Although the game was invented by Anglo-Americans whose roots came from Great Britain, it was soon the sport of choice for Irish and German immigrants who arrived in the middle of the nineteenth century. Additional essays consider the experiences of Jews, Slavs, Italians, Latinos, African Americans, and Asian Americans.

Despite cultural differences, they all had the shared experience early on of being shunned as "others," facing animosity or good-natured ribbing, depending on the source, from fans and opposing players. Germans faced a great deal of scorn during World War I but, surprisingly, not to the same extent during World War II.

Almost every region, nationality, or ethnic group has been the subject of separate volumes, but Baldassaro and Johnson provide a good overview under one roof here.

Other categories: Academic, Anthology, Essays

250. *The Baseball Talmud: The Definitive Position-by-Position Ranking of Baseball's Chosen People*, by Howard Megdal. New York: Collins, 2009.

Jews account for less than 1 percent of all Major Leaguers and only 3 percent of the general population in the United States. But those players have an especially loyal fan base, so when a new one makes it to the Show, it's a cause to celebrate, or *kvell*, as we say.

Megdal, who writes about baseball for several print and online publications, looks at each JML (Jewish Major Leaguer), through the 2008 season. He categorizes the players by their defensive positions, including left- and right-handed pitchers, both starters and relievers. The rankings are based on sabermetric statistics, with a little bit of humanity thrown in because numbers don't always tell the story. Some of these MOTS (members of the tribe) had but a cup of coffee in the Majors, so Megdal looks at their Minor League records and extrapolates what might have been, given the proper circumstances.

He closes with his all-time Jewish team, which includes Hall of Famers Hank Greenberg, Sandy Koufax, and Lou Boudreau, along with relative newcomers Ian Kinsler and Kevin Youkilis. Ryan Braun was a mere rookie when Megdal published his book; a revised edition will no doubt elevate his status.

Also by the author: *Taking the Field: A Fan's Quest to Run the Team He Loves* (2011)

251. *The Best Man Plays: Major League Baseball and the Black Athlete, 1901–2002,* by Andrew O'Toole. Jefferson NC: McFarland, 2003.

O'Toole assesses the progress—or lack thereof—made by African Americans over the years by focusing on six key figures in the annals of black baseball.

Rube Foster, whom the author deems more important than Jackie Robinson, created a league of their own for black athletes who were shut out of organized baseball. Satchel Paige, one of the stars of the Negro Leagues who eventually made it to the Majors, was the one of the faces and great personalities of the Negro Leagues. Larry Doby, the second African American to enter the Majors, never received his due, laboring in Robinson's shadow.

Curt Flood's contribution to all of baseball came not on the playing field, but through the courtroom. His refusal to be treated as a team's property paved the way to the multimillion-dollar salaries the players enjoy today. One of those to benefit was Dave Parker, a power hitter for the Pittsburgh Pirates and Cincinnati Reds who became the first African American millionaire in the Majors. But as an outspoken black man, he incurred the wrath of many so-called fans who were anxious to see him fail. The same could be said for Barry Bonds, whose treatment by the media — perhaps exacerbated by his behavior toward them, a chicken-and-egg situation — did not give him any benefit of doubt once the performance-enhancing drugs accusations started flying.

O'Toole concludes with a chapter warning that baseball needs to do more. The record for advancement into the front office is poor, and more opportunities need to be afforded to qualified black candidates.

Other category: Negro Leagues

252. *Beyond DiMaggio: Italian Americans in Baseball,* by Lawrence Baldassaro. Lincoln: University of Nebraska Press, 2011.

Going back through the popular magazines of the mid-1900s, it's not unusual to find passages that play on the stereotypes of various ethnicities. In a profile in the May 1, 1939, issue of *Life* magazine, one can find this seemingly complimentary remark in a profile of the Yankees' young star, Joe DiMaggio: "Although he learned Italian first, Joe, now 24, speaks English without an accent and is otherwise well adapted to most U.S. mores. Instead of olive oil or smelly bear grease he keeps his hair slick with water. He never reeks of garlic and prefers chicken chow mein to spaghetti." Can you imagine reading that kind of characterization today?

Baldassaro, a professor emeritus of Italian at the University of Wisconsin–Milwaukee, pays homage to the Italians who have had such an impact on the game including — besides the three DiMaggio brothers, Joe, Vince, and Dom, who contributed the book's foreword shortly before he died in 2009 — Ed Abbaticchio, regarded as the first Italian to play in the Majors; Tony Lazzeri, of the Yankees' famed Murderers' Row; Ernie Lombardi, who won the batting title in 1938 and 1942 despite being a slow-footed catcher; Phil Rizzuto and Yogi Berra, also from the Yankees; the Dodgers' Carl Furillo and Roy Campanella (Italian father); and more recent players like Tony and Billy Conigliaro, Ron Santo, Joe Torre, and Mike Piazza, to name just a few.

Other category: Pop Culture

253. *Brushing Back Jim Crow: The Integration of Minor-League Baseball in the American South,* by Bruce Adelson. Charlottesville: University of Virginia Press, 1999.

The Brooklyn Dodgers planned it out wisely when they assigned Jackie Robinson to Montreal in the International League. By doing so, they avoided subjecting him to the difficulties of playing in the Deep South, or, indeed, just about anywhere in United States.

The athletes included in Adelson's history were not so lucky. Many of them had grown up in the more progressive North or other places where segregation was not an issue. But when fan disinterest grew thanks to other leisure options, the Minor Leagues knew they had to adapt or die. They may have been vehemently opposed to black, but the love of green was more powerful.

One by one the leagues and teams began to sign players as novelty items to entice African American and white fans alike to come out to the ballpark. Some cities had an easier time of it; others, with strict antifraternization laws on the books, were much slower on the draw. Thus, each black player served as a pioneer in his own right.

The stories told by these men are surprisingly mixed. One would expect resistance from white players, whether a teammate fearful of the shame of losing their job to a black man, or an opponent wary of losing to an "inferior," yet there are also touching tales of increasing acceptance, camaraderie, and pride, both for these ballplayers and the larger African American community.

Other categories: Minor Leagues, Negro Leagues

254. *Few and Chosen: Defining Negro Leagues Greatness,* by Monte Irvin with Phil Pepe. Chicago: Triumph, 2007.

Triumph published a number of books in this series, primarily for individual teams under the lead authorship of an established star. Each volume followed a template, including anecdotes, statistics, and photos.

In this case, Irvin, who played with the Newark Eagles for eleven years before getting his big league break with the New York Giants, offers his choice of the top five players at each position. He also lists the best managers, owners, organizers, and pioneers, with the biggest nods going to Rube Foster, who was considered the father of the original Negro Leagues; Gus Greenlee, who brought black baseball back after Foster's initial attempts eventually failed; and Effa Manley, Irvin's boss in Newark and perhaps the most powerful female executive in all of sports.

The top team honor goes to the Pittsburgh Crawfords of the 1930s. With players like Satchel Paige, Josh Gibson, Oscar Charleston, and Cool Papa Bell, the Crawfords were comparable to the Yankees in terms of prestige and drawing power.

Other categories: Analysis, Negro Leagues

255. *"Get That Nigger Off the Field!" A Sparkling, Informal History of the Black Man in Baseball,* by Art Rust Jr. New York: Delacorte, 1976.

The ugly epithet has come from many a racist's lips, but the author first attributes its use in baseball to Adrian "Cap" Anson, the Hall of Famer who refused to participate in games with or against African Americans.

Rust focuses on some of the great black players with a combination of profiles, interviews, first-person accounts, and anecdotes from teammates, fans, and opponents.

The book is fairly light fare with plenty of photos, as it covers three eras designated by the author: the black baseball stars of the Negro Leagues; the accomplishments of players like Jackie Robinson and

Larry Doby, who broke the color lines in the National and American Leagues, respectively; and those athletes who came after, from Junior Gilliam to Frank Robinson, who gets extra props as the first black manager in the Majors. Then, for some reason left unexplained, Rust concludes with a brief chapter about contemporary (in 1976) Latinos such as Roberto Clemente, Felix Millan, Dave Concepcion, and Sandy Alomar, all of whom are worthy subjects, but they somehow seem out of place in such a book.

Rust was an unabashed fan growing up in New York, even though he couldn't come up with an answer when a teacher asked him how he could follow a sport that didn't allow his race to play. It's that fan's voice that adds a little twinkle to the stories.

Other category: Negro Leagues

256. *Only the Ball Was White: A History of Legendary Black Players and All-Black Professional Teams,* by Robert Peterson. New York: Prentice Hall, 1970.

Like Robert Whiting's books on Japanese baseball, Peterson wrote what many believe to be the seminal volume on the Negro Leagues, the one that opened the door for further academic studies. African American ballplayers before Jackie Robinson tended to get short shrift from fans and historians, but Peterson and authors like Lawrence Hogan, John Holway, and Larry Lester began to dig deeper, researching yellowing African American newspapers and seeking out former Negro Leaguers to give them proper credit and respect.

Unfortunately, since the mainstream press did not cover the Negro Leagues and even the black press didn't keep thorough records, a good deal of the information is anecdotal, but it's entertaining nevertheless. For example, Peterson includes in an appendix a register of players and officials from 1884–1950, a task that even the author admits is incomplete. Since then, research methods have improved to a point where many of these blanks can be filled in.

Other categories: Academic, Ethnicity, Negro Leagues

257. *Out of Left Field: Jews and Black Baseball,* by Rebecca T. Alpert. New York: Oxford University Press, 2011.

Alpert, an ordained rabbi and an associate professor of religion and women's studies at Temple University in Philadelphia, wrote this well-researched and scholarly history of the tenuous association of Jews into the world of black baseball and the Negro Leagues.

At once venerated for their business acumen and mistrusted as potential opportunists, a handful of Jews had major roles in the development of the sport, including Ed Gottlieb, Syd Pollack, and Abe Saperstein, the driving force behind the Harlem Globetrotters, as well as a handful of others.

The relationship between Jews and blacks — both groups frequent subjects of racist invective — made them tentative allies, but there were lingering doubts among the African American team owners as to the motives of these associates.

Alpert pays particular attention to "The Conflict over Baseball Comedy." The connection between Jews and the entertainment industry gave them an extra degree of authority. Pollack owned a team called the Ethiopian Clowns, which donned costumes and face paint to conduct their routines and play ball, which did not sit well with some members of the black community.

On the other hand, Alpert also pays tribute to the contributions Jews made in bringing an end to Jim Crow baseball, culminating with the signing and eventual promotion of Jackie Robinson to the Major Leagues.

Other categories: Academic, Ethnicity, Negro Leagues, Pop Culture

258. *Shut Out: A Story of Race and Baseball in Boston,* by Howard Bryant. New York: Routledge, 2002.

Imagine a Boston Red Sox team that included Jackie Robinson and Willie Mays in addition to stars like Ted Williams, Bobby Doerr, and Billy Goodman. But the team, owned by Tom Yawkey and led on the field and in the front office by Joe Cronin, was too blinded by

CHAPTER SEVEN

color — as opposed to being color-blind — to put their best product forward. Did such a pervasive attitude prevent them from making the Red Sox perennial pennant contenders?

That attitude didn't end after Pumpsie Green made Boston the last team have an African American player on its roster. Bryant reports that Boston's black players, like Reggie Smith and Earl Wilson — both of whom helped bring the team to a first-place finish in 1967 — endured shockingly backward treatment both within the organization and in Boston at large, with restaurants, bars, and hotels refusing them service. Ferguson Jenkins, Jim Rice, and Tommy Harper were denouncing New England's so-called sensibilities well into the 1970s.

Bryant, who received *Spitball* magazine's CASEY Award in 2002, points the finger of blame at the local media, who seemed uninterested in stirring up trouble in a town already beset with racial unrest. This makes his book a sort of hybrid, fitting just as well on the urban and civic studies shelves as in the sports section.

Other categories: Award Winner, Business

259. *When to Stop Cheering: The Black Press, the Black Community, and the Integration of Professional Baseball,* by Brian Carroll. New York: Routledge, 2007.

For many years, the Negro Leagues were a source of great pride to the African American community. The teams fielded some of the best athletes in the game, white *or* black, and for many fans of color this was literally the only game in town.

But at some point, according to the author, people began to question the justice involved in keeping players like Satchel Paige, Josh Gibson, and Cool Papa Bell out of organized baseball. Progressive thinkers of all colors argued for integration against overwhelming odds and intransigent racism.

The black press often went along with the status quo, since the teams were advertisers and the fans subscribers, but journalists such as Wendell Smith of the *Pittsburgh Courier* and Sam Lacy of the *Afro-American* newspaper chain, began a steady stream of agitation, politicking for Jackie Robinson to get his chance while at the same time preparing African American fans for the difficulties that lay ahead should the project fail. They constantly wrote about the progress that was demanded, even at the cost of sentencing the Negro Leagues to financial ruin. It was time to stop cheering for the present and prepare for the future.

Other categories: Media, Negro Leagues, Sportswriting

EVENTS

260. *56: Joe DiMaggio and the Last Magic Number in Sports,* by Kostya Kennedy. New York: Sports Illustrated, 2011.

The book industry is a sucker for anniversaries, and, of course, the higher the number the better. I suppose that an event's seventieth anniversary is pretty much the upper level for those who might re-member it taking place. In this case it's the celebration of DiMaggio's famed consecutive-game hitting streak.

These days, once a batter gets to thirty consecutive games with a hit, the media starts the countdown. In 2011 Andre Ethier of the Dodgers batted safely in thirty straight, leaving him still almost a month's worth of games short of DiMaggio's magic number.

Kennedy, a writer for *Sports Illustrated,* does a fine job in recreating the tension the Yankee Clipper must have felt as he approached the American League record of forty-one straight set by George Sisler of the Saint Louis Browns in 1922, and the Major League mark of forty-four by Wee Willie Keeler of the old Baltimore Orioles in 1897 (a National League team in those days). With those out of the way, it should have been smooth sailing for DiMaggio, but every day brought new demands, as America looked for some respite from the dark news that was unfolding in Europe and the Pacific.

The author presents the biography almost as a work of fiction, teasing the readers with cliff-hangers. He also includes interviews and research from contemporary sources that may strike some as extraneous, but it's just Kennedy's attempt to put DiMaggio's streak into perspective. With steroids casting a pall, at least for the time being, over recent records, *those* numbers have certainly become less magical.

Other categories: Auto/Bio/Mem, Pop Culture

261. *100 Years of the World Series, 1903–2004*, by Eric Enders. New York: Sterling, 2005.

This oversized volume succinctly sums up each of the Fall Classics through the Red Sox's storybook 2004 season. Most of the Series are wrapped up in two pages, and each includes a box of line scores.

The chapters are divided somewhat arbitrarily and follow a general time frame. Chapter 1 begins with the first World Series and concludes with the Black Sox scandal of 1919 and the acquisition of Babe Ruth by the Yankees. Chapter 2 continues through the end of World War II. Chapter 3 takes us up to the expansion era, while Chapter 4 wrings out the old and rings in the new after the end of the free-agent era in 1976–94, even though there was no Series in 1994. The fifth and final chapter is titled "Reign of the Sluggers." Cynics in the crowd, however, might suggest "Reign of the Steroids Users."

The photographs include a mix of classic historical shots along with a few new ones for the sake of variety. Another nice touch is the inclusion of the World Series program covers for each year. The first appendix includes World Series record holders and MVPs. But the second appendix offers a key selling point: box scores for each game.

100 Years is handsome addition to your library, but is one more example of a title that needs constant updating.

Other categories: Coffee Table/Gift, Pop Culture

262. *Baseball and The Blame Game: Scapegoating in the Major Leagues,* by John Billheimer. Jefferson NC: McFarland, 2007.

Unfortunately, in today's society people are always looking for someone else to blame their misfortunes on.

Most of the ballplayers discussed in Billheimer's book are just victims of timing. If a ball gets through Bill Buckner's legs during the regular season, it's no biggie. But in Game Six of the 1986 World Series with the Red Sox only one out away from winning their first World Series since 1918? Huge deal. And who can forget Merkle's Boner in 1908, when the New York Giants rookie failed to touch second base in an apparent win over the Chicago Cubs? That one has traditionally been cited as costing New York the pennant.

Billheimer parses similar events, including wild pitches, passed balls (Mickey Owen in the 1941 World Series), inopportune home runs (Thomson off Branca for the "shot heard 'round the world" in 1951), and dropped fly balls (Fred Snodgrass's World Series–losing error in 1912), among others life-altering miscues.

Nor do the managers, umpires, and even fans come away clean, although the author does have empathy for Steve Bartman, whom some folks blame for costing the Cubs the pennant in 2003 by hindering Moises Alou from potentially catching a foul ball. Billheimer seeks to establish whether that was justified at the time and, in fact, if the unfortunate incident was the deciding factor in the outcome. Most baseball-savvy people don't believe this was the case.

With the passage of time — not to mention the ability to go back and do research like this — some of Billheimer's arguments are stronger than others.

263. *Baseball Records Registry: The Best and Worst Single-Day Performances and the Stories Behind Them,* by Joseph J. Dittmar. Jefferson NC: McFarland, 1997.

One of the more unusual books regarding records, the *Registry* is not something to read through like a narrative. Rather it's something to savor, item by item.

Dittmar begins his opus with a 1901 game in which the Detroit Tigers scored ten runs in the bottom of the ninth against the original Milwaukee Brewers for a 14–13 win. And it goes on like that, chronologically, for another six hundred pages, featuring 226 I-never-knew-that moments that stood out over the next ninety-five years. The table of contents alone weaves a fascinating trail of the quirky items statisticians kept track of.

The author provides box scores for each game along with lively descriptions of the action and actors. He also thoughtfully offers several ways to locate these records via appendices that note performance highlights by game and by the specific record set, and he corrects some past mistakes he found in some of his sources.

Other categories: Analysis, Statistics, Trivia

264. *Baseball's Best: The M V Ps,* by Dave Masterson and Timm Boyle. Chicago: Contemporary, 1985.

Another sleeper in need of an update, this collection offers pretty much everything you need to know about the Most Valuable Players since the award was initiated in 1931, as well as a look at unofficial awards before then.

The authors include profiles of each of the honorees chronologically through 1984, along with details on how they earned the hardware. There's also a brief overview of the baseball season as a whole and a section on other top candidates for the award. What's missing, and would be appreciated in any future edition, would be the voting tabulations, to see just how close or far apart the races were.

The handy reference includes a number of appendices featuring such trivia items as M V Ps by team and position and predecessors to the current award, which is named in honor of Judge Kennesaw Mountain Landis, the sport's first commissioner. One item of curiosity is a section on "M V Ps of the Future," which examines ten high-level players from each league whom the authors predicted could win the award in the future. Although the list contained four future

Hall of Fame inductees, only one—Don Mattingly in 1985—would actually earn the prize, which just shows how difficult it is to win.

Other categories: Auto/Bio/Mem, Reference

265. *Baseball's Dead of World War II: A Roster of Professional Players Who Died in Service,* by Gary Bedingfield. Jefferson NC: McFarland, 2010.

I have always been about the veterans, especially those of the Greatest Generation. Bedingfield, a native of Great Britain, evidently feels the same: he hosts a website called Baseball in Wartime. This book is an extension of his appreciation.

Baseball's Dead feature profiles of the 127 players and umpires known to have died in, or as a direct result of, the war, beginning with Hugh P. Bedient Jr. in 1940, through Rodney L. Sooter in 1946, both of whom, coincidentally, perished as the result of non-combat-related plane crashes.

The servicemen are divided by branch, including army, army air force, navy, and marines, as well as the Canadian Army (represented by Donald A. Stewart). The author provides personal and athletic backgrounds for all, including statistics where applicable. Not everyone actually played professionally though; some were on their way before joining the armed forces, but most never advanced much above the lower rungs of the Minors. Of the group, only two made it to the Majors: Harry O'Neill, a catcher for the Philadelphia Phillies, who had a single appearance as a defensive replacement in 1939; and Elmer Gedeon, who played in five games for the 1939 Senators.

In addition to their baseball credentials, Bedingfield lists the players' military accomplishments, including ranks, companies, theater(s) of operations, and citations. It's a nice tribute to the men who made the ultimate sacrifice.

Other categories: Reference, Wartime Baseball

266. *Baseball's Pivotal Era, 1945–1951,* by William Marshall. Lexington: University Press of Kentucky, 1999.

Just as the golden age of the game is when *you* happen to think it is, the pivotal eras are similarly plentiful.

Marshall begins his book with an ending: World War II. The players who came back replaced the ones who had filled in during their absence and experienced a welcome return to normalcy.

It's hard to believe that so many major events took place in such a brief period. Take, for example, baseball's Mexican Revolution, in which several Major Leaguers who were fed up with dealing with the reserve clause thought they would take their talents south of the border. When things didn't go quite like they had hoped, they learned that Commissioner Landis had revoked their return privileges. This led to lawsuits as the players sought reinstatement, which eventually led Congress to hold hearings on the monopoly status of the national pastime.

Among the other events of the era: The Cubs' last World Series appearance, the beginnings of serious rumblings of union activity, the impact of television and other leisure activities on Major and Minor League attendance, and, of course, Jackie Robinson and the other African Americans who followed.

The author, a director of special collections and archives at the University of Kentucky Libraries, hits all the high points on the field, from the stars of the era to the exciting pennant races, including Bobby Thomson's "shot heard 'round the world." The result is a nice blend of academic and popular writing for which Marshall received SABR's Seymour Medal in 2000.

Other categories: Award Winner, Pop culture

267. *Bottom of the Ninth: Branch Rickey, Casey Stengel, and the Daring Scheme to Save Baseball from Itself,* by Michael Shapiro. New York: Times, 2009.

Whether it was opening the doors for African American players, developing plans for a farm system, or creating protective equipment, Branch Rickey was always thinking about new ways to improve the national pastime.

After the Dodgers and Giants left New York without a National League presence, several local movers and shakers set out to find a way to fill the void. With no established teams prepared to relocate to the Big Apple, Rickey—having worked most recently for the Pittsburgh Pirates—came up with the idea of the Continental League to add to, not compete with, the two established Major Leagues. The CL would consist of seven cities that had never had big league franchises, plus New York because, well, it was New York.

Shapiro covers the progress, or lack thereof, of the ambitious plan between 1958 and 1960, as Rickey and powerful local community leaders sought financial backing, battled resistance from the established teams, and threatened civil action that could have dismantled the protections the game had enjoyed through congressional interventions. Such an undertaking requires a huge amount of planning, and the author does not skimp on the details of the requisite political bargaining and backstabbing.

The CL ultimately failed to come to fruition, but it did lead to the 1961–62 and 1969 rounds of expansion, as well as New York's return to its rightful two-team place in the big leagues.

To be honest, there's not that much Stengel in here, except that he was gradually being phased out as the Yankees' manager. The "saving baseball from itself" in the title is also a tad hyperbolic, but *Bottom of the Ninth* gives a good report on a chapter in baseball history that seems to have slid under the table.

268. *Crazy '08: How a Cast of Cranks, Rogues, Boneheads, and Magnates Created the Greatest Year in Baseball History,* by Cait Murphy. Washington DC: Smithsonian, 2007.

Murphy, an assistant managing editor at *Fortune* magazine, seeks to convince a modern-day audience that the most exciting season in Major League history took place when their great- or even great-great-grandparents were kids. And she does it quite well. She ably captures the progress of the 1908 season, but it's the side stories that set this recap apart from less ambitious projects.

Six of the sixteen teams were still in the pennant chase with just a couple of days left to the campaign. Baseball had little in the way of entertainment competition, so the sporting eyes were glued to the newspapers and oversized live-action billboards that were constructed in major cities to provide fans with up-to-the-minute information.

The "time-outs" Murphy inserts between chapters can be either a distraction or a welcome diversion, such as the story of a female serial killer or the anarchist Emma Goldman, neither of which have anything to do with baseball, but they indicate some of the other crazy things that were going on in '08.

Murphy spins a lively story about the rough-and-tumble circumstances of early-twentieth-century baseball: pugnacious players who literally fought with opponents, umpires, and even amongst themselves; firetrap stadiums; gamblers; and the eternal battle by owners to control every aspect of the game.

This was the year of Merkle's Boner, the unfortunate late-season baserunning error the rookie committed, negating a win for his New York Giants over the Chicago Cubs. They subsequently lost the flag to the Cubs in a one-game playoff.

Even readers who already know the outcome will be caught up as Murphy's story builds to a frenetic climax, to such a degree that the World Series seems like an afterthought.

Other category: Pop Culture

269. *The Echoing Green: The Untold Story of Bobby Thomson, Ralph Branca, and the Shot Heard Round the World*, by Joshua Prager. New York: Pantheon, 2006.

Some fifty years after the fact, Prager, a multi–Pulitzer Prize nominee, went the supersleuth route to posit that Thomson benefited from a little extra help. No, not steroids, but an elaborate system of sign stealing the Giants employed throughout the season. The theory was that the team had a man in the stands who signaled to a man on the bench who relayed the information to the man at the plate. And while the late Thomson said others on the Giants may have taken advantage of the opportunity, he chose not to.

Prager first reported the scheme in a *Wall Street Journal* article in 2001—the fiftieth anniversary year of the event—which got a lot of tongues wagging. No way, said Thomson supporters, while Branca and Dodger fans felt somewhat vindicated. Of *course* the Giants won, they pointed out: they cheated. This opened up a hot ethical debate on the limits of sign stealing, with the consensus that it was perfectly fine to do it unaided by technology, from the confines of the dugout.

Other categories: Auto/Bio/Mem, Event, Pop Culture

270. *Eight Men Out: The Black Sox in the 1919 World Series*, by Eliot Asinof. New York: Holt, Rinehart and Winston, 1963.

This classic tale of deception on the diamond was one of the first examples of in-depth reporting on a specific event. *Eight Men Out* was the watershed book on the scandal, the starting point to which all subsequent books on the event refer and pay homage. It was also the basis for a fine feature film in 1988 by John Sayles, with memorable performances by John Cusack, David Strathairn, D. B. Sweeney, and others as members of the doomed octet.

Asinof, a former Minor Leaguer himself, dug at the truth and perhaps enhanced it a bit, according to his obituary in the *New York Times*. He brought to light the extent of desperation the eight members of that pennant-winning 1918 team felt in falling into the scheme, planning it out with gamblers, and executing—well, actually, *not* executing—their unexpected collapse against the underdog Cincinnati Reds.

How could such a thing happen? How could professional ballplayers who were heroes to kids in Chicago and across America stoop to such a heartbreaking crime, eliciting one of the most famous quotes in pop culture: the plaintive "Say it ain't So, Joe?" How could they destroy the faith of fifty million, as F. Scott Fitzgerald alluded to in *The Great Gatsby*?

Asinof offers a little bit of compassion as he points out how poorly the players, including Shoeless Joe Jackson, were paid by their penurious owner, Charles A. Comiskey, who was surely bound for the Hall of Fame prior to his banishment.

Other categories: Business, Auto/Bio/Mem

271. The *Final Season: Fathers, Sons, and One Last Season in a Classic American Ballpark, by* Tom Stanton. New York: Thomas Dunne/St. Martin's Press, 2001.

Whenever there's a documentary about the Brooklyn Dodgers, the final scenes usually include the demolition of Ebbets Field, with Frank Sinatra singing "There Used to Be a Ball Park Over There" as the wrecking ball crashes into concrete.

With the exception of Fenway Park and Wrigley Field, all of the old stadiums are gone, victims to crumbling urban infrastructures. Tiger Stadium was one of the last to go, and Stanton, a native of the Motor City and a lifelong fan, could not let the passing go without comment.

Armed with the knowledge that 1999 would be that final season at Tiger Stadium, Stanton made plans to attend each of the last eighty-one home games. He invites the reader to come along with his own family and introduces them to like-minded fans who are already mourning the loss of the beloved institution. As the death-watch advances, there's a sense of foreboding as the team and its followers struggle to come to grips with the inevitable: the Tigers needed to move on, just like the Dodgers did almost a half century earlier, because the neighborhoods were becoming too dangerous to attract an audience, and the trend was to build new "old" stadiums, which is kind of ironic, since the Tigers were leaving an old "old" stadium.

Fathers and sons are at the heart of the book: with the end of an era, what will Stanton and his own dad do to maintain their bond of baseball?

The Final Season received the 2001 CASEY Award from *Spitball* magazine and the Dave Moore Award from *Elysian Fields Quarterly*.

Other categories: Award Winner, Fandom, History/Team, Pop Culture

272. *The Forever Boys: The Bittersweet World of Major League Baseball as Seen Through the Eyes of the Men Who Played One More Time*, by Peter Golenbock. New York: Carol, 1991.

The Senior Professional Baseball League was a short-lived venture created with the idea that fans would still pay to see former Major Leaguers in competition. Wrong. Once the novelty wore off, the Florida-based league folded before the end of its second season. It's one thing to watch out-of-shape athletes running around for real stakes; it's another when they look more like your town's recreational softball league.

What was interesting was the love — the need — these former pros had for the game. They were simply unwilling to give it up, believing they still had enough to return to their former days of glory. It's worth noting that a handful did in fact return to the Majors after playing in the Senior League.

Golenbock followed the Saint Petersburg Pelicans, who finished first in the Northern Division and won the first and only SPBL championship. The author focused mainly on Bobby Tolan, the team's manager, as well as players such as Dock Ellis, Jon Matlack, Ron LeFlore, Steve Kemp, Milt Wilcox, and others, who reminisced about their time in the big leagues and what they hoped to accomplish with this last-gasp effort.

As the title states, it's a bittersweet story one almost wishes didn't provide the opportunity to be told: better to leave us with our memories of these athletes at their best.

Other category: Auto/Bio/Mem

273. *Game of Shadows: Barry Bonds, BALCO, and the Steroids Scandal,* by Mark Fainaru-Wada and Lance Williams. New York: Gotham, 2006.

Like Jose Canseco's tell-all *Juiced, Game of Shadows* sought to blow the lid off the dirty little secret of rampant performance-enhancing drug use. Unlike *Juiced,* this one was written by a couple of reputable journalists.

Fainaru-Wada and Williams — then investigative reporters for the *San Francisco Chronicle* — point to the Mark McGwire–Sammy Sosa spectacle as the watershed event in Bonds's psyche. He already had been recognized as one of the best of his generation, perhaps of all time, but his anger at the attention paid to McGwire, whom he considered an inferior, one-dimensional player, seemed to be the turning point in his decision to turn to pharmaceutical assistance.

Just as Canseco had claimed, the authors' note that the Giants management had no interest in pursuing the drug allegations, at least not while Bonds was doing so well and drawing fans to their new ballpark. The commissioner's office also turned a blind eye, putting off dealing with the problem as long as possible.

But with each passing year and each additional home run, Bonds's achievements raised eyebrows. How could someone this (relatively) old continue to improve, went the whispers?

The book tends to be a bit top-heavy with the technicalities of the investigations into BALCO — the company responsible for providing the drugs — and Bonds's trainer. This is where the authors show off their investigative chops.

One wonders what role Bonds's combative attitude toward the media played in their obsession to catch him in the act. Compare this with McGwire and Sosa, whose reputations as genial fellows made their fall from grace all the more disappointing. The reader comes to view Bonds as mean-spirited and misguided, but BALCO and its executives were the real villains.

Game of Shadows spent five weeks on the *New York Times* best-seller list.

Other category: *New York Times* Best Seller

274. *Hardball on the Home Front: Major League Replacement Players of World War II,* by Craig Allen Cleve. Jefferson NC: McFarland, 2004.

Much has been written about the relative quality of replacement players during the war years, but Cleve goes right to the source. He profiles and interviews nine men who were given the opportunity—regardless of the reason—to put on a Major League uniform, if only for a short time.

Did these players have any special feeling about taking the field while the men for whom they were filling in were overseas serving their country? Did they hear it from the fans? Were they determined to make the most of the opportunity in the name of freedom and to honor those in the military? Or did they not even give it a thought?

Most of the interviewees were Minor League veterans, toiling long and hard in the bushes, either before or after their call-up. A few enjoyed pro careers as long as fifteen seasons. And, to be fair, some of these players fulfilled their military obligations and were discharged or held jobs deemed essential and were therefore exempt; others were classified as unfit to serve.

In his introduction Cleve ponders what would have happened if World War II had shut down baseball completely, as the attacks on the World Trade Center did in 2001? What sort of impact might that have had on the nation's morale? If there was one good thing that came out of the war, it was that fans never had to contend with such a situation.

Other category: Wartime Baseball

275. *Heart of the Game: Life, Death, and Mercy in Minor League America,* by S. L. Price. New York: Ecco, 2009.

Price, a senior writer for *Sports Illustrated*, offers the devastating tale of thirty-five-year-old Mike Coolbaugh, who lost his life in an on-field accident in 2007, hit by a foul line drive while coaching first base for the Tulsa Drillers of the Texas League. He is portrayed as a genuinely nice guy, good husband, father, brother, and son, and the cover art of the book—a powerful-looking young man with his back to the camera, holding his two young boys in his arms—is truly heartbreaking.

But it's not just Coolbaugh's story. It's also the redemptive tale of Tino Sanchez, a catcher for the Drillers, who hit that fatal ball, as well as the families of both unlucky principals. It's the lingering specter of danger on the field, which led professional baseball to adopt a policy of having on-field base coaches wear batting helmets at all times. It is also a story of guilt and forgiveness, a rare, serious work in a genre generally known for more lighthearted fare.

Other category: Minor Leagues

276. *Home Run,* edited by George Plimpton. San Diego: Harcourt, 2001.

A perpetual all-star of sports literature, Plimpton assembled this tidy and fun collection of some of the most exciting and timeless pieces on baseball's power moments.

Some of the players selected, like Hank Aaron, Babe Ruth, and Sadaharu Oh, are recognized for their body of work over an entire career; others, like Mark McGwire, Roger Maris, and Bobby Thomson, for a special moment; and other for a combination of the two, like Reggie Jackson and Ted Williams. Their Boswells—and not necessarily Thomas, of *Washington Post* fame—are among the most recognized and honored names in the business: Robert Creamer writes about Ruth, Red Smith and Don DeLillo cover Thomson, and John Updike chronicles Williams's career-ending blast in the classic *New Yorker* essay "Hub Fans Bid Kid Adieu." Roger Angell takes a more general look at some famous sluggers in a brief piece. An excerpt from Malamud's *The Natural* falls on that old weepy baseball gambit of hitting a home run for that little sick kid in the hospital.

Any one story would be enjoyable, but combining them into one volume makes *Home Run* one of the better-crafted single-theme anthologies.

Other categories: Anthology, Sportswriting

277. *Hub Fans Bid Kid Adieu: John Updike on Ted Williams.* New York: Library of America, 2010.

Updike put the finishing touches on this tidy little book marking the fiftieth anniversary of his classic essay shortly before he died in 2009.

The piece was originally published in the *New Yorker* a few weeks after the end of the 1960 season — also the end of Williams's career. The story started out as standard assignment — perhaps not even a tribute when it was conceived — of the Splendid Splinter's final game. How could anyone have predicted that Updike's essay would come to be considered one of the most famous pieces of sportswriting? If the baseball gods preordained the improbable ending for Williams's career, did they also do the same to make sure Updike was in attendance?

The author supplements the original essay with footnotes, offering explanations and commentary on his original thoughts, describing more of the action and surroundings, and introducing a great word to the vernacular of the national pastime: *Schlagballbewusstein,* or "baseball consciousness." Whether this bit of retrospection takes anything away from *not* having the extra knowledge is impossible to say.

Following the essay, Updike adds a brief biographical chapter that brings Williams to the sad and ultimately bizarre end of his life.

Other category: Classic

278. *Last Time Out: Big-League Farewells of Baseball's Greats,* by John Nogowski. Dallas: Taylor, 2005.

Unfortunately, not everyone can go out on top like Ted Williams. Take Jackie Robinson, for example. He struck out to end the 1956 World Series against the Yankees and elected to retire shortly thereafter rather than accept a trade that would have sent him to the hated New York Giants.

Willie Mays had announced his plans to step down in the middle of the 1973 season. Traded to the New York Mets as a sentimental gesture the year before, the Say Hey Kid grounded out in the fourth game of the World Series against the Oakland A's, but he will more likely — and sadly — be remembered for stumbling around the outfield in the blinding California sunlight or on his knees at home plate, begging the umpire to reconsider an out call against teammate Bud Harrelson.

Nogowski tells of the swan songs of twenty-five legends, none of whom left under more heroic circumstances than Roberto Clemente, who gained his three thousandth hit on the last day of the 1972 campaign then died in a plane crash on New Year's Eve delivering humanitarian aid to the victims of an earthquake in Nicaragua.

Each chapter is introduced with a brief recap of the circumstances of that last appearance and concludes with the box score of the game and the player's all-time record. All of the players included in *Last Time Out* have been inducted into the Baseball Hall of Fame, with the notable exceptions of Pete Rose, who struck out in a pinch-hitting role, and Shoeless Joe Jackson, who went out with a double.

Other category: Auto/Bio/Mem

279. *Lights Out! The Wild Century-Long Saga of Night Baseball,* by David Pietrusza. Lanham MD: Scarecrow Press, 1997.

When Wrigley Field was retrofitted with lights for the 1988 season, the Cubs became the last Major League team to offer night games to its fans. Heretofore, the team had played all of its home games in the wilting Midwest summer heat, which some historians have offered as a reason for Chicago's inability to win a championship for so many years.

Pietrusza presents a straightforward story of early lighting experiments (Thomas Edison was involved in one project) that frequently ended in failure, philosophical objections ("Baseball was meant to be played in the sunshine, dammit!"), wartime interruptions, and financial realities — owners were worried they wouldn't be able to draw fans fatigued after a long day at work when, in fact, many patrons actually welcomed the opportunity to relax at a night game. While they may have been at a disadvantage in many respects, the Negro Leagues were ahead of their time, using portable light stanchions so they could add even more games to their already overloaded schedules.

Fun fact: the second of Johnny Vander Meer's consecutive nohitters came against the Brooklyn Dodgers in their first night game at Ebbets Field. Coincidence? Hey, the Reds played under the same conditions and *they* found a way to score six runs on eleven hits and win the game.

280. *Low and Outside: Baseball in the Depression, 1930–1939*, by William B. Mead. Alexandria VA: Redefinition, 1990.

Like the rest of America, baseball suffered during the country's worst economic crunch. Players' salaries were cut and executives looked for new ways to get fans to part with whatever diminishing disposable income they might have.

Desperation led to innovation, including the debut of night baseball, which was supposed to be a friend to the working man, offering some much needed entertainment after a hard day of work (or looking for work).

Full of pictures and profiles of some of the stars from that tenuous era, Mead's economical coffee-table book presents the best and the worst of the decade.

Of particular note are the chapters on the Saint Louis Cardinals, aka the Gashouse Gang, emblematic of the hardscrabble times and a welcome change from the more sophisticated cities that hosted Major League teams.

The end of the 1930s saw a changing of the guard, from stars like Babe Ruth and Lou Gehrig to a new generation led by Ted Williams, Joe DiMaggio, and Bob Feller. Gehrig, especially, gets the tribute treatment.

Low and Inside was part of a series of nine books published by Redefinition on various subjects, including baseball's early years, the inside game (also written by Mead), and other volumes focusing on a single defensive position.

Other category: Pop culture

281. *The Midsummer Classic: The Complete History of the All-Star Game,* by David Vincent, Lyle Spatz, and David W. Smith. Lincoln: University of Nebraska Press, 2001.

Just as the U.S. Supreme Court reconvenes on the first Monday in October, the annual MLB All-Star Game falls on the same spot on the calendar every year: the second Tuesday in July.

Three longtime SABR members collaborated on this large-format paperback about the annual affair, a 1933 invention of Arch Ward, the sports editor of the *Chicago Tribune*, for the Century of Progress International Exposition hosted in the city that summer, with the proceeds going to help retired ballplayers.

Although it was originally intended as a one-shot deal, the exhibition game proved so popular in bringing all these great players together that it became a staple of the baseball season with only a world war (1945) and a strike (1994) interrupting the flow.

Midsummer Classic covers every contest through 2000; two games were played each season from 1959–62. The volume contains a substantial recap, as well as rosters, box scores, and a play-by-play for each game. Additional sections offer a list of all 1,307 players who earned the right to call themselves All-Stars. There are also listings for the managers (the honors go to the two skippers whose teams appear in the previous World Series). There is also a section of career All-Star statistics. If that's not enough, two appendices give the results of the annual home run derby, a fan favorite that debuted in 1985.

The only drawback to *Midsummer Classic* is a dearth of pictures; a book like this cries out for the scrapbook treatment.

282. *The Miracle at Coogan's Bluff,* by Thomas Kiernan. New York: Thomas Crowell, 1975.

Kiernan, who earned his PhD in philosophy from Columbia University, combines a fan's memory with a scholar's thirst for answers in this recounting of the "shot heard 'round the world."

Miracle is, in a sense, two books. The first is the story of the 1951 season, which saw the New York Giants mount an amazing comeback to force a playoff against their archrivals, the Brooklyn Dodgers. Kiernan does not go into as much detail as Joshua Prager would in *The Echoing Green*, but that is secondary to the last half of the book, in which he interviews several of the key members of the Giants club some twenty years later for their thoughts on their baseball careers and what has been deemed one of the greatest games ever.

Among those sharing their recollections with Kiernan are man-of-the-hour Bobby Thomson, Bill Rigney, Alvin Dark, Monte Irvin, Wes Westrum, Sal Maglie, and Willie Mays, who lived up to his reputation as a wary and difficult subject. The author is not afraid to put each man on the spot. He grills the players for their thoughts about that fateful meeting with the Dodgers and what it has meant to them in the intervening years. For some, it was like walking on the moon: What do you do for an encore?

It's these personal moments that set *Miracle* apart from other accounts of one of the game's most dramatic moments.

Other category: Pop Culture

283. *Nobody's Perfect: Two Men, One Call, and a Game for Baseball History*, by Armando Galarraga and Jim Joyce with Daniel Paisner. New York: Atlantic Monthly Press, 2011.

On June 2, 2010, Galarraga, a pitcher for the Detroit Tigers, would have had baseball's nineteenth perfect game in the modern era (since 1900) if not for the blown call by Joyce, the first base umpire that day.

What made the story was not so much the injustice done, with demands for the umpire's job and a renewed call for reviewable instant replay, but the humanity of Joyce and especially Galarraga, the former for admitting his error rather than hiding behind his authority, and the latter for his forgiveness in losing one place in history but perhaps gaining an even greater one.

Both central characters had a long row to hoe to get to the top levels of their profession. Galarraga was one of the thousands of hopefuls from foreign countries seeking the promised land of Major League baseball. Joyce, on the other hand, was middle-America born and bred, and had his own obstacles to overcome. Fate put them on a convergent course in that auspicious game.

The language is a bit stilted at times: Galarraga's narrative is much more formal than Joyce, who tends to speak in incomplete sentences. But this is all just part of the charm of *Nobody's Perfect*.

Other categories: Auto/Bio/Mem, Umpires/Rules

284. *"On a Clear Day They Could See Seventh Place": Baseball's Worst Teams*, by George Robinson and Charles Salzberg. New York: Dell, 1991.

In baseball, conventional wisdom states that every team will win fifty games and lose fifty games; it's what you do with the rest that makes the difference. Robinson and Salzberg offer ten examples of teams that blew the majority of those remaining contests in spectacular fashion.

Beginning with the 1899 Cleveland Spiders, who went 20-134, and finishing with the 1988 Baltimore Orioles, who lost their first twenty-one regular season games, these guys could challenge Charlie Brown's ragtag *Peanuts* gang for worst team ever.

The 1962 Mets have always been the poster team for modern futility—even though the Spiders finished with the worst single-season performance of all-time—but it's always mentioned with affection rather than anger. The same could not be said years later. The team's won-loss record might have been better on paper, but the results of a last- finish in the face of higher expectations left a bitter taste in the fans' mouths.

The authors don't mean to be cruel; they acknowledge that some of these teams were victims of circumstances. Perhaps they were going through a rebuilding phase after several good seasons, such as the aforementioned Orioles, or perhaps injuries decimated the lineup, or the core of veterans was getting old all at the same time.

Even in the face of such ignominy, these wretched bands of brothers had a few bright spots, whether it was a player or two who stood out as an anomaly. One such is Steve Carlton, who accounted for 59 percent of the Phillies' victories in 1972 and emerged as the league's Cy Young Award winner. Maybe there were some promising future stars or even one or two outstanding games over the course of an otherwise miserable season. Even these clouds had a silver lining.

285. *Once Around the Bases: Bittersweet Memories of Only One Game in the Majors,* by Richard Tellis. Chicago: Triumph, 1998.

Unlike the subjects of Nogowski's *Last Time Out,* the subjects of *Once Around the Bases* did not enjoy Hall of Fame careers or *any* career to speak of, for that matter. They were the Moonlight Grahams of their times.

Of the forty players who still got to experience what many fans only dream of—appearing in a big league game—the most recognizable names are probably Bert Shepard, a World War II pilot whose leg was partially amputated by German doctors after his plane was shot down, and John Paciorek, brother of Major League veteran Tom; another brother, Jim, appeared in forty-eight games. Shepard fulfilled his objective when he pitched five and a third innings for the Washington Nationals—the more patriotic nickname for the Senators—against the Red Sox in 1945. Paciorek had a career day in his lone appearance: three hits in three official at bats, plus two walks and four runs scored against the Mets at the tail end of 1963, for a perfect 1.000 batting average. Unfortunately, a serious neck injury derailed his return to the Majors.

Tellis offers profiles for the rest of the young men who came so close but couldn't stay in the game due to various circumstances. If he ever publishes an update, he'll have to include Adam Greenberg, whose only trip to the plate for the Chicago Cubs in 2005 resulted in a beaning. As of this writing, he's still trying to mount a comeback.

Other category: Auto/Bio/Mem

286. *The Pitch That Killed: Carl Mays, Ray Chapman, and the Pennant Race of 1920*, by Mike Sowell. New York: Macmillan, 1989.

It is surprising that no one published a book on this sad topic prior to Sewell, considering the unique place Chapman has as the only Major Leaguer to have died on the field as a result of being hit by a pitch.

Mays and Chapman played during an era when ballplayers barely used gloves, much less any other kind of protective equipment. Baseballs were treated like gold and never taken out of play unless absolutely necessary. Add to the situation a pitcher known for doctoring the ball, which was already discolored from use, and having the game take place in the late afternoon of an overcast day and you have an accident just waiting to happen.

Then there's the contrast between the two principals: Mays was a surly fellow, known for brushing back hitters with aplomb, while Chapman was a generally nice guy, beloved by the Cleveland Indians fans and respected by his teammates.

Sowell soberly recreates the fateful event, with culminated with calls for Mays's suspension, if not arrest, and the mourning of Chapman and the fact that life—and the race for the pennant—go on.

If one good thing can be said to have come out of Chapman's death, it is that the rules were changed to put a new ball into use after it had become smudged or otherwise deemed unusable.

Other category: Auto/Bio/Mem

287. *Playing for Their Nation: Baseball and the American Military during World War II*, by Steven R. Bullock. Lincoln: University of Nebraska Press, 2004.

It seems that in every World War II movie, there's a scene in which a character — often on the verge of death, if not simple despair — asks how the Brooklyn Dodgers are doing. Legend holds that Japanese soldiers cursed the name of Babe Ruth as they roared into battle.

Such was the hold baseball had on our GI Joes, who needed that connection to something back home.

From FDR's green-light letter advocating to Commissioner Landis that the game continue for the sake of the nation's morale, to stars such as Ted Williams, Bob Feller, Warren Spahn, and Hank Greenberg, who lost prime playing time while they fulfilled their military service, Bullock follows the progress of the game during those turbulent war years.

While some ballplayers enlisted immediately after the attack on Pearl Harbor, others bided their time, waiting for their military call-up. In the meantime, they participated in charity events, war bond drives, equipment donations, and hospital visits to bring some cheer to America's fighting men.

Once inducted into the service, a number of athletes found time to play on company teams, giving their troopmates some respite with exhibition games. This morale-boosting theme is the main focus of *Playing for a Nation*, but the reality and necessity creeps in: with American drawn deeper into the fighting, the athletes — along with the rest of their fellow Americans — were called upon for more perilous sacrifice.

288. *Satchel, Dizzy, and Rapid Robert: The Wild Saga of Interracial Baseball Before Jackie Robinson,* by Timothy Gay. New York: Simon and Schuster, 2010.

Integrated baseball in the Major Leagues did not begin with Jackie Robinson. There were plenty of games between black and white teams, as well as a few instance of blacks playing *with* whites, thanks to the innovation of barnstorming: a collection of players making their way around the country following the regular season to pick up a few extra bucks. Most of these troupes were highlighted by a few All-Stars and supplemented with regular players. They would either compete amongst themselves or take on the best the local team town would have to offer.

Gay captures the excitement and frustration of African American players like Paige who were still waiting for the chance to prove their skills on the Major League level. Until then, they participated in these little affairs, which still served to spread their legends across the country.

A few of these headliners, such as Dizzy Dean and Bob Feller, were more progressive in their thinking and even argued for some of their Negro Leagues counterparts to join them in organized baseball. Dean demanded fair treatment for the black players on the tour, at least in terms of payment, but knew that this was not the stage on which to challenge Jim Crow.

The situation became even more exasperating after World War II, when African Americans, tired of being excluded despite their contributions to society, pushed even harder.

Other categories: Auto/Bio/Mem, Business, Ethnicity, Negro Leagues
Also by the author: *Tris Speaker: The Rough-and-Tumble Life of a Baseball Legend* (2006)

289. *Saying It's So: A Cultural History of the Black Sox Scandal,* by Daniel A. Nathan. Champaign: University of Illinois Press, 2002.

Almost immediately after the story broke that eight members of the Chicago White Sox had conspired to throw the 1919 World Series, the incident wormed its way into American culture. F. Scott Fitzgerald alluded to it in *The Great Gatsby,* and other novelists worked in references in their own stories of gambling and game fixing. Shoeless Joe Jackson became the symbol of the poor sap who was in way over his head and always regretted the way things turned out, but he was redeemed, at least fictionally, in W. P. Kinsella's story, which probably became even more imbued in pop culture by the film *Field of Dreams.*

Nathan discusses these and other aspects of how the legend of the Black Sox scandal evolved over the years, beginning with Asinof's seminal *Eight Men Out,* which was also turned into a movie, thereby introducing even more people to the whole sloppy affair.

The author also points out the seemingly unaffiliated consequences that resulted from the event, including serving as fodder for Henry Ford's anti-Semitic rants in the *Dearborn Independent,* blaming "too much Jew" for mucking up the national pastime and ruining things for true Americans.

One of my favorite lines—it pertains to a lot of books that seek to link baseball with other areas—can be found in the concluding chapter, in which Nathan admits: "Yes, narratives can be twisted into many shapes, used in various ways, made to serve a wide range of purposes. But in practice, there are limits" (216).

Other categories: Event, Fiction, Pop Culture, Scandal

290. *The Seasons: Ten Memorable Years in Baseball, and in America,* by Bill Gilbert. New York: Citadel Press, 2003.

Here's an icebreaker for your next party: When talking about baseball and the United States, which years do you think were the most important? Gilbert, who has several excellent sports and Americana titles to his credit, makes some valid arguments for his choices: In 1945 World War II ended and the regular players who had been called into service began to return to baseball action. In 1948 Truman defeated in Dewey and the Indians defeated the Red Sox. Three years later the United States entered into another armed conflict, but it was Bobby Thomson who hit the shot heard 'round the world.

In 1961 both Maris and Mantle took aim at Babe Ruth's single-season home run record while baseball went through its first round of expansion, just as Russia took aim at our shores and enacted a possible expansion plan of their own when they put missiles in Cuba.

Sports pundits said the Mets would win a World Series when man walked on the moon. In 1969 they were proved right. Gilbert also merits the 1975, 1980, 1995, 1998, and 2001 seasons as worthy of inclusion.

I have no quarrel with his selections, but if one looks hard enough, other years might have proved just as notable. 1947, anybody?

Other category: Pop Culture

291. *The Seventh Game: The 35 World Series That Have Gone the Distance,* by Barry Levenson. New York: McGraw-Hill, 2004.

There are few things more exciting in sports than the final game of a championship series. Broadcasters and writers open up the big bag of clichés to let us know "there's no tomorrow," among other pearls of wisdom.

Some clinchers have been stunning upsets: Bill Mazeroski's walk-off home run for the 1960 Pirates-Yankees meeting, or the Arizona Diamondbacks' Luis Gonzalez beating future Hall of Fame reliever Mariano Rivera in 2001. Others have been rather anticlimactic. Take, for example, the Cincinnati Reds' win over the Boston Red Sox in 1975 after Carlton Fisk's homer in the sixth game, or another Red Sox loss, this time to the Mets in 1986 after New York's improbable Buckner-aided win in Game Six.

In fact, after reporting on the ultimate games in chronological order, Levenson, founder and curator of the Mount Horeb Mustard Museum(!) in Wisconsin, rates the games for excitement beginning with five "stinkers" and fifteen "good ones" before wrapping up with his "fabulous fifteen." Tops on his list: The 1924 Washington Senators' 4–3 win in thirteen innings over the New York Giants, the franchise's lone world championship. You'll have to read the book to learn his rationale.

Other category: World Series

292. *The Short Season: The Hard Work and High Times of Baseball in Spring Training,* by David Falkner. New York: Times, 1986.

It is the best of times, it is the worst of times. Spring training has different meanings for different people. For the aging veteran and the borderline utility man, it's perhaps the last chance to hold one for one more season. For the high-profile Minor Leaguer, it's trying to go north with the parent club. For those secure in their station, it's a boring period, but at least the weather is nice most of the time and you can get in some golf and fishing.

The fans, on the other hand, are on vacation, pining for the opportunity to get close to their favorites in relatively confined settings in Florida and Arizona.

Falkner expresses this combination of laxity and anxiety in *The Short Season,* which was published at a time when free agency was relatively new and salaries were much smaller, so there was less at stake for both the ballplayer and his employer. Nowadays, there's more separation between the players and fans, but everyone still looks forward to that day on the calendar that notes when pitchers and catchers are scheduled to report.

Other category: Pop Culture

293. *Spalding's World Tour: The Epic Adventure That Took Baseball Around the Globe—and Made It America's Game,* by Mark Lamster. New York: Public Affairs, 2006.

Nowadays even kids on travel teams go all over the world for their competitions. No biggie. But think what it must have been like in 1888 for the first generation of professional ballplayers to circumnavigate the globe to bring America's national game to such exotic places as New Zealand, Australia, Samoa, England, and France, as well as other locales that had barely experienced Americans, let alone this strange concept of striking a ball with a bat.

Lamster conveys the excitement of all the parties as he recreates the promotional tour led by Albert Goodwill Spalding, the game's number one ambassador, and an All-Star team that included members of the Chicago White Stockings (now known as the Cubs) of Cap Anson, Tom Burns, and Ned Williamson versus another All-Star squad that included Ned Hanlon and John Montgomery Ward.

Spalding's World Tour is a testament to the imperialistic beliefs held by American leaders of the era and Spalding's desire to be considered the Johnny Appleseed of baseball, scattering its seeds all over the world.

294. *Spartan Seasons: How Baseball Survived the Second World War,* by Richard Goldstein. New York: Macmillan, 1980.

At the risk of sounding unpatriotic or insensitive, one of the most bizarrely entertaining periods in the national pastime came during World War II. Where else could you have a team like the Saint Louis Browns, one of the most unsuccessful franchises in all of sports, luck out to win its only pennant? When else could a sixteen-year-old pitcher be given the chance to play professionally against men twice his age? Or a one-armed outfielder (and was it a coincidence he wound up on the Browns)?

Goldstein captures the tenor of the mid-1940s in this lively book as he describes the feelings of the players who were deemed unsuitable for military service while at the same time hardy enough for a career in pro sports, however brief it may have been while the "real" athletes were away.

Beginning with FDR's green-light letter to Commissioner Landis offering the president's belief that baseball was good for the country's spirits during a dark period and should continue, *Spartan Seasons* recalls the relative difficulties the game endured: restricted travel and gas rationing that necessitated holding spring training in un-spring-training-like environments, and diverting materials, such as rubber, for military use, which had a subsequent impact on the quality of the ball. Even finding players to fill out Major and Minor League rosters proved a challenge.

Although Goldstein focuses on the home front, he nevertheless pays tribute to the ballplayers who served in the armed forces, such as Bob Feller, Ted Williams, and Hank Greenberg, among many others who saw combat, as well as those like Joe DiMaggio and others who played ball during their time in the service as a morale booster for the troops.

Other category: Pop Culture

295. *The Spitball Knuckleball Book: How They Are Thrown, Those Who Threw Them*, by Tom E. Mahl. Elyria OH: Trick Pitch Press, 2009.

This unusual coffee-table edition seeks to right the injustice of sweeping the practitioners of the now-illegal pitch under the metaphorical rug.

After a brief introduction on the origins of the spitter, Mahl profiles the twenty-three veteran hurlers who were grandfathered in and allowed to continue using the pitch once it was outlawed prior to the 1921 season.

Of course, that doesn't mean there weren't those outside that select group who didn't try to put a little something over on the umpires and hitters, including Hall of Famers Don Drysdale and Gaylord Perry. The latter gleefully lived off the reputation that he doctored the ball with a variety of substances. His antics on the mound before he threw still bring a chuckle to fans from that era.

Necessity being the mother of invention, those who couldn't throw an actual spitball developed a dry version, aka the knuckleball. The Mets' R. A. Dickey has been the most prominent practitioner of the pitch in recent years. Within that community resides an even smaller subset: those who employ the knuckle curve, which has fallen into disuse.

The final chapter describes how to throw both pitches and why they perform the way they do.

Other categories: Coffee Table/Gift, Instructional

296. *Streak: Joe DiMaggio and the Summer of '41*, by Michael Seidel. Lincoln: University of Nebraska Press, 2002.

You can't write about Joe DiMaggio without a major account of his fifty-six-game hitting streak in 1941. And you can't find a more thorough book on his accomplishment than Seidel's *Streak*, originally published in 1988.

In addition to the usual inside baseball material about individual games, impressions of fans, the media, and DiMaggio's teammates and opponents, Seidel reminds the reader that 1941 featured the last relatively peaceful summer before America's involvement in World War II. *Streak* includes a great deal of pop culture and history. This puts baseball into perspective while at the same time indicating how vital it was to the national sanity at a time when banner headlines spelled doom and gloom daily.

The book wraps up with an appendix of each of the fifty-six box scores, plus that of the fifty-seventh game, which ended one of the few records still considered unbreakable.

The 2002 edition contains an afterward that is almost worth the price—and of the additional purchase if you already have the first edition). Seidel discusses the backstory of finally getting a chance to speak with the great ballplayer himself. DiMaggio was a notoriously suspicious man, always worried about being taken advantage of, but once the author convinced him that he had only baseball in his mind, DiMaggio opened up.

Other category: Auto/Bio/Mem

Also by the author: It is perhaps fitting that Seidel also wrote a biography on DiMaggio's main rival in *Ted Williams: A Baseball Life* (1991).

297. *The Unforgettable Season: The Most Exciting and Calamitous Pennant Race of All Time*, by G. H. Fleming. New York: Holt, Reinhart and Winston, 1981.

Considered one the best one hundred sports books in a 2002 *Sports Illustrated* survey, *The Unforgettable Season* is a masterpiece of research and editing, especially since it was published before the Internet made such projects a relative breeze. Fans of media history and the English language will enjoy this mix of spot reporting, commentary, and feature writing, even if they aren't especially interested in the topic.

Fleming, a former professor of English literature in a Louisiana college, culled through microfilm and newspapers from more than twenty publications — most cities had multiple daily journals in a period before 24–7 radio and TV coverage — of the day to glean the best original recorders' accounts of that exciting race. It was made even more bizarre because of a literal misstep by New York Giants rookie Fred Merkle. He failed to advance to second base on an otherwise routine play, thereby negating the run that would have given his team the National League title.

At a time when the baseball fan can call up highlights or stories at the touch of a button, *The Unforgettable Season* is a cool reminder what patience fans had to have one hundred years ago, and how such delayed gratification might have made baseball even more exciting.

Other category: Pop Culture

298. *A Whole New Game: Off the Field Changes in Baseball, 1946–1960*, by John P. Rossi. Jefferson NC: McFarland, Publishers, 1999.

Those who are curious about the stories behind some of baseball's significant events will no doubt enjoy Rossi's history of baseball during the boomer era.

After the initial honeymoon period when players returned from World War II, baseball began to suffer as an industry. Americans became caught up with other leisure activities. The availability of television and air-conditioning meant people also had the choice of staying home, which presented its own situation in terms of how games were broadcast.

In addition, Rossi suggests that the dominance of New York's three teams had something of a negative impact on fans living outside the area. How much fun could it have been to watch the Yankees, Giants, and Dodgers win the pennant year after year?

All that had the consequent effect of making two-team towns untenable. The Braves were the first to go, moving out of Boston after the 1952 season, as did the Saint Louis Browns, who left for Baltimore, where they would be known as the Orioles. The Athletics quit Philadelphia for the greener pastures of Kansas City, Missouri, in 1955. And, of course, the Dodgers and Giants would leave New York in 1957. By 1960 the sixteen-team Majors were planning to add four new franchises, thanks in no small part to the failed challenge from the Continental League, the brainchild of former Dodger general manager Branch Rickey.

Rossi does not judge whether these transitions were good or bad for the game. They were just the natural order of things, the progress of the seasons.

Other categories: Academic, Classic, Popular Culture, Wartime Baseball
Also by the author: *The National Game: Baseball and American Culture* (2000); *The 1964 Phillies: The Story of Baseball's Most Memorable Collapse* (2005)

299. *World Series: An Opinionated Chronicle: 100 Years*, by Joseph Wallace. New York: Harry N. Abrams, 2003

Yet another in a long line of handsome commemorative books from Abrams, *World Series* capitalizes on a major event: one hundred years of the World Series. Well, strictly speaking, there were only ninety-eight, since there were no games played in 1904 or 1994.

As advertised, Wallace is quite free with his opinions, going a few steps beyond the standard recaps of the Fall Classics. In fact, he starts right off with his list of the ten best Series, beginning with the Twins' 1991 surprise victory over the Braves, and then ten worst: number one is the 1919 Black Sox Scandal—duh.

Since not all Series are deemed equal, Wallace expands more on the ones he feels offer more compelling stories than the rest, and the narratives of each are balanced nicely with the photographs. Most interesting for a book of this type is that Wallace includes no statistics of any sort. Refreshing.

He also offers a number of "Series Spotlights," as well as "Pull-outs" of oddball facts, quotes, story lines, and so on. His "Five Stages of Goatdom" play on the five stages of grief made famous by mortality expert Elizabeth Kubler-Ross. They even share the elements of denial, anger, and acceptance.

In a sense, aren't all books opinionated to a greater or lesser degree, simply by virtue of what authors choose to include and how they choose to present it?

Other categories: Coffee Table/Gift, World Series

300. *You Never Forget Your First: Ballplayers Recall Their Big League Debuts*, by Josh Lewin. Washington DC: Potomac, 2005.

I can't imagine anything more exciting than stepping up to the plate in your first Major League at bat and smacking a home run on the first pitch you see. Maybe Washington Nationals pitcher Tom Milone will discuss that feeling in Lewin's revised edition: Milone, the starting pitcher in the Nationals-Mets game of September 3, 2011, crushed his first offering for a three-run homer.

More than one hundred players, most of whom debuted after 1980, share their impressions as they discuss their first appearances. Lewin introduces each athlete—which includes Hall of Famers, All-Stars, and run-of-the-mill guys—with a brief background and box score of those first games, as well as the players' comments. This presents an interesting test in memory. With the passage of time, we tend to recollect events differently than they might have actually happened, sometimes exaggerating what actually occurred. With the box score right there, it's a bit harder to do so.

Other category: Auto/Bio/Mem

ORAL HISTORY

301. *A Bittersweet Journey: America's Fascination with Baseball,* by Rick Phalen. Tampa: McGregor, 2000

At some point, I would imagine even the most ardent fan looks at her relationship with the national pastime and wonders, what the *heck* am I doing? Isn't there some better way to spend my time?

Phalen came to this crossroads when he visited his old hometown to discover that the ballfield where he spent so many happy hours as a child was no longer there. Just like the line from the song "Big Yellow Taxi," they "paved paradise and put up a parking lot."

It had a profound effect on the writer, who embarked on a journey to discover just why the game is so important to so many people. Along the way, he interviewed some forty players, umpires, members of the media, and others who toiled in anonymity behind the scenes, seeking their insight and philosophy.

The product is somewhat uneven. Phalen's subjects possessed varying levels of skill, longevity, and success, and many of the questions posed have been addressed elsewhere, but they all have that same bittersweet quality of a shared experience by anyone involved in sports: you hope to enjoy it while you're doing it, you hope you had a career to be proud of even if you're not Hall of Fame material, and you're mostly sad when it's over and the real world comes a-knockin'.

Other categories: Academic, Auto/Bio/Mem

302. *Lasting Yankee Stadium Memories: Unforgettable Tales from the House That Ruth Built,* edited by Alex Belth. New York: Skyhorse, 2010.

In this first-person account, *Bronx Banter,* the popular blog that reports on the Yankees and the New York scene, features the observations of journalists and broadcasters who have covered the team over the years.

For some, the experience at Yankee Stadium was quite personal rather than business related. It was a clichéd first game, seeing-the-verdant-expanse type of thing. For others it was a childhood moment spent with family. For others still it might be a favorite player or an event marking a rite of passage.

More than fifty contributors from the New York and national media share their stories, including Bob Costas, Pete Hamill, Tony Kornheiser, Leigh Montville, Tom Boswell, Scott Raab, Charles Pierce, and Joe Posnanski. It's funny and touching to read these impressions. They're no longer professionals at this point, but simply fans.

Other categories: Anthology, Essays, Media, Sportswriting

303. *The Man in the Dugout,* by Donald Honig. New York: Follett, 1977

Thanks to fantasy baseball, millions of people have a chance to prove they could do the same job as a Joe Torre or a Bobby Cox. After all, they have all of the same information, the same statistics and analytics at their disposal.

Ah, but not so fast, pal. It takes more than just an accountant's mind to deal with the personalities, both from above in the front office and below in the dugout.

Honig, whose abbreviated career as a Minor Leaguer gives him an added measure of credibility on the subject, is one of the most prolific chroniclers of the game and the perfect writer to query the fifteen individuals included in his 1977 title. Some are familiar to just about any moderate fan: Walter Alston, who signed twenty-three one-year contracts and led the Dodgers both in Brooklyn and Los Angeles to seven pennants and four World Series titles; Joe McCarthy, leader of the Cubs, Yankees, and Red Sox, with nine pennants and an amazing *seven* world championships to his name; Bobby Brogan, a player on the Dodgers who, as a southerner was at first opposed to Jackie Robinson but soon had a change of heart; and Dick Williams, who took the Red Sox to within one game of the world championship in his first year with the team in 1967 and went on to have success with the Oakland Athletics and San Diego Padres.

Other skippers might be less familiar, but they still bring valuable points of view from their careers, which in this book range from the 1920s through the 1970s.

Other category: Analysis

304. *My Greatest Day in Baseball, 1946–1997,* as told to Bob McCullough. Dallas: Taylor Trade Publishing, 1998.

305. *My Greatest Day in Baseball,* as told to John P. Carmichael and other noted sportswriters. Lincoln: University of Nebraska Press, 1996.

In the movie *Field of Dreams*, a ghostly Moonlight Graham ruminates on how wonderful it would have been if he had gotten an opportunity to come up to bat just one time as a Major Leaguer, to prove he had played the game. No doubt that would qualify has his greatest day.

The theme—a staple of sports publications like *Baseball Digest* and the *Sporting News*—usually features brief interviews with a variety of players, from both the all-time greats and those who maybe had just one special moment. One would think it would be the latter group that would have better stories to tell, their highlights being fewer and farther between. When you're Willie Mays, how do you pick a single accomplishment? Even those like Hank Aaron, whom you would suspect to have no trouble picking their signature moments, might surprise the reader with something out of left field.

Carmichael's book was originally published in 1945, and so it includes long-ago players such as Babe Ruth, Dizzy Dean, Cy Young, Grover Cleveland Alexander, and dozens more. The McCullough publication features almost ninety subjects, mostly from the 1960s and on. So you'll have a Rick Aguilera moment — Game Six of the 1986 World Series — immediately following Aaron, who claims his greatest day actually took place some twenty years before he became the all-time home run king.

The stories are all fascinating and give an interesting insight into the importance placed on such events by the people who lived through them.

Other category: Auto/Bio/Mem

306. *The October Heroes: Great World Series Games Remembered by the Men Who Played Them,* by Donald Honig. New York: Simon and Schuster, 1979.

The Fall Classic presents a unique opportunity. Because it reaches a wider audience than a regular-season contest, a few lucky participants have the chance to shine on a grand stage. Some live up to expectations; others, perhaps hobbled by injury or just plain bad luck, come up woefully short. One example is Hall of Famer Dave Winfield, who had just one hit in twenty-two at bats in the 1981 beat-down by the Los Angeles Dodgers. For the regular Joes, the Series might become the answer to a trivia question. Al Weis, for instance, was a lifetime .219 hitter, but he batted .455 with a home run in the Mets' 1969 amazin' championship over the favored Baltimore Orioles.

The fifteen players included in Honig's oral history possessed a wide variety of talent. Three appeared in just one Series, including two players who were among the best of their respective generations: Lloyd Waner, a Hall of Famer, and Ted Kluszewski, a four-time All-Star. The third, Les Bell, a dependable member of the Saint Louis Cardinals, was hardly a household name. He played only five full seasons, but he batted .290 in the 1926 get-together with the

Yankees, which Saint Louis won on an ill-advised stolen base attempt by Babe Ruth to end Game Seven.

The remaining dozen subjects had the additional insight that only comes through repeat opportunities: pitchers "Wild Bill" Hallahan and Johnny Podres participated in four Series each for the Cardinals and Brooklyn Dodgers, respectively.

Only Tom Seaver and Gene Tenace appeared in games after 1970, playing to a younger, more hip crowd, with different expectations than their fan forefathers, so it's interesting to see the World Series evolve over the sixty or so years covered in *October Heroes*.

Other category: World Series

307. *This Side of Cooperstown: An Oral History of Major League Baseball in the 1950s,* by Larry Moffi. Iowa City: University of Iowa Press, 1996.

In this nostalgic volume, Moffi celebrates the players he favored as a kid growing up in Hartford, Connecticut.

While some of them were quite talented, the author had a special set of criteria for inclusion: they had to play at least one year during the fifties; they couldn't be the superstar, elite Hall of Fame guys; and they had to have made some contribution to the game, in his estimation, on or off the field. I'm sure if you spent some time on Baseball-Reference.com, you could do the math and see how many fell into that category, at least the contribution part, which seems a bit subjective.

His seventeen finalists include some All-Stars, a few power hitters (Roy Sievers won the American League home run and RBI titles in 1958), and some very good pitchers (Vern Law won the National League Cy Young Award for the world champion Pittsburgh Pirates in 1960). Their stories are probably typical of the era before big signing bonuses, multiyear contracts, and huge endorsement deals. It was both a prosperous and a tenuous time for America. The United States had finished with war for a while and was enjoying a degree of prosperity and relative calm, at last for some segments of society.

308. *A Brooklyn Dodgers Reader,* by Andrew Paul Mele. Jefferson NC: McFarland, 2005.

Anthologies are like free samples: They give you just enough of a taste to see if you like it, so that you can buy more. If you don't like it, you haven't really lost anything. *A Brooklyn Dodgers Reader* is a great example of this genre.

Mele has collected bits and pieces from books and newspapers capturing the essence of the team. His book is divided into roughly chronological chapters, but the majority of the stories come after Jackie Robinson's debut in 1947. A final few articles convey the combination of anger and sadness when the Dodgers left the borough.

The *Reader* consists of representative spot reporting and profiles of several of the boys of summer. Mele introduces each piece with a paragraph for context for his lineup of contributors, a who's who of New York and national sportswriting and reporting: Arthur Daley, Red Barber, Harold Parrott, Donald Honig, Jimmy Cannon, Dick Young, Red Smith, Shirley Povich, and, of course, Roger Kahn. Students of print journalism will no doubt find the manner in which the game was covered to be of interest. This was at a time when the city had several newspapers that were basically *the* source for the latest information. No ESPN Web Gems or MLB Network—actually, there wasn't that much television, period.

Other categories: Anthology, Sportswriting

309. *Can't Anybody Here Play This Game? The Improbable Saga of the New York Mets' First Year,* by Jimmy Breslin. New York: Ballantine, 1970.

In 1962 Jimmy Breslin, a legendary New York City columnist, followed the expansion team as it took its first faltering steps. Unlike the American League expansion draft the previous year, the eight National League teams put up only those players who were no longer of any value to them: stars on the downside of their careers, never-weres, and never-would-bes. So the team's struggles weren't a question of younger players undergoing growing pains, according to Breslin: these Mets just plain stunk. Not that New Yorkers really expected much. They were just happy to have a team in the National League again. Besides, if nothing else, the Mets were certainly entertaining in coming up with inventive ways to lose.

And don't forget Casey Stengel, fired by the Yankees in 1960 for the sin of turning seventy. He guided—if one could use that term—the Mets to a 40-120 record, which, though technically not the worst of all time, became the benchmark for futility in popular culture, as well as on the playing field. The Old Perfesser was pretty philosophical though, always looking ahead and waiting for his youth of America to mature into their place.

Originally published by the Viking Press in 1964, the book was reissued in 1969 with a new forward by Breslin to take advantage of the Mets success, although the timing was a bit off. He revised it that September, but had he waited just a few more weeks, Breslin could have included the unlikeliest of scenarios: a world's championship. Typical Mets luck.

Other categories: Classic, Pop Culture, Sportswriting

310. *The Complete Year-by-Year N.Y. Mets Fan's Almanac,* by Duncan Bock and John Jordan. New York: Crown, 1992.

Die-hard Mets fans shouldn't care that this book is more than twenty years old. The information and presentation make it a must-have, as Bock and Jordan cover just about everything you'd want to know about the team from 1962–91.

Each chapter features a year's worth of highlights—lowlights in the case of a few seasons—a monthly summary, and capsule profiles for the key players. There are a handful of annual team statistics and a look at the top players in the Minor League system as well. More detailed individual and team stats by year follow the narrative section.

Marginalia comes in the form of major (and a few minor) events in politics, medicine, and pop culture, which provides quite entertaining context for this stroll down memory lane.

But next time, fellows? More pictures please.

Other categories: Auto/Bio/Mem, Pop Culture, Reference, Statistics

311. *The Cubs: The Complete Story of Chicago Cubs Baseball,* by Glenn Stout, with photographs selected and edited by Richard A. Johnson. Boston: Houghton Mifflin, 2007.

312. *Red Sox Century: 100 Hundred Years of Red Sox Baseball,* by Glenn Stout, with photographs selected and edited by Richard A. Johnson. Boston: Houghton Mifflin, 2000.

313. *Yankees Century: 100 Years of New York Yankees Baseball,* by Glenn Stout, with photographs selected and edited by Richard A. Johnson. Boston: Houghton Mifflin, 2002.

What constitutes a good team history? For some it's a straight narrative, while for others it might be more of a photo album. Why not combine the best of both worlds, like Stout and Johnson did for the Cubs, Red Sox, and Yankees?

Is it any coincidence that these books feature three of the most popular franchises in the sports biz? While the Yankees were recurring winners, at the time of publication the other ballclubs were mired in decades-old streaks of futility: the Red Sox had not won since the First World War was winding down in 1918, and, as of 501's printing, the Cubs haven't played that late in the year since their 1908 team that featured "Tinker to Evers to Chance."

The books are presented chronologically, but not in any set length. Stout wrote most of narrative, but additional essays are provided for all three teams by some pretty famous writers: author Scott Turow, actress-director Penny Marshall, and columnist Mike Royko for Chicago; Charlie Pierce, Peter Gammons, and Howard Bryant for Boston; and Ira Berkow, David Halberstam, and Ring Lardner for New York.

Each of these would serve nicely as texts for college courses on the respective impact of baseball in three of America's most historic cities.

Other categories: Fandom, Pop Culture

Also by the authors: *Ted Williams: A Portrait in Words and Pictures* (1991); *DiMaggio: An Illustrated Life* (1995); *Jackie Robinson: Between the Baselines* (1997)

314. *The Dodgers Move West*, by Neil J. Sullivan. New York: Oxford University Press, 1987.

On the one hand, you have the Brooklyn fans, devastated by the abandonment by their beloved Bums, and ignorant of or uncaring about the political machinations between Dodgers owner Walter O'Malley and Robert Moses and the City of New York, which led to the team's move west. On the other hand, you have the optimistic fans in Los Angeles and Major League Baseball's powers that be, both of whom were anxious to see that relocation work and thereby open the door for more westward expansion (and the ensuing additional revenue).

But not so fast, says Sullivan.

Most books about the Dodgers concentrate on the former, the sense of loss suffered by the spurned supporters. *The Dodgers Move West* examines the situation from a different point of view.

Not everyone in Los Angeles was thrilled that the Dodgers were coming to town. There would be a lot of headaches before the dust literally cleared, not the least of which involved the many locals of Chavez Ravine who would be displaced by a new stadium.

Sullivan, who would publish a similar book — *The Diamond in the Bronx: Yankee Stadium and the Politics of New York* — in 2001, concentrates on the behind-the-scenes political gamesmanship between the Dodgers and city managements in both Los Angeles and New York.

Other categories: Business, Fandom

315. *Faithful: Two Diehard Boston Red Sox Fans Chronicle the Historic 2004 Season,* by Stewart O'Nan and Stephen King. New York: Scribner, 2004.

If it had been anyone else involved, one might chalk up a book like *Faithful* to dumb luck. But with Stephen King, you never know.

King and fellow novelist O'Nan had the good fortune to follow their beloved "Sawx" in the team's charmed year in which they impossibly came back from an impossible back-from-the-grave (another King specialty), down-three-games-to-none AL Championship series victory against their archrivals, the New York Yankees.

O'Nan seems to have done the lion's share of the work, writing on an almost daily basis about the ups and downs of the Red Sox throughout the season; King dropped in his opinions here and there. The style has been compared to a sports broadcast team, with O'Nan doing the play-by-play and King handling the color commentary.

It's a good partnership. What could have been a celebrity stunt — compare *Faithful* with Larry King's saccharine *Why I Love Baseball* — is instead a thoughtful and enjoyable conversation, although, at times, they *do* carry on like a couple of sports radio nerds.

The book was rushed to publication to take advantage of Boston's first world championship since 1918; otherwise, it probably would have waited till another year, like so many other Red Sox titles.

Other categories: Analysis, Fandom, World Series

316. *The Last Good Season: Brooklyn, the Dodgers, and Their Final Pennant Race Together,* by Michael Shapiro. New York: Doubleday, 2003.

The title of Shapiro's bittersweet and nostalgic tale is quite precise. Following their only world's championship in 1955, the Dodgers won the NL pennant the following year only to lose once again to their crosstown rivals, the Yankees (magnified by the only perfect game in World Series history, courtesy of Don Larsen).

It was all downhill from there as the Dodgers and their loyal fans, still uncertain of their conjoined future, sleepwalked through 1957, the Bums' last season in Brooklyn.

Perhaps more than any other team, the Dodgers were synonymous with community. Many of the players lived in the neighborhoods surrounding Ebbets Field, where they did business locally. That's why their departure was so devastating. There are still old-timers who count among their darkest moments the day their beloved Bums left for the West Coast.

But Shapiro's impending doom-and-gloom story casts aside such rose-colored memories. By 1956 many of the core Dodgers, including Jackie Robinson, Pee Wee Reese, Duke Snider, and Roy Campanella were on the downside of Hall of Fame careers. Combine that with middle-class flight to suburbia and you have a prescription for economic disaster. It's kind of ironic: a decade earlier, the Dodgers fought to bring Robinson to the Majors, but with the departure of white fans the team's management didn't believe African American and Hispanic residents could adequately support the team, although they would maintain the move as simply a matter of economics, not race.

Other categories: Business, Pop Culture

317. *The Little Red (Sox) Book: A Revisionist Red Sox History*, by Bill "Spaceman" Lee with Jim Prime. Chicago: Triumph, 2003.

There's no denying Bill Lee was one of the most colorful characters to wear cleats. He famously admitted to sprinkling marijuana on his pancakes, staged a one-man strike when a friend was traded, called his own manager a gerbil, and damned the Yankees and their owner as a bunch of storm troopers.

It comes as little surprise then that he would relish the opportunity to tweak his one of his former employers — in this case, the Boston Red Sox.

With the aid of Prime, who has several titles about the Red Sox to his credit, Lee offers his account of key moments from the team's history but adds a twist with his speculations: What if Babe Ruth had never been sold to the Yankees? What if the Sox had signed Jackie Robinson and Willie Mays when they had the chance rather than insisting they weren't good enough?

Lee has a lot of out-there notions, and his willingness to share them is a boon to all open-minded fans of the game.

Other categories: Analysis, Auto/Bio/Mem, Pop Culture

318. *Mile High Madness: A Year with the Colorado Rockies*, by Bob Kravitz. New York: Times, 1994.

I think I can say with little fear of contradiction that fans of any given hobby item of interest — be it comic books, television characters, presidents — enjoy a good origin story. There's something exciting about the work and thought processes that go into it.

The Colorado Rockies, along with the Florida Marlins, joined the National League in 1993. Kravitz, a sports columnist for the *Rocky Mountain News*, chronicled the team's baby steps in this low-key overview that, merely by dint of its *not* being about an established team, falls under the baseball-reading radar.

Goodwill abounds. Expectations are pretty low; the city is thrilled simply to have a big league team, and Kravitz does a good job reflecting the joys of this budding romance.

Everything goes into the record books when it's your inaugural season: the first hit, the first home run, the first win. And since this is the first go-around, everyone starts off fresh. No clubhouse politics or preconceived notions about the players, many of whom are getting their first chance to be regulars. Because Denver is the city with the highest elevation of any Major League city, fans witnessed an extra dose of offensive power, making instant folk heroes out of players like Dante Bichette, Andres Galarraga, and Charlie Hayes, all of whom might not have enjoyed the same success anywhere else.

Thanks to astute management, the Rockies would overachieve fairly early, making it to the NLDS after just two years, losing to the Atlanta Braves three games to one, and all the way to the World Series in 2007.

319. *The Million-to-One Team: Why the Chicago Cubs Haven't Won a Pennant Since 1945,* by George Castle. South Bend IN: Diamond Communications, 2000.

Add to that title the fact that the team from the North Side hasn't won a World Series in over one hundred years and you have an even more depressing situation.

So what's the explanation? Castle, who's written several books on baseball in general and the Cubs in particular, has a few pretty good theories. Take your pick: it could be the fact that prior to 1988 the Cubs were the only team without lights, meaning that all their home games were played in the daytime. This was great for most fans but not so good for the ballplayers who had to toil in the stifling Midwestern summer heat; in fact, it was a main theory for their collapse in 1969. Even when they finally installed lights, the Cubs still scheduled the majority of their contests as day games.

Team ownership passed from gum magnate Phil Wrigley to the Tribune Company in 1981. They quickly let it be known that having a pennant winner wasn't their top priority. Then there was the team's front office, which apparently did not look favorably on minorities; Hall of Famer Ernie Banks was the first black player, and he didn't debut until September 1953. Several of their managers — Leo Durocher, Dallas Green, Jim Frey, Don Zimmer — came up short in the strategy department, and prior to Durocher, the team tried a revolving college of coaches rather than name one man as field leader. That didn't work out too well. The coaches either battled to be top kick or ducked responsibility.

And don't forget the Curse of the Billy Goat, which has been the subject of several books.

Unlike other baseball books that need revising with the passage of time and the addition of new information, this one is still valid since the Cubs are still pennantless as of the time of this writing.

Other categories: Ethnicity, Pop Culture

320. *National Pastime: Sports, Politics, and the Return of Baseball to Washington, D.C.*, by Barry Svrluga. New York: Doubleday, 2006.

With all the machinations the Montreal Expos went through over their last couple of seasons, it's surprising there haven't been more books on this subject. For the last few years of their existence, the franchise constantly had the sword of Damocles over its head—hard to operate under that kind of pressure. Their ownership abandoned them, and Major League Baseball had the dubious responsibility of taking over until the situation could be resolved.

Resolution finally came with a much anticipated and much contested relocation to the nation's capital, and Svrluga, a sportswriter for the *Washington Post*, mixes the joy and anger in the nation's capital as politicians and baseball people wheeled and dealt while the players tried to go about their business. The frustration by the ballclub is, perhaps unsympathetically, humorous as they deal with one calamity after another and rush to prepare for the 2005 season. Simple things like working electrical outlets, bathrooms, and minor repairs seemed to elude resolution as part of the business-not-as-usual of the new Nationals.

Svrluga gives a bit of background on baseball in DC with the two incarnations of the Senators—also known as the Nationals from time to time—but the bulk of the book looks at the ballplayers on the 2005 squad. Contrary to my usual apolitical nature, however, I would have liked a bit more about the behind-the-scenes deals that brought the team to Washington and their new home.

Other category: Business

321. *New York City Baseball: The Last Golden Age, 1947–1957,* by Harvey Frommer. New York: Macmillan, 1980.

322. *The Era, 1947–1957: When the Yankees, the Giants, and the Dodgers Ruled the World,* by Roger Kahn. New York: Ticknor and Fields, 1993.

323. *Summer in the City: New York Baseball 1947–1957,* by Vic Ziegel with photographs from the *New York Daily News.* New York: Harry N. Abrams, 2006.

One of the problems baseball faced by the mid-1950s is that fans living in cities outside the New York area were, frankly, bored. Bored by the notion that either the Yankees or Dodgers or Giants, or some combination thereof, always seemed to be playing in the World Series. And while some claims just *seem* to be that way, in this case it was true. From 1947–57, the Yankees appeared in the Fall Classic nine times, winning seven. The Dodgers were their frequent victims, losing in five out of six matchups (kind of like the Washington Generals versus the Harlem Globetrotters, but without the yuks). The Giants won two pennants, losing to the Yankees in 1951 — no doubt they consider the Series anti-climactic after the shot heard 'round the world — and sweeping the Cleveland Indians in 1954.

This trio of veteran writers, however, put forth the argument that this was truly the golden age of baseball.

Frommer's contribution is straightforward and begins with an ending: the Dodgers preparing to leave their beloved Brooklyn because they were stymied in attempts to get a new stadium. He then informs his readers about what life was like in the postwar years and pays tribute to the first generations of black players before moving on to profile each team. Having set the stage, he concludes with a recap of the World Series matchups.

Kahn expands on his boys of summer theme to include the Yankees and Giants in the battle for the hearts and souls (and dollars) of the baseball-hungry public. His follows a more general chronology as he profiles the great players and colorful characters from each team. He has a way of squeezing the nostalgia out of each word, making readers of a certain age long even more fervently for youth lost.

Ziegel wrote for a couple of New York tabloids: the *Post* beginning in the 1960s and the *Daily News* from the mid-1980s until his death in 2010. He provides introductions for each year and adds additional text to supplement the original captions that ran with each photograph.

Too bad these three can't come as a boxed set. Each volume stands well alone, but together they would present a terrific united front.

Other categories: Coffee Table/Gift, Fandom, Pop Culture, Photography

324. *Now I Can Die in Peace: How ESPN's Sports Guy Found Salvation, With a Little Help from Nomar, Pedro, Shawshank, and the 2004 Red Sox*, by Bill Simmons. New York: ESPN, 2005.

325. *Feeding the Monster: How Money, Smarts, and Nerve Took a Team to the Top*, by Seth Mnookin. New York: Simon and Schuster, 2006.

The Red Sox's first championship since 1918 created a boom in books about the Boston franchise, both new titles as well as reissues of older ones.

Two of the better, more pensive offerings include Simmons's anecdotal fan-point-of-view and Mnookin's deeper analysis of a *Moneyball* approach to building a championship team.

Simmons's style is what I can only describe as stream of consciousness: he begins a thought then thinks of something else and has to immediately explore it in a side note (because he might forget what he was trying to say, and it takes too long to look at footnotes at the bottom of the page or flip back and forth to endnotes anyway). He obviously has a lot of ancillary thoughts, since there are more than five hundred of these things in a 350-plus-page book.

Simmons, a former *Boston Herald* writer, certainly has the background to report on a personal level. He's not like an author for hire who chases the flavor-of-the-month topic, so his stories, beginning six years prior to the momentous 2004 campaign, seem more earnest.

Mnookin, who grew up in Red Sox Nation and graduated from Harvard, deconstructs how the Red Sox front office, including Theo Epstein, the thirtysomething boy wonder general manager, assembled the "idiots" who would become champions. Then there's the obligatory historical background about how great the team used to be before they sold Babe Ruth. With his departure, the Sox went into a decline then resurged during the Ted Williams, Dom DiMaggio, and Johnny Pesky era. That was followed by another decline because they couldn't bring themselves to sign black players, then by gradual resurrection until they became perennial postseason contenders, if not American League champions.

You read Mnookin's book, which spent a couple of weeks as a *New York Times* best seller, for the head; you read Simmons's for the heart.

Other categories: Analysis, Fandom, Pop Culture

326. *Out of Left Field: Willie Stargell's Turning Point Season*, by Bob Adelman and Susan Hall. Pittsburgh: Proteus, 1980

Willie "Pops" Stargell was the Paul Bunyan of the Pittsburgh Pirates. He could create fear in the hearts of opposing pitchers while still in the on-deck circle, using a sledgehammer to warm up instead of a baseball bat.

Stargell enjoyed his best season in 1973, finishing second for the National League MVP award as the Pirates struggled to an 80-82 record. It was the first year after the death of his beloved friend and teammate, Roberto Clemente, so the team was operating under a huge practical and emotional burden from the start. But Stargell took a leadership role on the field and in the clubhouse, which would set the Pirates up for several great seasons to come, culminating in a world championship in 1979, when he finally did receive the recognition he so richly deserved as cowinner of the NL MVP award.

The book was years ahead of its time. If this scenario had taken place now, Stargell and the Pirates would no doubt be the subject of a reality TV series, which is exactly the flavor of *Out of Left Field*.

It consists of narrative, interviews, and lots of photos, all of which contribute to the book's cinéma vérité feel (enhanced by the lack of editing out blue language — reader beware). An author's note at the outset reveals the candid nature of the work, which was technically unauthorized despite the apparently unlimited access Adelman and Hall seem to have had.

Other category: Auto/Bio/Mem

327. *Pinstripe Empire: The New York Yankees from Before the Babe to After the Boss*, by Marty Appel. New York: Bloomsbury, 2012

After landing a job as a teenager with the New York Yankees answering Mickey Mantle's fan mail, Appel served as public relations director for the Bronx Bombers from 1973–77 and has maintained his association with them ever since. This put him in a unique position to write the first definitive history of the franchise since Frank Graham's *The New York Yankees: An Informal History*, published seventy years ago as part of the Putnam series of team overviews, which means much of the material has never been presented in such a formal manner. A special introduction by Frank Graham Jr. goes a long way in giving *Pinstripe* an unofficial seal of approval.

The project was both a labor of love and an awesome responsibility, and it can probably be summed up by paraphrasing from Ernest Thayer's classic poem: "There was ease in Appel's manner as he stepped into his place; / There was pride in Appel's bearing and a smile on Appel's face." These were almost surely his feelings toward having published such an impressive volume about the organization that has been his personal and professional locus for most of his life.

This contribution to the baseball literary canon is a massive one, weighing in at nearly six hundred pages; fans of both baseball history and the Yankees will wish it was longer. The bibliography alone is more than a dozen pages and serves as an excellent resource for further reading about one of pro sports' most storied teams.

Other category: Pop culture

328. *Superstars and Screwballs: 100 Years of Brooklyn Baseball,* by Richard Goldstein. New York: Dutton, 1991.

The Brooklyn Dodgers were a baseball Janus. For most of their existence, save for a couple of blips in 1916, 1920, and 1941, they were mired in the lower half of the eight-team National League. Sure, they had some colorful characters, including Babe Herman, who hit .393 in 1930 and *still* didn't win the batting title; Dazzy Vance, the ace of the pitching staff; and Casey Stengel, who got his managerial start with the Bums in 1934. Yet overall success never was one of their hallmarks. But give them credit for trying new things, such as night baseball and — the biggest game changer of all — the introduction of African Americans to the Major Leagues. Is it any coincidence that their best years came after Jackie Robinson joined the team in 1947? That's where most of the superstars that the lend the book its title enter into the equation; Robby was surrounded by the likes of Duke Snider, Pee Wee Reese, Gil Hodges, Roy Campanella, and Carl Erskine, among others.

The Bums may have been the most beloved Major League franchise of all time. Oh, you can have your Yankees, with their constant pennants and World Series appearances, but come on, isn't that kind of boring? Nestled in the heart of Flatbush among their fans, the team became a pop culture icon.

Of course, for the baseball-loving residents of the Borough of Kings, the crusher came when the front office decided that, in the expansive era of the 1950s, it was no longer economically viable to remain ensconced in tiny Ebbets Field, and the threat to take their ball and play elsewhere unless they got a nice shiny new ballpark was met with stony indifference by city leaders.

Goldstein, a longtime writer for the *New York Times* and other city publications, explains the mythos and bathos behind the team in an entertaining and educational manner.

Other categories: Auto/Bio/Mem, Business, Fandom, Pop Culture

Also by the author: *You Be the Umpire!* (1993); *An American Journey: My Life on the Field, in the Air, and on the Air* (with Jerry Coleman, 2008)

329. *The Teammates: A Portrait of Friendship*, by David Halberstam. New York: Hyperion, 2003.

The premise of Halberstam's last baseball book would make for an excellent, if extremely sad, buddy movie. Dom DiMaggio and Johnny Pesky, two members of the Boston Red Sox from the forties and fifties, and now well into senior citizenry, drive from San Francisco to Florida to bid goodbye to their teammate, Ted Williams. Bobby Doerr, the fourth musketeer, was unable to make the trip because of his wife's illness, but they all have the same shared experiences. They were all young men once, at the peak of athletic prowess, with few cares after the war was over.

Unlike most ballplayers who go their separate ways after retirement, these gentlemen remained in close contact. And like any friendships, there are lulls and silences even when they were physically together. The affection and mutual admiration, however, was always there.

But old age catches up, even for ex-stars. Williams died shortly after the visit and DiMaggio passed away in 2009. As of this writing, Pesky and Doerr were 92 and 94, respectively. Death is indeed the great equalizer.

Halberstam captures each man's then-and-now story in an eloquent, bittersweet approach in this slim volume, and the final leave-taking between the buddies is truly heart-rending.

The Teammates spent thirteen weeks on the *New York Times* bestseller list.

Other categories: Auto/Bio/Mem, Classic

330. *The Washington Senators*, by Shirley Povich. New York: Putnam, 1954.

Povich began his career in journalism as a teenager back in 1922 and spent the next seventy-plus years associated with the *Washington Post*. So who better than to write the definitive history of the franchise than him?

Unfortunately, the lean years outweighed the good ones, which came early on. The Senators, who were officially known as the

Nationals from 1905–55, won back-to-back pennants in 1924 and 1925 and once again in 1933, though they lost all three World Series, twice to the New York Giants. Povich spends much of his narrative accentuating the positive while acknowledging the negative honestly and without the kind of denigration so popular in contemporary writing.

The book was reissued in 2010 by Kent State University Press and contained a foreword by Richard "Pete" Peterson, who served as editor of the Writing Sports Series and offers a great backstory of the original Putnam series and the republishing efforts of the Southern Illinois University Press's Writing Baseball series. One of the purposes of the project, which began in 1997, was to bring back some of the literary classics so that they could be enjoyed by a new generation of readers. Eight of the original fifteen volumes—one for each of the original 16 Major League teams with the exception of the Philadelphia Athletics—were reprinted between SIUP, Northeastern University Press, and Kent State University Press. All serve as great representations of the excellent writing of the day.

Other category: Classic

331. *The Worst Team Money Could Buy: The Collapse of the New York Mets,* by Bob Klapisch and John Harper. New York: Random House, 1993.

If there's any book that screams for a revision, it's this deconstruction of how the New York Mets threw beaucoup bucks at free agents and made some blockbuster deals that should have all but guaranteed a postseason berth. And this was with a payroll of $45 million, less than the cost of one Jason Bay these days.

This is what happens when you put a no-nonsense manager like Jeff Torborg in charge of a bunch of nonsense-loving young men. The lineup included some of the biggest busts in free-agent history. After the book came out, Bobby Bonilla offered to show Klapisch the Bronx, and not as his tour-guide. Vince Coleman never lived up to his promise due to injuries, although he did manage to injure a little kid by throwing firecrackers into a crowd of fans in 1993.

Eddie Murray would be elected to the Hall of Fame, but he was a real curmudgeon to the press. Bret Saberhagen, only three years after winning a Cy Young Award, appeared in just seventeen games before going down with a sore arm. Anthony Young began a losing streak that would end at twenty-seven the following year. And Dwight Gooden continued his descent into baseball hell. So instead of running away with the NL East division, and perhaps more, the Mets finished in fifth place with an abysmal record of 72-90.

Klapisch and Harper, writers for the two New York City tabloids at the time, present here an anatomy of a failure, with all the health problems, distractions, and stupid shenanigans that doomed the Mets to becoming one of the biggest disappointments of all time.

Maybe the authors could be persuaded to revisit their project, with a then-and-now section featuring the team's fortunes during the late 2000s.

Other categories: Business, Pop Culture

332. *The Year the Expos Finally Won Something,* by Brodie Snyder, illustrated by Aislin. Toronto ON: Checkmark, 1981.

The maternal side of my family hails from Montreal, so after the Mets my favorite team was the Expos. So I'm pretty much a sucker for any book — and there are precious few — about the team. As of this writing Jonah Keri, author of *The Extra 2%: How Wall Street Strategies Took a Major League Baseball Team from Worst to First,* is working on a history of the franchise.

Snyder, a longtime sportswriter for the *Montreal Gazette,* provides an entertaining, lighthearted look at the Expos' ups and their singular down, the final game. He profiles the members of the team, followed by a journal for the 1981 campaign, when a midseason strike caused the cancellation of some fifty-four games. The Expos had the second-best record in the National League East, primarily because they played six more games than the leading Saint Louis Cardinals, dropping five of them.

Montreal ended up losing to the Dodgers in the NLCS on a game-winning ninth-inning home run by Rick Monday, and it was basically all downhill from there, despite a few good seasons in the early 1990s.

Aislin, aka Terry Mosher, a popular political cartoonist for the *Gazette* and other Canadian publications, provides the illustrations.

Also by the author: The *Year the Expos Almost Won the Pennant!* (1979)

WOMEN

333. *Breaking into Baseball: Women and the National Pastime,* by Jean Hastings Ardell. Carbondale: Southern Illinois University Press, 2005.

There is a scene in *A League of Their Own* in which an errant pregame warm up toss rolls to an African American woman who happens to be standing far down the line in foul territory. When the catcher, standing fairly close by, asks her to toss it over, the fan rears back and fires a strike to the pitcher, who is standing much farther away. Despite her obvious talent, there was no spot for her in the league.

That's the basic premise in Ardell's book about the role of women in the game. Despite their affection, their knowledge, and their talents, they have had difficulty finding a place in the national pastime.

Ardell traveled across the country looking for stories; fortunately for us readers, she found plenty of them. Although their roles were limited, women were indeed present: in the press box, as umpires (Pam Postema), as owners (Effa Manley and Joan Payson), and even as participants (Ila Borders played with men on an independent league team, and the Colorado Silver Bullets, a team comprised totally of women, also toured for a couple of years).

Although there is a degree of dismay, the book is mostly upbeat, as the women share their love of baseball and Ardell remains confident that somehow, someday, a woman will participate in a Major League game.

The book is part of the Southern Illinois University Press Writing Baseball series.

Other categories: Auto/Bio/Mem, Pop Culture

334. *No Girls in the Clubhouse: The Exclusion of Women from Baseball,* by Marilyn Cohen. Jefferson NC: McFarland, 2009.

In the early days of the game, if women played at all, it was amongst themselves and was considered more of an amusement than serious athletic activity. Then one day a nineteen-year-old named Jackie Mitchell struck out Babe Ruth *and* Lou Gehrig in an exhibition, which infuriated Commissioner Kennesaw Mountain Landis so much that he officially decreed no woman could ever be involved in organized—that is, professional—baseball. According to Cohen, a professor of sociology and urban studies, that's not fair. She avers that women deserve the chance to compete, and not just in aberrational situations like the All-American Girls Professional Baseball League, which began during World War II but faded out by the mid-1950s.

No Girls in the Clubhouse looks at the advances made by women on the field, as opposed to the front office or the press box—which have their own exclusionary histories to consider—from lawsuits that enabled girls to play in little league and high school, to the Colorado Silver Bullets, a women's team competing against men on an exhibition basis, to Ila Borders, a pitcher who played with the independent league Duluth Superior Dukes in the late 1990s.

Other category: Pop Culture

335. *Women at Play: The Story of Women in Baseball,* by Barbara Gregorich. New York: Harcourt Brace, 1993.

Even before *A League of Their Own* was released in 1995, Gregorich published this collection of profiles and history about the role of women as participants in the national pastime.

This small, stylish volume divides the history into four categories: the early years, when women formed their own recreational teams shortly after the invention of the game; the bold years, which reflected the unbridled optimism of the Roaring Twenties; the league years, which is the largest chapter and deals with the All-American Girls Professional Baseball League and many of its players; and the modern years, in which women sought more of a place in the men's game. Because of its publication date, it does not consider that women would eventually play with and against male athletes.

With a bit of expansion, the league years could be its own book. There have, in fact, been several books on the AAGPBL published since *A League of Their Own* premiered. In covering the league years, Gregorich interviews several standouts who gush about the fun and freedom of competing for the fans.

Other categories: Auto/Bio/Mem, Pop Culture

Also by the author: *She's On First: A Novel* (1987)

336. *Women in Baseball: The Forgotten History*, by Gai Ingham Berlage. Westport CT: Praeger, 1994.

While *Women at Play* and *Breaking into Baseball* took a generally populist and lighthearted approach to the subject, Berlage's *Women in Baseball* carries a more scholarly and pessimistic view.

Berlage concentrates on the exclusion foisted on women by the lords of baseball, led by Commissioner Landis, who decided he would protect womanhood by forbidding them to play. I'm sure the fact that his edict came in the aftermath of a day on which a teen-aged Jackie Mitchell struck out Babe Ruth and Lou Gehrig in an exhibition game was mere coincidence. Not.

The author, a sociology professor who wrote frequently about women in sports, chides this segregation, pointing out that women have been part of the game since its inception. The contributions of women, however, have mostly gone unnoticed — for example, those of ladies like Alta Weiss and Lizzie Murphy, both of whom played on men's semipro teams in the early 1900s. But here's the rub: no one could figure out a way to allow women to play in the professional game.

Like Gregorich, Berlage devotes a good portion of her book to the accomplishments of members of the All-American Girls Professional Baseball League.

Other category: Pop Culture

8

Instructionals

Those who can, do; but those who can, also teach. It might not be practical to learn a physical activity from a book, but that doesn't mean you can't find something helpful from instruction manuals.

The books in this category were written by a variety of sources: players, managers, and teachers, among others. Some are geared toward the athletes and contain detailed how-to information, including frame-by-frame photographs and charts depicting proper defensive play. Others are intended as guides for those who would coach younger players.

But there's more to the game than the mere physical. All the strength and agility in the world won't help a player who has a poor attitude. This is why books that teach a good mental approach are so popular.

337. *The Baffled Parents Guide to Great Baseball Drills*, by Jim Garland. Camden M E: Ragged Mountain Press, 2002.

Players come and go. Gloves, bats, and other items of equipment evolve over the years. But the skills needed to succeed in the game have remained basically the same for more than a century.

According to Joe Riggins, the fictional manager of the Durham Bulls in the film *Bull Durham*, baseball is a simple game: you throw the ball, you hit the ball, you catch the ball. *Great Baseball Drills* gives parents the ways to practice those concepts without much ado for individuals, small groups, and full teams. All ages and skill levels, from beginner to advanced, are included and indicated as such, so the kids shouldn't be bored. The diagrams are exceedingly helpful, even for those who aren't Connie Mack or Rod Dedeaux.

Garland, a veteran educator and coach, breaks down the material for on-the-field use and helps the parent-coach handle the philosophical aspects of teaching the kids the right way to play the game, which, let's face it, can be challenging regardless of whether the kids are more like the Bad News Bears than little league champs.

338. *Base-Ball: How to Become a Player,* by John Montgomery Ward. Philadelphia: Athletic, 1888.

I don't know where people get the notion that the early ballplayers were all a bunch of dumb hicks. Granted, John Montgomery Ward was quite atypical. Not only was he a college graduate, he was also a practicing attorney. All this gave him the background needed to be a leader in the short-lived Players' League, an attempt to collectivize profits and share them among the players.

Ward's *Base-Ball* was the first player-written overview of the game. He leads off with a brief chapter on baseball origins and history — brief because, really, how many years had the game been around at that point? Next, he goes into an analysis of the requirements for each defensive spot. "Second base," he writes, "is the prettiest position to play of the entire in-field" (84). The few illustrations are charmingly anachronistic, probably because the fielders didn't wear gloves. There are also bits of advice regarding general strategy and training habits.

The book was republished as a facsimile edition in 1993 by the Society for American Baseball Research and is available for free online reading from several sources.

Other categories: Auto/Bio/Mem, Classic, History

339. *Baseball: How to Play the Game: The Official Playing and Coaching Manual of Major League Baseball,* by Pete Williams. New York: Universe, 2011.

This large, colorful volume encompasses the fundamentals of the physical, if not quite mental, game as played on the field. Basic instruction is offered along with helpful tips for batting, pitching, and fielding from such Major Leaguers as Mark Teixeira, John Lackey, Jason Marquis, Tim Hudson, Ivan Rodriguez, and many more.

The photos go a long way in teaching readers the right baseball fundamentals and skills as well as what *not* to do. There is also a section on some of the basic rules that are inevitably misunderstood and confusing, such as the balk, the infield fly rule, obstruction, and interference, along with a few other scenarios that frequently serve as a source of commentary among the broadcasters and sportswriters.

Situational baseball is briefly discussed, but more serious attention will no doubt be addressed in a subsequent manual.

340. *Baseball: Individual Play and Team Play in Detail,* by W. J. Clarke and Frederick T. Dawson. New York: Scribner, 1915.

One of the fascinating things about this nearly one-hundred-year-old volume is how little the basic strategy has changed. Obviously the objective also remains the same: score more runs than the opposition.

The book is written in exacting detail and formal language, with detailed instructions for each position. Pitchers are even instructed on how to throw "out-curves," "out-drops," and "slow balls."

One wonders what players from that era would think of today's gloves, which make their fielding gear look like shreds of cardboard. There is also tutoring on batting and base running, followed by team plays that are illustrated by rudimentary but still recognizable diagrams.

The book was written by a couple of college professors — Clarke was the head coach for the Princeton University baseball team, and

Dawson was general athletic coach of Union College — so it's perfectly rational to find a chapter devoted to "Hints to College Players." His first suggestion: "Have regular hours for study. If these are to be at night, have them in the early part of the evening. 'Think baseball' after you have prepared your other lessons." Other nuggets: "Keep a note-book and put down in it the mistakes you have made, also the mistakes others make" and "Avoid tobacco. It can't do you any *good*" (179–83). Some things never change.

341. *Batting*, by F. C. Lane, reprinted by the Society for American Baseball Research. Lincoln: University of Nebraska Press, 2001.

Lane, the editor in chief for *Baseball* magazine for almost thirty years, compiled this tidy little volume on the intricacies of offense.

Batting was first published in 1925 as a collection of articles compiled for the magazine, and featuring some of the top hitters of the day, such as Ty Cobb, Rogers Hornsby, and Babe Ruth. The majority of tips seem to lean toward the game's psychological issues, like "When the Fans Razz," "How Mental Impressions May Help or Harm the Batter," "Where Other Interests Intrude," and "Batting Slumps and How to Cure Them."

There are lots of theories on the offense side of the program. Some may strike the readers as common sense, others as mumbo jumbo, but one has to remember that this instructional was originally published more than seventy-five years ago.

The 2001 reprint edition is a bit dense with text, but it has a better design overall. Perhaps including photographs or diagrams would have gone a long way toward making *Batting* more readable and aesthetically pleasing to a modern audience. Still, if you can get beyond the these little inconveniences, you'll be rewarded with a keen insight into the game as it was played by some of the most proficient hitters of their time and of all time.

Other categories: Auto/Bio/Mem, History

342. *How to Pitch*, by Bob Feller. New York: A. S. Barnes, 1948.

This slim volume is beautiful in its simplicity. Feller, the premier pitcher of his generation, imparts his considerable skills as he covers every aspect of the position briefly and succinctly. The illustrations — especially the close-ups of the grips for various pitches — really help him get his point across.

Feller's father famously used a portion of the family's farm to build a baseball field. Not everyone has that luxury, but the future Hall of Famer offers instructions for a simple but effective homemade practice strike zone and home plate setup.

He also knows that you have to be an all-around athlete to succeed, so he gives tips on batting and fielding as well.

Other category: Auto/Bio/Mem

343. *The Mental Game of Baseball: A Guide to Peak Performance*, by H. A. Dorfman and Karl Kuehl. South Bend IN: Diamond, 1989.

A perennial favorite among coaches, parents, and players, *The Mental Game of Baseball* offers the ability to prepare, as much as possible, away from the field through positive approaches and visualization — tools often employed in the field of hypnosis. The authors take a relaxed approach as they try to put the user-reader at ease in an area that calls for a combination of relaxation and aggressiveness.

The book is divided into two basic areas: general suggestions that apply to the game as a whole, and area-specific ideas for pitching, batting, fielding, and base running. All of the latter contain shared themes, but by separating them out, Dorfman, an educator who later found great demand as a sports psychologist, and Kuehl, a baseball "lifer," make it as easy as possible for the reader to find a connection.

Also by the author: *The Mental ABC's of Pitching: A Handbook for Performance Enhancement* (2000); *The Mental Keys to Hitting: A Handbook of Strategies for Performance Enhancement* (2001)

9
International

Baseball may have gotten its start as America's national pastime, but it is no longer the product of the United States alone. The game is now played all over the world on every level, from youth to national amateur squads to professional teams. Naturally, there are several books that highlight this spreading of the wealth to foreign shores.

344. *Baseball without Borders: The International Pastime,* edited by George Gmelch. Lincoln: University of Nebraska Press, 2006.

According to a press release issued by Major League Baseball, almost 30 percent of major leaguers were born outside the United States. With more and more players imported, it's important to understand where they are coming from—literally and figuratively—and what baseball is like in their corners of the world.

While the fundamentals of the sport are the same, the culture and history are different in each part of the world and deserve to be recognized. This collection of sixteen essays from an array of scholars covers the major areas, such as Japan and the rest of Asia; Latin and Central America and Canada; Europe, especially Great Britain, Holland, and Italy; and Australia.

How did these nations come to receive *our* national pastime and what did they do to put their own stamp in the game? Why does it flourish in some places but not others? What role does economics play? It's obvious that in some of the poorer countries, baseball serves as a way out, but what about the industrialized nations?

Like many essay collections of its kind, *Baseball without Borders* serves as an excellent introduction and a launching point for supplemental investigation.

Other categories: Academic, Anthology, Ethnicity, History, Pop Culture

345. *Blue Jays 1, Expos 0: The Urban Rivalry That Killed Major League Baseball in Montreal,* by David Luchuk. Jefferson NC: McFarland, 2007.

The rivalry mentioned in the title is not one of those regional exhibition contests or even interleague play, such as the Mets playing the Yankees or the Cubs facing off against the White Sox. It is much more about municipal and provincial politics.

The author ponders if the plight of the Montreal franchise, irreparably comprised following the 1994 strike, was exacerbated by off-field events involving Canadian federal and Quebecois provincial governments, misappropriated funds, and under-the-table deals, issues that usually come in under the United States' radar.

Luchuk sets his narrative during the 2002 season, with both the Expos and Blue Jays beset by their individual problems, despite their host cities' long history in the game. The Expos were one of the teams under consideration for contraction and were eventually taken over by Major League Baseball—this created its own conflict-of-interest issues—until its eventual relocation to Washington DC in 2005.

Although the book's narrative unfolds month by month, there is a lot of backstory exposition for each team that makes the narrative a bit choppy, as it flits around from the games and players to the fate of the Expos to the political angle. Still, if the reader can parse it out, *Blue Jays 1, Expos 0* makes for a unique study of baseball to the north.

Other categories: History, Politics

346. *Diamonds around the Globe: The Encyclopedia of International Baseball,* by Peter C. Bjarkman. Westport CT: Greenwood Press, 2005.

There is no question that baseball is no longer just America's national game. It has become a global enterprise, played in dozens of nations on six continents. And who knows: maybe some research team is even playing a version in the Antarctic.

Bjarkman, a writer who specializes in Latin American baseball, expands his vistas with this six-hundred-plus-page reference. He leads off with a section on Cuba, the country on which much of his other writings focus, and he moves on to Canada, Japan, Puerto Rico, Venezuela, the Dominican Republic, Mexico, the Caribbean, and the Pacific Rim.

Each chapter offers a brief history of how baseball came to the individual country. Usually, it happened via American military forces, touring Major Leaguers on goodwill missions, or travelers who brought the game back with them after visiting America. Bjarkman also pays tribute to some of the key figures from these countries who excelled locally or made the big jump to the Major Leagues, a huge accomplishment at any time but especially significant going back fifty years or more.

Since no baseball encyclopedia can be considered complete without lists and statistics, Bjarkman includes local champions and individual leaders as well as how teams fared in various international competitions. Appendices include an international baseball timeline of greatest moments and a now-outdated roster of members of the International Baseball Federation.

Other categories: History, Reference

Also by the author: *The Encyclopedia of Major League Baseball* (in American and National League editions, (1993); *Baseball with a Latin Beat: The History of the Latin American Game* (1994); and *Smoke: The Romance and Lore of Cuban Baseball* (with Mark Rucker, 1999)

347. *The Northern Game: Baseball the Canadian Way,* by Bob Elliott. Toronto ON: SportsClassic, 2005.

Baseball hasn't historically been considered the Canadian game (depending on who you ask it's either ice hockey or lacrosse), but there have been more than 230 Major Leaguers since 1869 who were born in our neighbor to the North.

Elliott, a baseball writer for the *Toronto Sun* and a member of the veterans committee of the Hall of Fame, presents the sport in all its maple leaf splendor, from the first recorded Canadian pitch in 1838 to circa 2005.

As a half Canadian on my mother's side, I can be a bit prideful. Sure, we have our stars, like Ferguson Jenkins, Larry Walker, Eric Gagne, and Ron Taylor, who not only compiled a perfect 0.00 ERA for two World Series winners (the Cardinals in 1964 and the Mets in 1969), but also went on to become the team physician for the Toronto Blue Jays.

Maybe it's because of the harsher climate, and this may be totally jingoistic, but Canadians just might enjoy and appreciate the game a bit more *because* they don't take it for granted. The book's dust jacket even depicts a well-used baseball nestled in a snow bed. Elliott's book is full of this kind of light-heartedness as he spends as much time on the little leaguers and older amateurs as he does on the big leaguers.

One appendix contains a roster of all Canadian-born Major Leaguers. Others consist of the nation's all-time Major League leaders; All-Star teams by province, and yes, they're all accounted for; a list of every player on Team Canada; and a list of Major League award winners, including the James "Yip" O'Neill Award, handed out by the Canadian Baseball Hall of Fame in honor of the first star of the game, who just happened to be born in Ontario. In 2012 Elliott became the first Canadian to win the Spink Award, presented by the Baseball Writers' Association of America for contributions to baseball writing.

Other categories: History, Reference

348. *Pitching in the Promised Land: A Story of the First and Only Season in the Israel Baseball League,* by Aaron Pribble. Lincoln: University of Nebraska Press, 2011.

In 2007 Boston businessman Larry Baras came up with the idea to combine two of his passions: baseball and the Holy Land. He put together a group of advisors that included some pretty prominent names in the game, among them economist Andrew Zimbalist; former Yankees public relations head Marty Appel; Minor League owner Marvin Goldklang; former Major Leaguers Ron Blomberg, Art Shamsky, Ken Holtzman, and Steve Hertz, who would manage some of the teams; and former U.S. ambassador to Israel Daniel C. Kurtzer, who served as commissioner for the fledgling league.

Pribble, a former Minor Leaguer who had pursued a career as a high school teacher, was drafted as a pitcher for the Tel Aviv Lightning, one of the six IBL franchises. He efficiently weaves into his narrative the growing pains shared by everyone involved in the form of late paychecks, poor field conditions, and general apathy in the local media.

Pribble also writes about the ambivalence of being an unaffiliated Jew visiting the land of his religious heritage and thinking about the sociopolitical issues of the region for the first time.

Pitching is a sweet story of young — and not-so-young — men trying for one more season in the sun, or as a last-ditch attempt to garner attention and prolong a career in the game.

Other category: Auto/Bio/Mem

349. *Playing America's Game: Baseball, Latinos, and the Color Line,* by Adrian Burgos Jr. Berkeley: University of California Press, 2007.

The designation *America* does not mean just the United States or even North America, according to Burgos, an assistant professor of history at the University of Illinois at Urbana-Champaign. As the title implies, baseball belongs to *all* the Americas, Central and South included.

Baseball has been played in those nations since the late 1800s, as Burgos explains in his mostly standard history. But he wants to clear up a few issues that have long been a source of confusion and, to some, annoyance. For one thing, *Latino* is not a catchall for every player of Hispanic descent. Each country has its own proud heritage, with great players coming from just about every nation that plays the sport.

Another debate has been about who had a harder time breaking into the Majors: African Americans or Hispanics. The author contends that although black athletes indeed had a lot to deal with, they at least had communities in baseball towns where they could find some small comfort; Latinos rarely had that kind of support system when they began to arrive in larger numbers in the 1950s. They often struggled with a double whammy: dark complexions and unfamiliarity with the English language.

A less-enlightened print media of the day often reported a Latino player's interview answers in dialect, which had the effect, intended or not, of making the player look stupid. Some managers demanded an English-only clubhouse. This was a source of frustration and tension for players who were having a difficult enough time adjusting to a new culture, from ordering food in the few restaurants that would accept them to dealing with their new Anglo teammates. Burgos notes the ethnic makeup of the pressroom is still basically the same as it was in generations past: white and male.

Other categories: Academic, Ethnicity, History

Also by the author: *Cuban Star: How One Negro-League Owner Changed the Face of Baseball* (2011)

350. *Through a Diamond: 100 Years of Japanese Baseball*, by Kerry Yo Nakagawa. San Francisco: Rudi, 2002.

Japan has been crazy for baseball ever since a teacher from America brought the game to their shores more than one hundred years ago. And like others who immigrated to America, the Japanese

Americans took up the game as a way of assimilating into the culture of their new homeland. Even during their heinous confinement in internment camps during World War II, they continued to play the national pastime. When World War II ended, the U.S. military sponsored tours by American All-Star teams to boost morale in a devastated Japan, leading to a renewed interest—organized play had been suspended in the interim—as well as creating a bridge between former enemies.

In addition to the overarching impact on the community as a whole, Nakagawa, a writer and director of the Nisei Baseball Research Project, profiled some of the pioneering figures, including Masanori Murakami, the first Japanese national to reach the majors, as well as Ryan Kurosaki and Don Wakamatsu, the first *sansei* and *yonsei* (third- and fourth-generation American, respectively), to reach the game's highest level.

Then there was the journey of Hawaiian-born Wally Yonamine, the first *nisei* (second-generation American) to play professional ball *in* Japan. Although he did not garner the same attention as Jackie Robinson, Yonamine was met with similar racial taunts and death threats.

Through a Diamond was written before Ichiro Suzuki spearheaded a new wave of Japanese players in the Majors. Their exploits might call for a new edition in the near future.

Other categories: Auto/Bio/Mem, History

351. *You Gotta Have Wa: When Two Cultures Collide on the Baseball Diamond*, by Robert Whiting. New York: Macmillan, 1989.

This is the first and perhaps still the best book about pro baseball in Japan, especially as it pertains to American expatriates trying to hang on for one more big paycheck. Whiting, who fell in love with Japanese baseball while stationed there during a stint in the military—and has lived there on and off ever since—is considered the go-to guy on the subject, introducing the dedication and hardworking perfectionist philosophy to a wider readership many years before the presence of Japanese players in the Major Leagues became commonplace.

Wa is the concept of sublimating individuality for the greater good of the team, a notion American players sometimes had difficulty gleaning, a la Tom Selleck's character in the feature film *Mr. Baseball*.

Whiting follows several ex–Major Leaguers, including Leon Lee, Randy Bush, and current Major League manager Charlie Manuel, as they attempted to deal with isolation from the familiar, with mixed results. *Wa* is an eye-opening look at the game that proves that there's more to baseball than the American way.

Other category: History

Also by the author: *The Chrysanthemum and the Bat: The Game Japanese Play* (1977); *The Meaning of Ichiro: The New Wave from Japan and the Transformation of Our National Pastime* (2004)

10

Minor Leagues

From a tiny acorn grows a mighty oak.

There's a reason the Minor Leagues are collectively called the farm system. That's where the overwhelming majority of Major Leaguers are planted and raised. Only a handful of players have entered the Majors without playing a single day beating the bushes.

If you're lucky enough to have a big league affiliate in your town, the love affair can be both short and long. Likewise, books about the Minor Leagues can be happy, such as when celebrating a history, or sad, like when a player fails to live up to his potential and leaves the game without fulfilling his promise.

Some volumes speak of an entire league or a specific franchise, but they almost always feature a special affection for and a glimpse of small-town Americana.

352. *Baseball's Fabulous Montreal Royals: The Minor League Team That Made Major League History,* by William Brown. Montreal QC: Robert Davies, 1996.

Montreal may have appeared on America's radar thanks to Jackie Robinson, but as the author points out, baseball had been a part of that charming Quebec city since 1897. Brown, a freelance broadcaster and reporter, regales the reader with anecdotes and highlights prior to and after Robinson's brief stay there.

Although by no means the most popular sport north of the border, Montrealers enjoyed spending parts of their summers in Delorimier Stadium, watching the next best thing to Major League baseball—presented in both English and French, for an additional kick. The Dodgers' AAA franchise played there, featuring some of its up-and-coming stars, including future Hall of Famers Don Drysdale, Roy Campanella, and Tommy Lasorda, among others.

Most of the players would say they loved their time in Montreal and how well they were treated by the fans. But just as the Dodgers had abandoned Brooklyn for the warm climate of southern California, so would operations cease in Montreal, moving their affiliate to Spokane, Washington. Fortunately, it wouldn't be all that long before baseball returned to town, with a big league franchise this time.

Other categories: History/Team, International

353. *The Brooklyn Cyclones: Hardball Dreams and the New Coney Island*, by Ben Osborne. New York: New York University Press, 2004.

Brooklyn, one of the largest cities in the United States, had been without a professional baseball team since the Dodgers skipped town after the 1957 season. So it was with a great huzzah when it was announced that the New York Mets would field a low-level Minor League affiliate beginning in the summer of 2001.

Just think of what it would mean to civic pride, to the community in which the new ballpark would be situated, right in the middle of one of the most historic recreation spots in America: Coney Island, home of Astroland, Nathan's Famous, and the legendary roller coaster for which the team was named. Local, national, and even international media marked the event with great fanfare.

But what did situating the team there actually accomplish? How did it affect the local residents who had for years been in the throes of a poor economy? Promises were made in terms of jobs and the ancillary benefits local business would receive from the increased traffic a professional ballclub was sure to bring. This urban study is as much at the heart of Brooklyn resident Osborne's book as the game on the field, and it proves that having a team to represent you is great, but it doesn't solve all your ills.

Other categories: Analysis, Business, History

354. *The Encyclopedia of Minor League Baseball,* second edition, edited by Lloyd Johnson and Miles Wolf. Durham NC: Baseball America, 1997.

Anyone interested in MiLB (as opposed to MLB) would do well to peruse a copy of this indispensable out-of-print reference that covers the bush leagues dating back to 1883. You'll find standings for each league along with their Major League affiliations, statistical leaders, All-Stars, and managers.

The Golden Age of MiLB is generally set in the late 1940s to early 1950s. There were more than sixty leagues and scores of teams, from Abbeville AL to Zebulon NC, in practically every state of the union, as well as in Canada, Cuba, the Dominican Republic, Mexico, Panama, Puerto Rico, and Venezuela.

With the Majors experiencing turmoil in the mid-1990s, fans discovered the minors, which provided a simpler—and cheaper—brand of baseball. The release of *Bull Durham* has also been credited with a resurgence of interest in the Minor Leagues.

If you are patient and go through this generally straightforward reference book, you will be rewarded with little gems buried within, such as a "This Date in Minor League History" for each season, where you'll find little-known facts such as Major League stars making their professional debuts in the Minors, statistical feats, and obituaries for those whose MiLB accomplishments just couldn't seem to get them over the top and into the Show.

Other categories: History, Pop Culture, Statistics

355. *The Last Best League: One Summer, One Season, One Dream,* by Jim Collins. Cambridge MA: Da Capo Press, 2004.

There's a magical place in New England where the best college-age amateurs gather each summer, many picking up wooden bats for the first time. It is the Cape Cod League, an elite collection of ten teams where athletes vie for a chance to make it to the pros; one out of six signs a contract, according to Collins, who follows the fortunes of the Chatham A's in this charming little tale.

These young men are embraced by the local community. They work day jobs, live with host families, and build relationships with admiring fans, as well as, in some cases, more personal ones with the young ladies in town. Collins gives the folks who organize the leagues and open their homes and hearts as much credit as he does the players. They do it for the love of the game, the clichéd-mom, apple-pie, small-town Americana with which baseball has always been associated.

No doubt the majority of players in each season's Cape Cod League realize they won't be advancing beyond high-level amateur and semipro situations, but it's a time for one last free summer before the burdens of the real world take hold.

The Last Best League makes for ideal summer vacation reading, especially if you happen to be in the Cape Cod area. By the way, if the premise sounds familiar to movie fans, it should. A similar theme was screened in the 2001 feature film *Summer Catch*, starring Freddie Prinze Jr., Jessica Biel, and Brian Dennehy. Collins maintained he came up with idea first.

Other categories: Fandom, Pop Culture

11

Pop Culture

Baseball encompasses so many other parts of American culture: music, movies, art, poetry, and even cooking.

This section offers suggestions on some of the most beautiful art and photography titles. Many seek to kill two birds with one stone, mixing illustrations with literary passages, either from general works or those about baseball itself. You'll also find books that deconstruct baseball movies, either from a sports or cinematic point of view.

All the books listed here share a common theme in that they are wholly about baseball; that is, they don't just mention it in passing or include it as one of several themes. On the other hand, you'll find there's a tendency toward repetition. Many of the books use the same pieces of art, authors, or stories as being representative of the best literature on the game.

356. *101 Baseball Places to See Before You Strike Out,* by Josh Pahigian. Guilford CT: Lyons Press, 2008.

It would be easy to cop out and mention all thirty major league ballparks, but that would be lazy. Instead, Pahigian mixes it up.

Sure, there are some big league venues — how could you *not* include Yankee Stadium, Fenway Park, and Wrigley Field? But there are also institutions honoring the lives and careers of Ty Cobb, Bob Feller, Yogi Berra, the Negro Leagues, and, of course, the mother of all sports museums, the Baseball Hall of Fame in Cooperstown.

Hungry? There are plenty of places to grab a bite that are either owned, operated, or merely bear the name of some top personalities: Boog's Barbecue (as in Boog Powell) in Maryland, Ozzie's Restaurant and Sports Bar in Saint Louis, and Nolan Ryan's Waterfront Steakhouse and Grill.

You can even make a pilgrimage to the gravesites of Babe Ruth, Jackie Robinson, and Ted Williams, whose last stop was the Alcor Life Extension Foundation in Scottsdale, Arizona, which supposedly still serves as the repository of his severed head.

As for the truly oddball, Pahigian includes Chicago's Billy Goat Tavern, where the curse that still follows the Cubs originated; the old Cook County Criminal Courts building, where eight members of the Chicago White Six stood trial for allegedly throwing the 1919 World Series; and the site in Burlington County, New Jersey, which provides the special mud used by Major League Baseball to take the sheen off of new balls.

Also by the author: *The Seventh Inning Stretch* (2010); *The Ultimate Baseball Road Trip: A Fan's Guide to Major League Stadiums* (with Kevin O'Connell, 2012)

357. *Are We Winning? Fathers and Sons in the New Golden Age of Baseball,* by Will Leitch. New York: Hyperion, 2010.

This sweet and sentimental story of the relationship between the author and his father centers around a game between the Saint Louis Cardinals and their hated rivals, the Chicago Cubs. To be honest, prior to reading it I didn't have much use for Leitch. The iconoclast was the founding editor of *Deadspin*, a gossipy blog that seems to take glee in knocking sports icons off their pedestals. He almost came to blows with Buzz Bissinger (author of *Three Nights in August*) over the contempt in which the latter held the blogosphere due to its own general lack of respect for the journalistic profession.

But it is a kinder, gentler Leitch the reader will find in *Winning*. He obviously loves the game—and his father—even if it is difficult for men to express such things.

Baseball is no longer the romantic rose-colored commonality

shared by generations. The book's dust jacket reveals an unfortu-nate reality: as a result of high ticket prices and a sense of restless-ness over the national pastime, the fans just aren't coming out like they used to.

Leitch tries to address some of these issues in between reporting on the game and the tacit understanding that, in his case, the love between father and son need not be acknowledged by mere words.

Other category: Fandom

358. *Baseball: A Literary Anthology*, edited by Nicholas Dawidoff. New York: Library of America, 2002.

Perhaps the best of its kind, *Baseball: A Literary Anthology* is a one-stop sampling of some of the best writing about baseball.

The more than seventy pieces included — almost all from the twentieth century — run the gamut of literature: fiction, nonfic-tion, poetry, song, and more. The usual suspects — found in just about every volume of this nature, since their work is so well-re-spected — constitute the centerpieces for this volume. There are book excerpts from Jim Bouton, Roger Kahn, Bernard Malamud, Philip Roth (but from *Portnoy's Complaint* rather than *The Great American Novel*), and Don DeLillo.

There are columns from the great sports journalists of their day, such as Red Smith, Jimmy Cannon, Heywood Broun, Jerome Holtzman, and Wendell Smith.

There are also some nice surprises, just to keep things fresh: Horrormeister Stephen King writes earnestly about his son's little league team; Carl Sandburg contributes a poem and a personal essay; and William Carlos Williams and Robert Frost also contribute poems. Molly O'Neill, a food editor and sister to former Major Leaguer Paul, offers a family story that just might embarrass her little brother.

The only misgiving I have is that I wish it were longer. The 720-plus pages were probably the limit of realistic publishing and mar-keting capabilities.

Other categories: Anthology, Auto/Bio/Mem, Classic, Essays, Fiction, History

359. *The Baseball: Stunts, Scandals, and Secrets Beneath the Stitches*, by Zack Hample. New York: Anchor, 2011.

Hample, the world's foremost published authority on how to snag a ball at Major League stadiums, goes the whole nine yards in analyzing just about everything there is to know about one of the prime pieces of sports equipment.

He's done an impressive amount of research, and he discusses the legends and lore of the horsehide — now cowhide — including how it's made, where it's made, and how physics makes it do the crazy things it does.

Hample also refers to his previous work, offering tips on how to legally acquire a souvenir at the ballpark short of paying for it, suggesting the best places to hang out during batting practice, and the etiquette of requesting a ball from a player. Ever the model of politeness, Hample, in a lengthier-than-most acknowledgments section, goes so far as to thank, by name, each of the 1,169 players and coaches who gave him a ball over the years. This is a craftsman at work, ladies and gentlemen.

The most entertaining part, however, might be Hample's lists and trivia, especially "Foul Balls in Pop Culture," in which a ball is used as a plot device in movies and on TV.

360. *A Baseball Album*, by Gerald Secor Couzens. New York: Lippincott and Crowell, 1980.

What sets this combination memoir, history book, and anthology apart is that its author was such a young man at the time of its publication — at least judging by his picture on the dust jacket. Usually you'll have an older person at the helm offering his or her own memories of the subjects gleaned over several decades.

Couzens's book runs the gamut in terms of age-appropriateness. The chapters are brief and fairly general in this hodgepodge of wildly disparate topics. Chapters include examinations of a handful of elite pitchers (Rube Marquard, Carl Hubbell, and Sandy Koufax), catchers, infielders, and outfielders. He also touches on superstitions, African Americans in the game, Japanese baseball, umpires, managers, and even the team doctor, who rarely gets credit in baseball books.

The anthology includes previously published pieces from contributors such as Commissioner Bowie Kuhn, sportswriters Leonard Koppett and Robert Lipsyte, author Ed Linn, and historian Harold Seymour.

The format of the book might be a bit jarring—it's as if Couzens was keeping an actual scrapbook and then rearranged the entries to form some topical cohesion—but that's part of the charm.

Other categories: Anthology, Auto/Bio/Mem, History

361. *Baseball and American Culture: Across the Diamond,* edited by Edward J. Rielly. New York: Haworth Press, 2003.

This anthology is a perfect fit for inclusion in the book you're now reading. Divided into five broad categories—"The American Fan"; "Baseball Inclusivity"; "Money, Managing, and Myth"; "Baseball and the Arts"; and "Baseball and Resolution of Conflict"—it contains a smorgasbord of topics ranging from a narrow focus ("On Fenway, Faith, and Fandom: A Red Sox Fan Reflects") to one of broad consequences ("Baseball and Blacks: A Loss of Affinity, a Loss of Community"). You've got your movies, your poetry, your segregation issues, your religion, your labor relations, your politics, and so on.

Most of the essays are written by scholars, but that doesn't mean the articles are necessarily scholarly. Of special note is Rob Edelman's section on "Politics, Patriotism, and Baseball On-Screen," in which he discusses, among other things, how one can tell the good cinematic guys from the bad. Simple, of course: if they love baseball, they're on the right side.

Another item that's a bit out of the ordinary is Loren Coleman's "Boys of Summer, Suicides of Winter: An Introduction to Baseball Suicides." Unsettlingly, there are more than one might think. Another favorite of mine is Roberta Newman's "Here's the Pitch: Baseball and Advertising," which links the two industries back the late nine-teenth century, hawking everything from underwear to cigarettes to cereal.

Other categories: Academics, Anthology, Commentary, Essays

362. *Baseball and the Mythic Moment: How We Remember the National Game,* by James D. Hardy Jr. Jefferson NC: McFarland, 2007.

Memory is a funny thing. Two people can experience the same event yet recall it completely differently. For example, Bill Buckner, the first baseman for the Boston Red Sox in 1986, probably has a dif-ferent take on Mookie Wilson's grounder in Game Six of that year's World Series than does the New York Mets outfielder. The same is undoubtedly true for fans of both franchises.

Hardy's book is full of such examples. Some are important on a national level, such as Lou Gehrig's "Luckiest Man" speech. They have become part of the nation's cultural fabric. Others may not be as grand to America as a whole, but to the faithful followers of a specific player or team, even for one year, they are no less a marker.

The cover of *Baseball and the Mythic Moment* indeed recreates one such moment that is still talked about sixty years later. Ask any serious fan of the game to define "The Catch." Just those two words and you'll hear about Willie Mays's mad dash to snare a far fly ball off the bat of the Cleveland Indians' Vic Wertz in the 1954 Fall Classic.

Hardy concludes with a fascinating chapter about the impact of television on perception. Before TV, tales of derring-do were in the purview of the radio announcer, or, going back even further, the sportswriter. Like the stories of our ancient ancestors, they were passed down from generation to generation. Now, thanks to advanced recording technology, we will always be able to see and marvel at a hobbled Kirk Gibson coming off the bench to hit a game-winning home run-someday, perhaps, in 3-D. Which method is better? The author leaves that to the reader to decide.

363. *Baseball Archaeology: Artifacts from the Great American Pastime*, with photographs by Bret Wills and text by Gwen Aldridge. San Francisco: Chronicle, 1993.

Most books like this focus on items from a single source, such as the Baseball Hall of Fame or a private collection. This slim large-trim paperback combines the best of both worlds.

Starting with baseball's pioneer days — with balls and bats that appear positively primitive — these are indeed fossils that represent the evolution of the game no less than primitive tools and cave drawings tell the stories of our earliest ancestors.

The items are grouped by purpose as well as specific eras in the game: for instance, gloves, bats, catchers' equipment, uniforms, and hats Even the trophies that were awarded to the game's premier players and the tickets have a place here. There is relatively little in the way of traditional collectibles here, though. Yes, there are some photographs of old cards and pennants, but the focus is on what the athletes left behind.

Other categories: Coffee Table/Gift, History

364. *Baseball as America: Seeing Ourselves Through Our National Game*, Washington DC: National Geographic Society, 2002.

Sponsored by Ernst and Young, Baseball as America was a travelling exhibition featuring items from the Baseball Hall of Fame that visited cities across the country for several years in the early 2000s. It was a godsend for those for whom a trip to Cooperstown was not feasible.

One of the best books of this kind — it's very similar in scope and presentation to the Ken Burns and Geoffrey C. Ward cohort to the *Baseball* miniseries in terms of written material and illustration — this coffee-table edition, issued as a companion volume to the exhibit, covers dozens of facets of the game, including photos, artwork, memorabilia, and more.

The stories, poems, and anecdotes are provided by a wide range of contributors, many of whom aren't generally known for their association with the game. Television journalist Tom Brokaw, for example, writes about how soldiers in World War II played baseball during respites from battle to maintain their connection to home. His essay is sandwiched between a photo of the famous green-light letter from president Franklin Roosevelt to Commissioner Landis urging that baseball should continue for the sake of the nation rather than shut down for the duration, and a piece by commissioner Bud Selig following the return of baseball after September 11, 2001.

That's just a small sampling of the menu. While there is certainly the standard fare from familiar names in the baseball cosmos, there are some surprises as well, such as writer Michael Chabon's article on the connection between fathers and sons after receiving a modest gift of some old baseball cards from his dad; singer Paul Simon's paean to Joe DiMaggio; and comedian Bob Newhart's sketch on why nobody will ever play baseball.

Other categories: Anthology, Classic, Coffee Table/Gift, Essays, History

365. *Baseball Diamonds: Tales, Traces, Visions, and Voodoo from a Native American Rite*, edited by Kevin Kerrane and Richard Grossinger. Garden City NY: Anchor, 1980.

Another in a fine line of anthologies that delve into the literary, this collection is an expanded version of *Baseball I Gave You All the Best Years of My Life*. Here, dozens of essays and poems on a variety of topics are divided into general categories, including the early stages of the game, ballplayers, ballparks, and "Baseball Math and Abstract Games."

Many of these pieces are extremely personal and reflect the contributors' experiences with the game, either as a participant, a child, or an observer, although there are a handful of items from people who actually cover baseball from the point of view of a professional, such as Roger Angell. Short fiction is interspersed with these memoirs and essays, but the reader might have trouble differentiating between them, since there is nothing in the way of contributor identification.

A book like *Baseball Diamonds* might strike some as a bit hard to get through, but, as with the source of its inspiration, it's worth the effort.

Other categories: Anthology, Essays

366. *Baseball I Gave You All the Best Years of My Life*, fifth edition, edited by Richard Grossinger and Lisa Conrad. Berkeley: North Atlantic, 1992.

Baseball books don't get much more literary than this. The fifth edition is culled from previous versions, which, in turn, were adapted from *Io*, a college publication.

The dozens of contributions lean heavily toward poetry. A sprinkling of essays recalls childhood and adult experiences of going to the game or watching a beloved hero at work. *Baseball* also features a small selection of illustrations, including several photos of players from the fifties through the seventies on vacation, one of which captures a young Grossinger posing with New York Yankee pitchers Don Larsen and Maury McDermott circa 1956. Another apt chapter features an ersatz All-Star team comprised of literary figures in a pre-Photoshop collage.

A highbrow book such as this is definitely a challenge for those unfamiliar or uncomfortable with such an approach to expressing one's fandom, but it's worth the effort to see how the other half cheers.

Other categories: Anthology, Classic, Commentary, History

367. *Baseball . . . The Perfect Game: An All-Star Anthology Celebrating the Game's Greatest Players, Teams, and Moments*, edited by Josh Leventhal. Minneapolis: Voyageur Press, 2005.

A latecomer to the genre that concentrated on the turn of the twenty-first century, this graphics-heavy edition features some of the greatest writers on the game as well as the people, places, and things on which they report.

Most come from previous works: Jim Brosnan leads things off in

"Opening Day," taken from his memoir *The Long Season*, followed by passages from Doris Kearns Goodwin's *Wait 'Til Next Year*, Eliot Asinof's *Eight Men Out*, and Eric Rolfe Greenberg's *The Celebrant*.

Other contributors include Robert Creamer, Ty Cobb, Marty Appel, Jules Tygiel, Jane Leavy, John Thorn, and actress Tallulah Bankhead, among several others. Each excerpt—as well as the accompanying photos—fits perfectly with such issues as the World Series or "What Makes a Great Hitter?" an essay by one of the greatest of them all, Ted Williams.

This is not a straight-ahead chronology, as one might expect given the book's overarching mission statement. Nor, at just over two hundred pages, is it an especially large book. But good things sure do come in small packages.

Other categories: Anthology, Auto/Bio/Mem, History, Sportswriting

368. *Birth of a Fan*, edited by Ron Fimrite. New York: Macmillan, 1993.

Do you remember when you became a baseball fan? Did a family member take you to see your first professional game? Were you handed a ball, bat, or glove and guided gently—or kicking and screaming—onto a field?

Ron Fimrite, a writer for *Sports Illustrated*, put the question to a bunch of his contemporaries. Their answers, some straightforward and others roundabout, make up the roster for this collection of original essays.

This is an all-star lineup, including such heavy hitters as Roger Angell, Roy Blount Jr., Robert Creamer, Frank Deford, Mark Harris, and George Plimpton, among others. For some of them it was love at first sight from the moment they stepped out of the stadium's corridor to encounter the biggest expanse of greenery they had ever seen. For others it could simply be the time spent with family or friends and the longing to replicate the moment by returning to the game.

In reading these essays, you get the impression that the ladies and gentlemen who shared their intimate thoughts and memories became award-winning writers because they all were failed athletes. The playing field's loss is, in this case, the readers' gain.

Other categories: Anthology, Essays, Fandom

369. *The Book of Baseball Lineups,* by Nicholas Acocella and Donald Dewey. Secaucus NJ: Citadel Press, 1996.

The authors put together almost one hundred lineups in this neat little paperback encompassing the entertaining, educational, funny, and thought provoking. Many names will be unfamiliar to most fans, but they made major contributions to the game nonetheless.

You might expect to find Babe Ruth in the category "Most influential—on the field," but what about Dickey Pearce? Doesn't ring a bell? Don't fret. Each lineup includes a cogent explanation or justification for inclusion. In this case, Pearce, who appeared in fewer than forty games over two seasons in the late 1870s, was responsible for situating the shortstop position in its present-day location between second and third bases. As for "Most influential—off the field," you have Jumpin' Joe Dugan, whose late-season trade to the pennant-bound Yankees in 1922 raised such a ruckus that Commissioner Landis instituted a midseason trade deadline that is still in effect.

There is the standard fare, such as youngest, oldest, all-time bests and worsts, and lineups consisting of players whose names share a theme such as colors or food. The real fun, however, is in the oddities, such as a team comprised of players who were traded several times during a single season—Dave Kingman played on four clubs in 1977—or the more morbid "They died with their spikes on," a lineup of athletes who passed away during their playing days, led by Hall of Famer Roberto Clemente, who perished in a plane crash delivering humanitarian aid to earthquake victims in Nicaragua after the 1973 campaign.

Other categories: History, Trivia

Also by the authors: *The Ball Clubs* (1996); *The Biographical History of Baseball* (2002)

370. *The Cambridge Companion to Baseball*, edited by Leonard Cassuto and Stephen Partridge. New York: Cambridge University Press, 2011.

Another excellent collection of essays on myriad topics that share a connection with baseball, the *Companion* includes some themes rarely found in a single volume from such a distinguished panel of contributors.

Topics range from the symbiosis baseball shared with wars, the movies, literature, urban planning and economic development, statistics (in the form of sabermetrics), international relations, and the mass media.

Many of the essays continue the theme with brief "interchapters," which add a bit of nuance to the article preceding it. For example, David Venturo writes about "Baseball and Material Culture," the activity of collecting and accumulating stuff, so he adds a brief follow-up on perhaps the holy grail of baseball collectibles: the Honus Wagner T-206 card. Similarly, Masaru Ikei's "Global Baseball: Japan and East Asia" is followed by Cassuto's comparison of the impacts of Ichiro Suzuki, the first big-name position player from Japan to compete in the Major Leagues, with Roberto Clemente, the first Puerto Rican superstar.

To paraphrase Forrest Gump, *The Cambridge Companion* is like a box of chocolates. You never know what you're going to get, but chances are you're going to enjoy it.

Other categories: Academic, Anthology, Essays, History

371. *Cubs by the Numbers: A Complete Team History of the Chicago Cubs by Uniform Number*, by Al Yellon, Kasey Ignarski, and Matthew Silverman. New York: Skyhorse, 2009.

This book represents yet another way to rank players: by uniform number. The authors offer their opinions on the best players to don Cubs' flannel, from jersey number 1 (Jose Cardenal, he of the oversized Afro) to 99 (Todd Hundley in 2001). It's purely a subjective system, since the authors don't go by stats alone; being a colorful character counts for a lot.

More than 1,300 players who wore the Chicago uniform through 2008 are present and accounted for here. Two of my favorite features address the most obscure player to wear each numeral and "guys you never thought of as a member of the Cubs who wore #xx," which consists mostly of late-season call-ups, rookies, or familiar names who may have played briefly with the team.

Although technically there are numbers involved, this is not a statistics-based book; it's more anecdotal and a lot of fun, primarily for fans of the individual teams. This is one of a series of similar titles by Skyhorse for other teams, including the Mets, Yankees, and Red Sox).

Other categories: History, Pop Culture, Trivia

372. *Cult Baseball Players: The Greats, The Flakes, The Weird, and The Wonderful*, edited by Danny Peary. New York: Simon and Schuster, 1990.

Yeah, yeah, everybody loves Mantle and Mays and Koufax; everybody loves a winner. But you don't need to be a football hero to get along with the beautiful girls. Wait, sorry—wrong metaphor.

Peary has collected the thoughts of almost sixty writers on the players included here, but for every Duke Snider, there's a Moe Berg; for every Fergie Jenkins, there's a Zeke Bonura.

The only one who's conspicuous in his absence seems to be Charlie Brown's idol, Joe Shlabotnick, who batted .143 in the Green Grass League.

Other categories: Auto/Bio/Mem, History, Trivia

373. *The Cultural Encyclopedia of Baseball*, by Jonathan Fraser Light. Jefferson NC: McFarland, 1997.

This massive undertaking of almost nine hundred pages is truly an "everything you always wanted to know" type of book. In fact, you will find things here that you probably had never even associated with baseball, but now that it's there it may very well lead to further investigation.

There are many items that can be found in other books and in greater depth, certainly when it comes to players, managers, executives, and teams, but on the other hand I can't remember anywhere that addresses asterisks, defamation, glove oil, glasses, or attorneys — Light's day job is that of an employment attorney — just to name a small fraction of the interesting tidbits you will find within. He even manages to find an entry for "Z": the last stanza of Ogden Nash's baseball poem, "Line-Up for Yesterday." It's almost like the food replicator in *Star Trek*: if you can think of it, chances are you'll find something written about it in Light's *Cultural Encyclopedia*. The reader can flip to about any page at random and find an interesting or unexpected item, which might even be the best way to approach this coffee-table edition.

Don't be daunted by the cover price, which, at seventy-five dollars, is expensive even for a McFarland title; you can pick up a used copy for about a third of that online.

Other categories: Anthology, Coffee Table/Gift, History, Reference

374. *Fantasyland: A Season on Baseball's Lunatic Fringe*, by Sam Walker. New York: Viking, 2006.

Fantasy baseball has always been around, in one form or another, whether it's a tabletop game, a dice-and-card setup, or merely flipping baseball cards in ersatz competitions.

I wonder if the group of writers and journalists that assembled at New York's La Rotisserie Française restaurant in 1980 could have envisioned a time when their private little creation would explode into a multi*billion*-dollar industry. These days, there are more magazines targeted at fantasy baseball aficionados than the general fan population.

Walker, a writer for the *Wall Street Journal*, took up the challenge to join one of the most serious of these competitions, the Tout Wars, a private league designed for the fantasy baseball elite. His book reads like an espionage thriller. He assembles his team of experts, including a statistician and a baseball savant, and uses his own sources to suss out inside information and find out which players are hot, who is injured, and who might be on his way to the Minors. The most innocuous rumor can send these competitors into paroxysms of joy or despair, especially as the season winds down. It seems a lot more people are rooting for individuals rather than the whole team, and even then just for certain statistics.

As much as I cringe over that old Jacques Barzun quote about knowing baseball, a paraphrase is appropriate here: those who want to know the hearts and minds of fantasy baseball nuts had better read *Fantasyland.*

Other categories: Fandom, History

375. *From Abba Dabba to Zorro: The World of Baseball Nicknames,* by Don Zminda. Morton Grove IL: STATS, 1999.

From the sublime, like the Yankee Clipper, The Iron Horse, and Dizzy, to the ridiculous Death to Flying Things, this book covers the sadly bygone era of the colorful appellation.

This slim, no-frills paperback includes great nicknames because somebody has to bestow the monikers, right? Some are personal, coming early in life from family members (Carlton "Pudge" Fisk, Dave "Boo" Ferris) as well as from teammates. According to legend, Babe Ruth called younger guys Kid and older guys Pops because he could never remember their real names.

Back in the day, nicknames were often based on characteristics — a player's ethnicity or religion or handicap — that we might now consider politically incorrect. Yet many of these athletes considered these as badges of honor and good-natured acceptance. Italian players, for example, were often called Dago, including Joe DiMaggio, who used it self-referentially. Mike Epstein, a slugger in the 1970s, was known as SuperJew, while Hank Greenberg and, most recently, Ryan Braun, were both called the Hebrew Hammer.

Nicknames were also conferred according to geography (the Duke of Flatbush, the Fordham Flash), animals (Harvey "the Kitten" Haddix), personality (Johnny "Grandma" Murphy), even cartoon characters (Henry "Bam Bam" Muelens). Then there are the opposites: quiet guys are called Chatty, bald players called Curly, and heavy players were often Slim. Umpires receive nicknames, too, but many were probably too profane to make it into the book.

As is usually the case in books of lists, there are plenty of theme teams, such as the All-Food Team, led by Pie Traynor, Mark "Big Mac" McGwire, and others. One notable sports personality who is conspicuous in his absence: ESPN host Chris "I Have a Nickname for Everybody" Berman.

Other categories: History, Reference, Trivia

376. *The Great God Baseball: Religion in Modern Baseball Fiction,* by Allen E. Hye. Macon GA: Mercer University Press, 2004.

Social commentators decry that we put our sports heroes on too high a pedestal, that we make them out to be almost godlike, and then when they fail we suffer a crisis of faith.

Hye, a professor of German and Danish (of all things), analyzes the religious components of nine novels. Each takes up its own "inning," and most will be familiar to many readers.

Frankly, more than a couple of these titles might stretch the overarching theme. Although there are no doubt spiritual motifs in *Shoeless Joe,* can they be defined as *religious?* But, hey, I'm for anything that makes the reader think, and *The Great God Baseball* will certainly do that.

As if to show that academics needn't be too stuffy, Hye offers a series of "Extra Innings," that features "Baseball in the Bible," as well as a quiz on "Religion as Baseball" and an All-Religious Name Baseball Club, which includes the likes of Preacher Roe, Bubba Church, Eddie Priest, and, of course, Jesus Alou.

Other categories: Academic, Essays, Fiction

377. *Guys, Dolls, and Curveballs: Damon Runyon on Baseball,* edited by Jim Reisler. New York: Carroll and Graf, 2005.

One does not normally associate Citizen Runyon with baseball. His racket was more attuned to the squared circle of the sweet science whence he derived material for the colorful characters that populated his fiction, such as Nathan Detroit and "Nicely Nicely" Johnson of *Guys and Dolls* fame.

However, as a young scribe gainfully employed under the protectorate of the Hearst syndicate, young Master R. turned many a purple phrase as he offered his fanciful and felicitous reportage on some of the biggest icons of the game. Among them were Big Bam and the Georgia Peach, and others who were just plain oddballs, like Charles "Victory" Faust, who sought an audition with Mugsy McGraw's Jints on the say-so of a boardwalk swami who predicted a Christy Mathewson–like future for him. McGraw was so taken with the brashness of the odd little fellow that he signed Faust as a good-luck totem.

Other meanderings by Runyon contemplated events on the field, both great and small, as well as the 1919 Black Sox scandal, which must have been a bit of an albatross around his neck since mastermind Arnold Rothstein was a boon buddy.

Let us have no disillusionary thoughts about the colorful colloquy Runyon's work engenders. It's well worth the time spent trying to decipher the writer's reportage of the sports story circa 1925.

Other categories: Anthology, Essay, Sportswriting

378. *How to Talk Baseball,* by Mike Whiteford with illustrations by Taylor Jones. New York: Dembner, 1987.

This amusing little paperback is just the thing to entice those who might otherwise have no interest in the game. There are no long-winded explanations or definitions from Whiteford, a sportswriter for the *Charleston Gazette*: just some basic terms, illustrated by Jones's caricatures.

The author picks a handful of figures who have made an eternal impression on baseball through their contributions on the field, in the front office, or behind the microphone or typewriter, the latter of which is a nice touch since their words have had a major impact in how fans perceive the game. A few might strike the less casual reader as curious: pitcher Dennis Eckersley? manager Charlie Dressen?

Similarly, the baseball terms listed are a mix of the essential and the anachronistic, which is also fine, given the game's long history. But this definitely isn't *The Dickson Baseball Dictionary*, nor need it be to be appreciated.

Other category: Reference

379. *Joy in Mudville: The Big Book of Baseball Humor*, edited by Dick Schaap and Mort Gerberg. New York: Doubleday, 1992.

With your favorite team in the cellar or player on the disabled list, you could use a good laugh, right? Have I got a book for you!

Beginning with the classic "Casey at the Bat," and a few knock-off versions, *Joy in Mudville* features such well-known humorists, sportswriters, and authors as Mitch Albom, Robert Coover, Calvin Trillin, Russell Baker, Ogden Nash, Damon Runyon, Tony Kornheiser, Garrison Keillor and James Thurber, among many others. Likewise, the dozens of cartoons come from the pencils and inkwells of some of the medium's most recognizable practitioners, including Arnold Roth, Jules Feiffer, Gary Trudeau, and Charles M. Schulz.

Within these pages you'll find Frank Sullivan's eternally relevant "The Cliché Expert Testifies on Baseball," as well as excerpts from Neil Simon's *Brighton Beach Memoirs*; Ring Lardner's "Alibi Ike" and *You Know Me Al*; and George Plimpton's *Sports Illustrated* story "The Curious Case of Sidd Finch." And if Casey Stengel's 1958 appearance before Congress wasn't written as a comedy routine, it should have been; the transcript is included.

Like an adroit pitcher-catcher battery, Schaap—the broadcast journalist and writer—handles the words while cartoonist Gerberg takes care of the illustrations, including several of his own. Together they produced a perfect game.

Other category: Anthology

380. *Little League, Big Dreams: Inside the Hope, the Hype, and the Glory of the Greatest World Series Ever Played,* by Charles Euchner. Naperville IL: Sourcebooks, 2006.

As I have said elsewhere in this book, I have a problem with the use of words like *best* and *greatest*. While they might apply to a specific moment or person, that moment or person just might not stand the test of time.

Such is the case with *Little League, Big Dreams*. It is included in this list of must-reads as an example of how simple themes can get away from their intended purpose in the wrong hands of a writer who tries perhaps a bit too hard to make a fit.

It's great to give kids the big league experience—how exciting it must be to be interviewed on television by former Major Leaguers asking your opinion, and to have thousands of fans screaming your name. But the flip side is the unyielding pressure, exacerbated by just that constant media attention.

Euchner writes what is at once an homage to the kids and a commentary on youth sports, with grown-ups, as usual, being the ones who muck it up.

Was the 2005 Little League World Series truly the greatest ever? Was it any more exciting than previous events? If so, was that due in part to the media hype? Depends on whom you ask. For those directly involved, it probably was a fantastic experience. But those who participated prior to or after 2005 might have a different opinion.

Other category: Media

Also by the author: *The Last Nine Innings* (2002)

381. *The Meaning of Nolan Ryan,* by Nick Trujillo. College Station: Texas A&M University Press, 1994.

Trujillo, an associate professor of communications studies at California State University, Sacramento, portrays Ryan as a paragon of American values, almost a hero from the movie westerns, forthright and unstinting in his devotion to hard work and fair play. There's even a photo of him in a cowboy motif.

He divulges an amazing amount of meaning in his book about the then future Hall of Famer. Published the year after Ryan retired, the book searches for what his long, steady, record-breaking career meant to a variety of segments within the larger baseball society. For Rangers fans, it was pride in the fact that the Alvin, Texas–born pitcher had come home. For older folks, he was proof that age is no impediment to success. The list goes on.

While a chapter focuses on what he meant to the team with whom he closed out his illustrious career, these sentiments could be applied to any he was a member of post-Mets, since he never had a chance to blossom with them. Ryan meant a lot to his opponents too; every time he took the mound, it meant increased revenue at the ballpark.

Ryan's career also posited a different way of evaluating performance. Although he won 324 games, he also *lost* 292 and established the Major League mark for most lifetime walks. But he played on some poor teams, like Walter Johnson, who excelled on the mostly underperforming Washington Senators.

Other categories: Analysis, Auto/Bio/Mem, History

382. *The New Baseball Reader,* edited by Charles Einstein. New York: Viking, 1991.

Here's a novel idea: an anthology of anthologies. In this case, Einstein cannibalizes his own series of *Fireside Books of Baseball* for the best of the best, so to speak.

The usual suspects are once again represented here, but there are plenty of new kids on the block to keep things from getting too re-petitive. Instead of John Updike's paean "Hub Fans Bid Kid Adieu," you have his seldom seen "Tao in The Yankee Stadium Bleachers." Instead of a Roger Angell piece, you have one from Zane Grey; rather than a Roger Kahn nod to one of the boys of summer, there's a hint from Heloise on how to keep your baseball cap clean and fresh.

Categories include profiles, fiction, spot reporting, history, poetry, autobiography, and "general." Einstein presents the pieces—which date back to the late 1800s—in a very democratic, if uneven, man-ner: alphabetical according to the contributor. This actually adds to the enjoyment in that you don't get bogged down with five straight pieces of biography or statistics. He also introduces each piece with a few explanatory lines to put it in context, a helpful touch that's missing from many books of this kind.

Other categories: Anthology, Essays

383. *Play Ball!: The Story of Little League Baseball,* by Lance Van Auken and Robin Van Auken. University Park: Pennsylvania State University Press, 2001.

Little League has certainly come a long way since it was devised by Carl Stotz, a lumberyard clerk who had an epiphany while tossing the ball around with his nephews in Williamsport, Pennsylvania, in 1938. Wouldn't it be great, he thought, to have a place for kids to play together in an organized situation against other teams in nearby towns, with real fields, uniforms, and umpires?

Lance Van Auken, then the director of media relations and com-munications for Little League Baseball (he was named vice presi-dent of communications in 2008), and his wife, Robin, lovingly assembled this commemorative edition of the game's place in this nation's culture. Both Van Aukens served as little league volunteers for several years.

Rich with photos, *Play Ball!* shows us a slice of Americana that has endured and thrived, even through wars, recession, and other tough times.

I doubt Stotz could have envisioned how his idea would have

mushroomed over the next seventy years, expanding into an global phenomenon, culminating with an internationally televised Little League World Series. Who knows: maybe he might think the current situation, with prime-time coverage and little boys and girls receiving full-on rock-star treatment, has taken his original concept a bit too far.

Other categories: Coffee Table/Gift, History, Juvenile, Reference

384. *Red Sox University: Baseball's Foremost Institution of Higher Learning,* by Andy Wasif. Chicago: Triumph, 2009.

New England has several fine academic institutions: Harvard, Yale, MIT, and many others. Add to that list *Red Sox University,* where a fan can get practical examples of how baseball incorporates biology, history, architecture, political science, economics, health, and even religion and philosophy. Each course in Wasif's fun book is admittedly Red Sox–centric, but that's the way fans are anyway: the world revolves around their team, but they're willing to learn anything as long as it pertains to their interests.

The book is sprinkled with lots of sidebars and fillers because you know what people's attention span is like these—oh, look, a chicken. For example, there are several key terms, such as "Future Yankee [loo'zah] n.—any good, young player on a small-market team who is looking to make way more money than he could possibly get staying where he is" (53). It's funny because it's true.

In this day when college can set you back upwards of sixty thousand dollars a year, the $14.95 you'd spend on *Red Sox University* is certainly a bargain and the education you get from it will last a lifetime, unlike that math course you took, which you no doubt have forgotten by now.

Other categories: Analysis, Fandom, History/Team
Also by the author: *Red Sox Fans Are from Mars, Yankees Fans Are from Uranus: Why Red Sox Fans are Smarter, Funnier, and Better Looking (In Language Even Yankee Fans Can Understand)* (2010)

385. *Sometimes a Fantasy: Midlife Misadventures with Baseball Heroes,* by Jeff Guinn. Fort Worth: Summit, 1994.

Playing fantasy baseball just isn't challenging enough for some people. They actually want to play the game, advanced age, weight, or lack of any discernible skills notwithstanding.

Fantasy camps were created to fill this need. Many are offered under the auspices of Major Leagues teams, where middle-aged fans with a chunk of disposable income can spend a week schmoozing with some of their favorite players. I myself took advantage of such an opportunity with the Yankees several years ago and found it a life-changing experience. My knees still haven't recovered from that week of catching. This book should be required reading for anyone thinking about going, just as a cautionary tale.

Guinn, a journalist in Texas, participated in a Cubs-themed camp and chronicled the event in painstaking detail. It's a hoot to read descriptions his fellow campers; the aches and pains of playing again after so many years away from the diamond; and interacting with former Cubs like Ernie Banks, Ferguson Jenkins, Joe Pepitone, and Jimmy Piersall, among others. It's cool to find other nuts like you out there, but discovering that the ballplayers are regular guys, with their good qualities and bad, just might make you grow up, even if you want to maintain that little piece of your innocent childhood.

Other categories: Auto/Bio/Mem, Fandom, History

386. *The Summer Game,* by Roger Angell, Lincoln: University of Nebraska Press, 2004.

387. *Why Time Begins on Opening Day,* by Thomas Boswell. Garden City NY: Doubleday, 1984.

As the Most Interesting Man in the World might say, I don't often read the *New Yorker,* but when I do, it's because it contains another Roger Angell essay.

Angell has been covering the game for that publication since 1962, and in the introduction to this collection of columns he thanks his lucky stars that he was free from the tyranny of daily deadlines. It gave him the chance to provide his long, thoughtful word paintings about more than just the score or another ballplayer profile.

The Summer Game was on the *New York Times* best-seller list for five weeks in 1972. It includes samples from his first decade at the *New Yorker,* but any one of his other collections — *Five Seasons, Late Innings, Season Ticket,* or *Once More around the Park* — would have worked just as well for inclusion in *501.* In 2001 Angell also collaborated with pitcher David Cone, then a member of the Yankees, on *A Pitcher's Story,* another thoughtful look at the craft with one of the game's craftier practitioners.

Boswell, a *Washington Post* sports columnist since 1984, has likewise published several collections of his work. *Why Time Begins on Opening Day,* although published two years after *Why Life Imitates the World Series,* is more representative and includes pieces from other sources, including *Inside Sports,* a popular magazine of the eighties and nineties, and another piece that was published in *Playboy* (with no pictures, of course).

While Angell is more verbose by dint of his freedom of space, Boswell comes across as concise, tight with a phrase but nevertheless managing to charm the reader by making some of the most mundane topics interesting.

Other categories: Anthology, Essays, Sportswriting

388. *The Summer That Saved Baseball: A 38-Day Journey to Thirty Major League Ballparks,* by Brad Null and Dave Kaval. Nashville TN: Cumberland House, 2001.

Kudos to these two young men who decided to share their last free summer together following college graduation by embarking on a cross-country trip to see each team play on its home turf. They fulfilled a dream shared by many baseball fans, but who lack the organization skills or stick-to-itiveness to pull it off.

The Summer That Saved Baseball covers a lot of territory — more than sixteen thousand miles, actually — as the authors describe their 1998 experience in journal-like fashion. They also kept a tally of all their expenses along the way. It's amazing how many teams were so accommodating in providing free tickets (twenty-four out of thirty), parking, concessions, and souvenirs, not to mention all the assistance Null and Kaval received along the way in the way of free room and board from friends and family. I'll have to try this ploy sometime.

They evaluate the quality of each locale, offering bits of history and trivia. There is relatively little about the actual games they saw, which is fine. The real stories are the people they met along the way and the theme of bonding over baseball.

Other categories: Analysis, Fandom, History, Travel

389. *Willie's Time: A Memoir,* by Charles Einstein. New York: Lippincott, 1979.

You could say the title of Einstein's book has two meanings. On the one hand, we're talking about the career of the Say Hey Kid. On the other hand, we're talking about America from 1951–73. The dust jacket depicts the ballplayer in the center of a collage that features photos of John F. Kennedy, Dwight D. Eisenhower, Nikita Kruschev, Martin Luther King Jr., Frank Sinatra, and other representatives of those years. It's as if everything revolves around the Hall of Famer.

Einstein, who served as the ghostwriter for Mays's 1955 autobiography, *Born to Play* (one wag reviewer posited that Willie had never actually read the thing), employs the unusual device of dividing the chapters by presidents, as if to mark the social progress of the country as Mays begins as a rookie during the Truman administration and completes his journey during the Nixon years.

There's not so much on-the-field information here, but that's okay; there are plenty of other books that extol Mays's athletic prowess. This is more about the *author's* memories, and as such is subject to interpretation and questions by the reader. Einstein shows a different side of Mays: less formal, more involved in life outside the ballpark, but never simple. He could be a difficult person to read. Mays once told a reporter he would like to be a manager someday, and then shortly thereafter told someone else he *wouldn't* want such a responsibility. Willie was indeed a complex individual.

Einstein provides a contemplative look at how much the country changed from the innocence of the postwar years through the Vietnam era.

Other category: History

ACADEMIC

390. *Extra Innings: Writing on Baseball,* by Richard Peterson. Champaign: University of Illinois Press, 2001.

Peterson, a professor of English, parses literary writing — as opposed to newspaper and magazine reporting in this entertaining and educational historiography.

In the nonfiction portion of the book, he refers to the early works by Albert Spalding and Alfred Spink, pointing out how much topics and styles had changed by the era of Harold Seymour, David Q. Voigt, and Benjamin Rader, who wrote for a more scholarly audience. Fiction gets a separate treatment, as Peterson distinguishes between the requirements needed for novels versus short stories; later works in both styles featured a more gritty realism than had been the custom in the Jack Armstrong–type stories of the early twentieth century.

Finally, Peterson offers some tongue-in-cheek advice on "How to Write a True Baseball Story": stay away from the Black Sox (done to death); toss in some real-life players; make the protagonist a pitcher, since he's already the center of attention; and use a colorful nickname.

Extra Innings is a great starting point for those interested as much in the process as the product.

Other categories: Analysis, Fiction, History, Pop Culture
Also by the author: *Growing Up With Clemente* (2009); *The Pirates Reader* (2007); *The St. Louis Baseball Reader* (2006)

391. *Imagining Baseball: America's Pastime and Popular Culture,* by David McGimpsey. Bloomington: Indiana University Press, 2000.

There are plenty of books that deconstruct the popular works on baseball literature. McGimpsey does all that and more in this scholarly yet accessible collection of essays based on specific themes: baseball and the generations; baseball and exclusion; and baseball and community.

McGimpsey offers some examples to prove his various points, including novels and television episodes that are certainly not on the beaten path, for example *The Fan, All G.O.D.'s Children,* and *Dr. Quinn, Medicine Woman.* Of course, there's plenty of room for the old favorites; one unique and welcome component is his assessments is the necessary differences between the written and film version of some of the classics, including *Bang the Drum Slowly* and *The Natural.*

It is worth pointing that McGimpsey, who writes poetry, fiction, and criticism on pop culture, is a professor at Concordia University in Montreal. Does this make any difference in his credibility? On the one hand, he is an outsider, going so far as to refer to the game as "America's pastime." On the other hand, that distance may give him an objectivity that often comes with a fresh viewpoint.

Other categories: Analysis, Fiction

Also by the author: *Dingers: Contemporary Baseball Writing* (2007)

392. *The Physics of Baseball,* second edition, by Robert K. Adair. New York: Harper Perennial, 1994.

All right, so maybe this falls into the scientific realm, in which I am merely a passerby, but if someone could ever rework this into a "Physics of Baseball for Dummies," I'd be all over it.

Adair, who served physicist to the National League from 1987–89 (who knew such a position even existed?) endeavors to explain what happens when the ball leaves a pitcher's hand, or when the bat meets the ol' horsehide, or how outfielders judge the path of fly balls.

Unfortunately for me, Adair—Sterling Professor of Physics at Yale University—uses phrases like "Reynolds numbers" and "Magnus force" and a dizzying array of charts and formulas in his book. A. Bartlett Giamatti, in a blurb of Adair's work, called it "A brilliant book . . . written in a clear, elegant style." I can go for the "elegant" part, but clear?

If you have the patience and curiosity, as I wish I did, I'm sure you'll find *The Physics of Baseball* quite illuminating. I can almost see Mr. Spock reading it and murmuring, "Fascinating." Put *that* as a blurb, Dr. Adair!

Other categories: Analysis, History

393. *The Tao of Baseball: Entertaining and Thought-Provoking Commentaries on the National Pastime,* by Gō. New York: Simon and Schuster, 1991.

There aren't many books that might change the way you think about the game, but this is certainly one of them.

Gō—the nom de plume for Canadian author Gordon Bell—makes his case by comparing just about every conceivable action on the field in terms of yang and yin.

In two dimensions, the ball itself is the perfect symbol to represent the traditional black-and-white icon. Yang, the white part, represents the positive force: light, birth, youth, and winning. Yin, the black portion, is negative, representing darkness, death, and loss. Like Newton's third law of motion, each action has an equal and opposite reaction.

The author—who is described on the book cover as an "artist, writer, philosopher, and baseball fan"—breaks the Tao into its eight trigrams, or fundamental components. Each one has its unique properties, such as father, mother, first son, first daughter, and so on, which he uses to further describe each defensive position and spot in the batting order. The trigrams are also used to compare balls, strikes, and outs from the offensive and defensive points of view. Bottom line: one man's ceiling is another man's floor.

You don't have to know Buddhism or Zen concepts to appreciate Gō's comparisons, but you do have an open mind. It would be interesting if some brave ballclub would adopt *The Tao of Baseball* as its playbook, a sort of philosophical answer to *Moneyball*. I've heard of monks playing soccer, but can't you just picture them on the diamond?

394. *Watching Baseball, Seeing Philosophy: The Great Thinkers at Play on the Diamond*, by Raymond Angelo Belliotti. Jefferson NC: McFarland, 2008.

Look hard enough and you can find a way to link any seemingly disparate items. That's the case with this volume, which compares several well-known ballplayers and managers with their philosopher counterparts.

Belliotti, a distinguished teaching professor of philosophy at SUNY Fredonia, sees similar qualities between these two groups: Ted Williams is paired with Albert Camus; Satchel Paige with Marcus Aurelius; Joe DiMaggio with Friedrich Nietzsche; Joe Torre with Aristotle; Jackie Robinson with Antonio Gramsci; Mickey Mantle with Saint Thomas Aquinas; John Franco with William James; and Billy Martin with Niccolo Machiavelli (now *that* makes sense). To be honest, there are a few guys on the athlete side of the equation I wouldn't have thought to describe as great thinkers; has Jose Canseco even heard of Immanuel Kant? Is Belliotti stretching things a bit? Perhaps, but it's certainly fun to read his defense of his selections.

The comedian Steve Martin had this joke about studying math and philosophy: the math you'll forget in a year, but just one philosophy course can screw you up for the rest of your life. Here's hoping it doesn't have that effect on your baseball enjoyment.

Other category: Anthology

395. *The Whole Baseball Catalog: The Ultimate Guide to the Baseball Marketplace*, edited by John Thorn and John Carroll. New York: Simon and Schuster, 1990.

396. *The New Baseball Catalog*, by Dan Schlossberg. New York: Jonathan David, 1998.

Similar in format and philosophy to the popular hippie publication *The Last Whole Earth Catalog*, this entertaining offering from Thorn and Carroll offers a variety of information to a wide cross section of fans. The editors include sections on training equipment, history, memorabilia, broadcast media, books, film and video, and the early versions of fantasy baseball. Check out the photo on page 283 to see what passed for state of the art in laptop computers in 1990.

Schlossberg offers a similar almanac-type book devoted to people (both on the field and behind the scenes), places, and things under the umbrella of the national pastime.

The presentation is somewhat haphazard. Supplementing the general entries are lots of factoids and fillers to please all manner of readers. Such a format allows them to pick and choose how deeply they wish to dive into the information pool.

The chapter on "The Language of Baseball" is a lot of fun, with its backstories on team and player nicknames. Other chapters focus on superstitions and traditions, fans, other leagues in other lands, equipment, ballparks, and trades, among other things.

In both cases, a fair amount of the listings are out of date, but overall even that information would be useful for researchers who want to know what the zeitgeist was like not all that long ago.

Other categories: History, Reference

397. *Women Characters in Baseball Literature: A Critical Study*, by Kathleen Sullivan. Jefferson NC: McFarland, 2005.

Those who read baseball fiction or watch feature films know that the female characters basically fall into fairly strict categories: the seductress, such as Memo Paris and Harriet Bird in *The Natural* and

Lola in *Damn Yankees* and *The Year the Yankees Lost the Pennant*; the evil-doer, a la Rachel Phelps in the film *Major League*; the nurturer, like Ethel in The *Monty Stratton Story* or Aimee in *The Winning Team*; or the disbeliever, usually a mother who doesn't want her son to waste his time but eventually comes around—think Ma Gehrig in *The Pride of the Yankees* or Ma Stratton in *The Stratton Story*).

Sullivan, a lecturer at the University of Texas at Arlington, further classifies them in terms of the goddesses of mythologies, primarily those who nurture others and those who exert their own personalities and desires. Her novels of choices include the aforementioned *Natural* as well as the *Southpaw* series by Mark Harris, but they extend beyond the classic texts, introducing her readers to an exciting variety of heretofore underrated works, including *She's on First* by Barbara Gregorich; *Rachel, The Rabbi's Wife*, by Sylvia Tennenbaum; *The Sweetheart Season*, by Karen Joy Fowler; and *Things Invisible to See*, by Nancy Willard.

The issue I have with such books, however, is that sometimes the analysis runs too deep. Do the writers really sit and figure out that scenario X represents concept A? If they do, fine. After all, literary scholars and teachers need something to talk and write about. But sometimes a cigar is just a cigar.

Other categories: Analysis, Women

ART AND PHOTOGRAPHY

398. *The Art of Baseball,* by Shelly Mehlman Dinhofer. New York: Harmony, 1990.

Dinhofer, director and curator of the Museum of the Borough of Brooklyn, assembled more than 125 iconic pieces representing some of the best-known figures in the genre of baseball art, both as subjects and artists.

Among the many painters and illustrators you'll find in this slim coffee-table book are Norman Rockwell, Joseph Christian Leyendecker, Andy Jurinko, Lance Richbourg, Elaine de Kooning,

Roy Lichtenstein, and Robert Riggs, who contributes a dramatic four-page pullout of Jackie Robinson doing what he does best: creating havoc for the opposition.

Dinhofer describes the various styles and backstories for many of the items in her book. While examples of sculpture and folk art are included, they definitely take a back seat to paintings and other paper-based pieces.

The chapters follow the progress of both baseball and schools of art. Illustrations were used by the print press of the mid- to late nineteenth century when photography wasn't common or practical. In the days of Babe Ruth, artists like Leyendecker provided heroic portraits for magazine covers. The postwar era gave artists the means to experiment with new media and styles. But the chapter I found most unusual was the one depicting the role of government, which sponsored various programs during the Great Depression that gave artists employment. This had the consequent benefit of providing wonderful images for generations to come.

Other category: History

399. *Ballet in the Dirt: The Golden Age of Baseball,* by Neil Leifer. Los Angeles: Taschen 2007

Leifer began taking pictures professionally for the Brooklyn Dodgers at the age of seventeen. Throughout his five-decade career — he caught the shutterbug while in high school — he has taken some of the most iconic photos in sports history, not the least of which was the famous shot of Juan Marichal hitting catcher John Roseboro over the head with his bat in a 1965 game between the Los Angeles Dodgers and San Francisco Giants.

Leifer's best baseball work, which appeared mostly in *Sports Illustrated,* was collected and published by Taschen, which specializes in gorgeous, if pricey, art volumes. The original cover price was $400, but you could also buy limited editions for $700 and $1,000.

The sections are divided into general categories, such as "Heroes", "Rivalry", and "World Series," and the black-and-white and color photographs capture some of the great players of the 1950s through the 1970s, including Roberto Clemente, Mickey Mantle, Willie Mays, Hank Aaron, Stan Musial, and Sandy Koufax in a combination of action, candid, and posed situations. It's amusing to see the captions translated into German and French; you wouldn't think there would be much interest in baseball in those European nations.

Other categories: Coffee Table/Gift, History

400. *Baseball,* by David Levinthal. New York: Empire Editions, 2006.

This collection of photographs, taken by the artist on a large-format Polaroid camera, is eerily reminiscent of *The Twilight Zone.* The subjects—miniature toys that represent some of the greats of the game—are silent, out of focus, in shadows, or shot at odd angles. You almost expect them to come to life after the lights have been turned off and everyone's gone home.

Among the scores of legends Levinthal shot are Joe DiMaggio, whose classic figure adorns the cover of this handsome coffee-table edition, Babe Ruth, Tom Seaver, Joe Morgan, Sandy Koufax, and Reggie Jackson. See Carlton Fisk frozen in midwave, Yogi Berra jumping into the arms of Don Larsen at the end of the pitcher's perfect game in the 1956 World Series, and Jackie Robinson stealing home in another Fall Classic.

Levinthal has said he tried to evoke a Normam Rockwell–Edward Hopper look in his work. He purchased the models from hobbyist shops and painstakingly posed them to obtain the desired effect and emotion through his camera, which was about the size of a refrigerator. And rest assured, there is a lot of emotion here, even if the objects are inanimate.

Other categories: Classic, Coffee Table/Gift

401. *Baseball*, photographs by Walter Iooss Jr. and text by Roger Angell. New York: Harry N. Abrams, 1984.

Another in a short list of coffee-table books that feature a single photographer, *Baseball* highlights the work of Iooss, a longtime staffer for *Sports Illustrated*. He may not be a pioneer on the level of a George Brace or a Charles M. Conlon, but his work is nevertheless evocative and dazzling, whether it's an extreme close up of a posed subject, a batter laying down a bunt, or a manager deep in thought (or arguing with an umpire).

At the outset, the book juxtaposes a double-page spread of a little leaguer, just at the beginning of what will hopefully be a lifelong love affair with the game, with members of the famed Three-Quarter Century Club, a group of senior softball players, clad in white and still acting like little boys. From there we attend spring training. There's a balance of lightheartedness and tension as players vie for a spot on the roster. Then we wrap up with the Fall Classic, with teams and fans jubilant in victory. In between are more than one hundred classic Iooss shots, taken mostly during the sixties and seventies.

That Angell contributes the text is another indication that this publication is something special. He incorporates his praise for Iooss into a broader personal essay on his association with the game, in which he describes iconic photography as necessary in providing lasting evidence of the game's exceptional moments.

Other category: History

402. *Baseball: A Celebration!*, by James Buckley Jr. and Jim Gigliotti. New York: Dorling Kindersley, 2001

Another in a line of books produced to mark—and perhaps take advantage of—the new millennium, *Baseball* is a history told through hundreds of snapshots. Most are in black and white, but, as if to note the progress in photographic technology, color begins to slowly make its way into the baseball world.

While the emphasis is obviously on the illustrations, Gigliotti's essay on "Baseball Photography" explains the evolution of the use of the camera to capture the action of the game on the field and, in some cases, of private life as well, as players became more accessible in the era before free agency.

It's not just familiar shots of Lou Gehrig making his famous "Luckiest Man" speech, or Babe Ruth's last appearance at Yankee Stadium, or Carlton Fisk directing his 1975 World Series home run. It's also the misty-eyed little leaguer gazing ruefully into the distance after a loss, or the group of African American fans waiting outside Ebbets Field in the late 1940s for a glimpse of Jackie Robinson. *Those* are the moments we remember above all because they have personal meaning for us.

In his introduction, Buckley writes about his own family's long-standing love of the game and that the hundreds of photographs — offered in chronological sequence — do not just mark the passing of time, "but the passing of the story of baseball from one generation to the next" (8).

Other categories: Coffee Table/Gift, History

403. *Baseball: A Treasury of Art and Literature*, edited by Michael Ruscoe. New York: Macmillan, 1993.

The large format goes a long way in appropriately presenting impressive illustrations and artwork, including full-size reproductions of magazine covers such as the *Saturday Evening Post*.

As in several baseball books, the editor uses the popular technique of separating similar components into innings based on a common topic; this volume begins with "The Roots of the Game" and concludes with "You Can Look it Up." The chapters in between offer excerpts from books, as well as poems, songs, and speeches.

The dozens of photographs, toys, advertisements, and paintings and illustrations — beginning with the 1844 painting *Boy with Ball and Bat* — that separate the texts come from some of the most famous artists in the genre: Norman Rockwell, Edward Laning, Andy

Jurinko, Michael Heslop, Mike Schacht, and several others. Photos of the plaques for all the Hall of Famers through 1992 make a fitting coda to the book.

Many of these items can be found in other anthologies and collections, but the presentation here is truly worth the time spent.

Other categories: Anthology, History

404. *Baseball: The National Pastime in Art and Literature,* edited by David Colbert. New York: Time Life, 2001.

This is quite the double play combination. The illustrations and texts are symbiotic, each serving as a commentary on the other.

Some of baseball's most beloved stories and poems are to be found in this oversized collection, including excerpts from Doris Kearns Goodwin, Stephen King, Pete Hamill, Roger Angell, Mark Harris, Eliot Asinof, W. P. Kinsella, and dozens more from the masters of fiction and nonfiction.

The art—in such forms as the cartoons of Arnold Roth, *Saturday Evening Post* covers by Norman Rockwell and J. F. Kernan, and a pastoral scene by Currier and Ives, among many other familiar images—depicts the strength of athletes and the beauty of all participants in the game, including the fans.

The editor purports to follow a relatively chronological pattern, beginning with the first stumbling steps of childhood participation and ending—well, it doesn't really end, does it? (Grantland Rice's eulogistic poem to Babe Ruth notwithstanding.)

Other categories: Anthology, Coffee Table/Gift

405. *Baseball in America.* New York: Collins, 1991.

In the 1990s Collins produced a popular series of large photography books on a single theme, such as *A Day in the Life of America* or *A Day in the Life of Italy,* among many others. This is the baseball version, with fifty leading photographers given free rein to express their thoughts about the national pastime through pictures.

It begins in childhood, either sitting on a parent's knee at the ballpark or taking that first uncertain swing at an oversized plastic ball with an oversized plastic bat. All too soon, it's time to put aside childish things. The stakes get higher and the action more intense, as the athletes move on to high school and college, followed by the Minor Leagues, and then, finally and with great luck and determination, the Major Leagues. There are also salutes to the ballparks and the family, friends, and fans who cheer them on.

The photography matches the increasing drama with intense action shots and evocative angles. Several pictures require two pages to adequately express the emotion. Then — just like the other books in the series do — things slow down as the day draws to a close. The players retire and return home; fans find other amusements, such as town softball; and the sun sets over America.

Each picture is identified by location, which spans the country from the congested streets of New York City, where grown men still play stickball, to the deserts of Arizona where Native American children play in the shadows of Monument Valley. Credit is also given to each photographer. Captions accompany many of the photos to set up the circumstances of the shot, but most require no explanation.

Other category: Fandom

406. *Baseball's Golden Age: The Photographs of Charles M. Conlon*, by Neal McCabe and Constance McCabe. New York: Harry N. Abrams, 1993.

A master behind the lens in the early days of sports photography, Conlon's work artistically presented the rough-and-tumble life of the pro player in the first quarter of the twentieth century. The photos in this coffee-table edition were culled from some eight thousand negatives and primarily feature the biggest names in the game at the time, including several shots of Babe Ruth, Lou Gehrig, Cy Young, and Ty Cobb.

The majority of the photos are headshots depicting serious fellows; you might expect them to be more joyful, given their profession.

Others are action shots, remarkable in that era when photographers were actually allowed to work on the field during games.

The editors made some stunning choices. Some of my favorites are shots of the same player taken years apart in a virtually identical pose, as if to mark the passage of time. Even as young men, they seem old, which is part of the beauty as well as the melancholy.

One of the book's highlights is a four-page gatefold featuring Conlon's iconic extreme close-ups — a style rarely used at the time — of some of the 1927 Yankees. Most of the nearly two hundred photos in this edition come with comments by the artist about his subject — or comments from the subject about what he was thinking at the time the picture was taken.

Other category: History

407. *The Boys of Spring: Timeless Portraits from the Grapefruit League, 1947–2005,* by Ozzie Sweet. Wilmington DE: Sports Media, 2005.

408. *Mickey Mantle: The Yankee Years: The Classic Photography of Ozzie Sweet,* by Ozzie Sweet. Richmond VA: Tuff Stuff, 1998.

In these two coffee-table books Sweet, whose work was a staple of SPORT magazine for many years, offers a couple of theme-based collections.

He seems to enjoy photographing his subjects from below, as if to make them seem larger than life and to put them on a pedestal. These shots incorporate a solid background of slightly oversaturated blues, oranges, and lilacs.

The *Mantle* book follows the Commerce Comet from his debut in 1951 through his retirement in 1968 and includes his statistics for each season. Most of the shots in both books are posed, as if for publicity stills, including a series Sweet shot for *Boys Life* magazine in the 1960s, with Mantle and his son, Mickey Jr. While Sweet's technique is evocative of the era, his habit of posing everything just so detracts slightly: we want more spontaneity in our baseball.

The majority of what we see in *Mantle* depicts him as a man apart, although there are a few with teammates like Roger Maris, Whitey Ford, and Billy Martin. Particularly appealing is a nice black-and-white set taken during a laid-back spring training fishing trip.

Several of these shots also wind up in *The Boys of Spring*, which also features Sweet's signature color stylings. The players interact with fans during a period in the season when access was relatively unfettered. Then there are those of the athletes at rest and play, fishing, hanging around the hotel pool — in short, acting like the young men they are.

The chapters, like the preseason itself, are pretty loose. The photos are arbitrarily collected for batters, pitchers, managers (with a special nod to Ted Williams, who led the Washington Senators in their final year in the nation's capital), and training rituals.

Larry Canale, editor in chief of *Antiques Roadshow Insider*, contributed the text for both books.

Other categories: Auto/Bio/Mem, History

409. *Classic Baseball Photographs, 1869–1947*, by Donald Honig. New York: Viking Studio, 1994.

Honig photoanalyzes scores of classic and generally heretofore unseen sepia-toned images from baseball's past in this large-format edition.

The snapshots are divided into three distinct, albeit somewhat arbitrary, time frames, beginning with the first twenty years of the twentieth century. Despite the title's claim, the only shot from the 1800s is a group photo of the 1869 Cincinnati Reds.

Most of the earlier pictures are either formally posed or intended to depict action. A two-page spread of the 1907 New York Yankees in civilian dress during spring training looks more like a bunch of gangsters than ballplayers, although the two don't have to be mutually exclusive.

Few of the early players actually look like *young* men. A classic shot of a sweater-clad Honus Wagner crouching over a bunch of bats, lost in thought, makes him look well passed middle age, while Christy Mathewson warming up radiates a sense of youthful strength and grace.

Most of the shots highlight the stars of their respective eras, including Ruth, Gehrig, Cobb, Feller, and the rest of the usual suspects. All exude an elegance and simplicity—obviously the technology was not yet available for special effects like time-lapse and multiple exposures.

The photos were taken by the pioneering sports lensmen of the eras, but many other contributors are lost to time, destined to be forever anonymous.

Other categories: Coffee Table/Gift, History

410. *Diamonds Are Forever: Artists and Writers on Baseball,* edited by Peter H. Gordon. San Francisco: Chronicle, 1987.

Published as a companion book to a popular traveling exhibit, *Diamonds* offers images that will be familiar to lovers of both art and baseball.

The program, produced by the New York State Museum under the auspices of the Smithsonian Institution Traveling Exhibition Service, included paintings, drawings, photographs, sculpture, and other items chronicling myriad aspects of the national pastime.

The book is organized like a lineup, leading off with "The Place," the ballparks that host the games. Up next is a section on "The Equipment," with interpretations of balls and bats. In the three slot is "The Players," with portraits of actual and fictional ballplayers.

Batting cleanup is "The Action," in which artists render the beauty, speed, and grace of the sport. And "Something Else," which serves as a catchall category, rounds out this abbreviated team.

Although *Diamonds* features a few pieces of sportswriting—mostly in the form of poetry—it's the illustrations that are the selling point. Many of the items included are just part of the artists' catalogues but will serve as a good launching point for future investigation of their work.

· Other categories: Coffee Table/Gift, History

411. *Heart of the Game: An Illustrated Celebration of the American League, 1946–1960,* by Andy Jurinko. Wilmington DE: Sports Media, 2004.

Jurinko, who died in 2011, considered the era of his youth and early adulthood before the dilution of expansion to be his golden age. In tribute to those players, he published this stylish history of the American League for the fifteen years following World War II.

The impetus for the book, Jurinko explains in a note preceding Robert Creamer's introduction, was a gift from his wife of *The Baseball Encyclopedia.* He studied the old Macmillan classic for months, choosing the players he would eventually paint and include in *Heart of the Game.* He supplemented the 385 thumbnail headshots with 135 larger pieces to form this elite group, along with an additional 70 action shots.

One representative from each team was picked for special attention, which is provided in the form of reproductions of feature articles from *SPORT* Magazine, including Ted Williams, Minnie Minoso, Bob Feller, Al Kaline, Mickey Mantle, Vic Power, Brooks Robinson, and Harmon Killebrew. The publisher took special pains to note that, for the sake of flavor and authenticity, the original language from the text remained intact, however politically incorrect it might appear to modern readers.

The project — which took ten years to complete — was put on hold by the attacks on the World Trade Center, just a few hundred feet from Jurinko's home and studio.

Other categories: Auto/Bio/Mem, History

412. *The Immortals: An Art Collection of Baseball's Best,* by Dick Perez with text by William C. Kashatus. Exton PA: Brilliant Graphics, 2010.

If money was no object, everyone would own a copy of this massive homage to the greatest players in the game created by baseball artist nonpareil Perez.

The 550-plus-page coffee-table edition — printed on heavy, glossy paper for a finer touch — was published in three formats, ranging in price from a relatively modest $199 to $1,500 for a deluxe edition that included an original watercolor painting signed by the artist. This version actually sold out.

Perez's work is instantly recognizable to baseball art fans. With text contributed by Kashatus, the author of several books on the national pastime, Perez devotes several pages to most of those enshrined in the Hall of Fame. The players are compartmentalized by era, with numerous images per athlete.

In addition to his stand-alone artwork, Perez produced an annual series of Diamond King cards for Donruss from 1982–96, which are reprinted in *The Immortals*.

Other category: Memorabilia

413. *The New Yorker Book of Baseball Cartoons*, edited by Robert Mankoff with Michael Crawford. Princeton NJ: Bloomberg Press, 2003.

Some people read the *New Yorker* for the stimulating articles. Me, I go straight to the funny pages.

Mankoff, cartoon editor for the magazine, and Crawford, a frequent contributor, have collected years' worth of amusing and thought-provoking material, including some of their own illustrations.

The cartoons range from topical — the Yankees losing a World Series? Horrors! — to the ironic, to simple sight gags, to plays on words. Regular readers will recognize the publication's stable of contributors such as Charles Addams, Mischa Richter, Lee Lorenz, Charles Barsotti, and George Price. These names might not mean much by themselves, but just do an Internet search for samples of their work and you'll find yourself saying "Aha!"

This isn't as serious a title as most of the other books included here, but it's just plain fun. And isn't that what baseball should be about?

Other category: Anthology

414. *New York Yankees 365,* by the Associated Press. New York: Harry N. Abrams, 2009

One evening, when I was a kid no older than ten or so, my family had dinner at a delicatessen. I was restless and got up to wander around the establishment and came across a display for the New York Mets. Not realizing this was actually a large page-a-day calendar rather than a book of coupons, I began merrily tearing off sheet after sheet. Who had the discipline to stop at one?

That's pretty much the sentiment I feel when it comes to books like *New York Yankees 365,* one of several handsome page-a-days from Abrams. Each book includes a photo and appropriate caption, anecdote, or quote. The problem is, it's impossible not to look ahead. Needless to say, the Yankees edition might be of interest only to those who follow the team, although they're so steeped in history and tradition that it's difficult to imagine anyone strenuously objecting.

Other category: History/Team

415. *The Perfect Game: America Looks at Baseball,* by Elizabeth V. Warren. New York: Harry N. Abrams, 2003.

Many books of baseball art and photography focus on the great athletes. But for Warren, a former curator for the American Folk Art Museum in New York City, it's the artists who are the stars.

This colorful coffee-table edition, which served as an unofficial catalogue for a thirteen-month exhibition hosted by the museum in 2003–4, has the feel of a well-done arts-and-crafts show, and includes examples of woodworking, metallurgy, quilting, painting and drawing, needlework, as well as other styles and media.

Among the topics represented are ballclubs from various locations and generations, as well as several works depicting the Negro Leagues; bats and balls as artwork; signs; tabletop games; and other articles representing aspects of the sport.

In the book's introduction, Warren stated that her goal in offering *The Perfect Game* was to introduce baseball fans to the world of folk art and show them that "there is another way, beyond the relics and collectibles of the past, to look at the history of their beloved sport" (11).

Other categories: Coffee Table/Gift, History

416. *Sandlot Peanuts,* by Charles M. Schulz. New York: Holt, Reinhart and Winston, 1977.

The *Peanuts* gang enjoyed a typical suburban middle-class childhood circa the 1960s. And what's more suburban than sandlot baseball? Although Lucy was constantly making a fool of Charlie Brown with that darned football and there were a few nods to ice-skating and hockey, baseball was Schulz's sport of choice.

It was never overtly expressed, but most of the games came against unorganized neighborhood teams. And except for that one little gambling scandal, there were no adults around to muck up the fun. Charlie Brown managed the group as well as pitched, and his misadventures would rival those of some professional teams.

Their best player was a dog. Literally. The few wins they managed over the years came almost exclusively via forfeits. The second baseman was encumbered by a security blanket, and the catcher was a Beethoven prodigy. And, of course, Charlie Brown was routinely flipped and stripped of clothing by line drives back through the box. But you have to him credit; no matter how bad things got, he never gave up, which is a great lesson, whether or not that was Schulz's intention. In 2010, Wezen-ball.com even published an incredibly detailed three-part deconstruction, "Calculating Charlie Brown's Wins, Loses, and Other Stats," as gleaned from the strips from 1951–70."

Not all the baseball action — and there were more than six hundred daily and Sunday strips about the game — centered on the kids' play. Some featured actual players, including a remorseful nod to the San Francisco Giants' Willie McCovey in the 1962 World Series. And, as could be predicted, Charlie Brown's own hero, Joe

Shlabotnik, was the worst player in the pros, but that didn't matter to the funny round-headed kid, who is the very definition of a faithful fan.

Other category: Coffee Table/Gift

417. *Smithsonian Baseball: Inside the World's Finest Private Collections,* by Stephen Wong. New York: Smithsonian, 2005.

Some fans collect items about a specific team or player. Others will focus on one specific item, like bats or yearbooks, or perhaps a specific era. One thing they all have in common, though, is that they love to share and talk about their avocation. The more exotic the item, era, or topic, the better, and some of those lucky enough to have the necessary disposable income are featured in *Smithsonian Baseball*.

There are several handsome examples of board and action games dating back to the late 1800s. Some collect nineteenth-century equipment or lobby cards from movies. Some go after items that are personal. One gent, for example, collects bricks and pieces of concrete.

Wong, who spent more than two years researching and writing this colorful coffee-table edition, analyzes more than twenty different collections (including his own), filling the book with hundreds of photos. Each chapter bears the name of the individual collector and the items in which he or she specializes. Penny Marshall, director of *A League of Their Own*, for example, has a penchant for odd items that carry a baseball theme, such as a thermometer distributed as a promotional item by a meat market that bears an image of Lou Gehrig, and a checkers table made with baseball bat legs signed by Christy Mathewson. Many of these items have not been seen for decades.

Interspersed within the chapters are helpful hints on assembling your own collections. And since these are high-end collectibles we're talking about, Wong attempts to teach the reader how to make sure you get what you're paying for when it comes to the genuine articles.

418. *Willie Mays: Art in the Outfield,* by Mike Shannon. Tuscaloosa: University of Alabama Press, 2002.

Elite athletes are often compared with artists, and Willie Mays was a virtuoso at the plate, in the field, and on the base paths.

Shannon, editor of *Spitball* magazine and the author of several excellent books on baseball writing, combines a brief biography with forty examples of paintings, sketch art, mixed media, and photography arts depicting the Say Hey Kid.

I may not know art, but I know what I like, and my favorite piece is Robert Hurst's acrylic on canvas *Study in Black and White*, which features a colorized Mays sitting next to a black-and-white Mickey Mantle. Mays has his arm draped around his counterpart's shoulder as Mantle looks off into the distance, perhaps an indication of white America's ambivalence over civil rights. In another portrait with what could be seen as a similar theme, Mays is leaping out of the way of a brushback pitch. Another reminder of my youth comes from Mike Petronella's caricature, *Capping a Career*, reminiscent of the work of Bruce Stark for the *New York Daily News* in the 1970s.

Shannon pays proper respect to all the contributors in addition to providing details about each piece in an extensive biographical section. In 2011 The Suffolk, New York, Y-JCC self-published *32@75*, a similar, albeit much smaller, book about Sandy Koufax.

Other categories: Auto/Bio/Mem, History

419. *Yankee Colors: The Glory Years of the Mantle Era,* with photographs by Marvin E. Newman and text by Al Silverman. New York: Harry N. Abrams, 2009.

The tradition of excellent art books published by Abrams continues with this collection of photos concentrating on the New York Yankees in the World Series from 1955–64. Although there is plenty in the way of action shots, the more human aspects of the ballplayers come through with candid photos taken in the locker room, Yankee Stadium at night, and in spring training. There are also a couple of shots of Mantle as fashion plate; he and Billy Martin are so natty they could have been models for clothing advertisements of the day.

Contrary to the impression given by the title, a sizeable portion of the photos, especially from the 1950s, are in black and white. In fact, these might be even more artistic than the others, given the technical requirements to produce quality shots in the predigital age. In addition, while this is indeed the Mantle era, the wealth is spread around quite a bit, with many shots featuring his teammates and opponents.

Newman, a contributing photographer for *Sports Illustrated* during the period, certainly moves around a lot: he shoots from vantage points on the field, to the wells set aside for lensmen, to the deepest parts of the stadium as he mixes with the fans. All of this gives *Yankee Colors* a different look from others photo books, as does the combination of game-time drama—especially during the heightened national attention of the World Series—and lighthearted camaraderie.

CARDS AND COLLECTIBLES

420. *300 All-Time Stars Baseball Cards*, by the editors of *Consumer Guide*. Lincolnwood IL: Publications International, 1988.

Rather than take the standard year-by-year approach, this one starts with the athlete and goes from there.

The players are divided by era, with the stars—as of 1988—leading off, followed by their counterparts from the 1950s through the 1970s, before concluding with the "stars of yesterday."

Each page features an individual player, with biographical information, a career stats line, color photos of two or three representative cards, as well as a brief list of additional cards with their 1988 values. Those who were considered at the time to be the stars of today also have recent cards from each of the big three companies: Topps, Donruss, and Fleer.

421. *Cardboard Gods: An All-American Tale Told Through Baseball Cards,* by Josh Wilker. New York: Seven Footer Press, 2010.

Unlike Jamieson's *Mint Condition,* Wilker writes from a very personal viewpoint. Although just past the golden age of card collecting, Wilker links his fascination with the hobby to an awkward childhood; he started collecting as a sort of defense mechanism against his crumbling family unit.

His relationship with his cards—and with the Boston Red Sox—is almost like a Rorschach test, in that he sees certain moments from his adolescence reflected in the faces staring back at him, or looking off into the distance.

The book is an extension of his blog, *Cardboard Gods,* where he opines about the cards of his youth and the memories they bring to mind.

422. *The Complete Book of Collectible Baseball Cards,* by the editors of *Consumer Guide.* New York: Beekman House, 1985.

Naturally, books like this can never be complete, at least until baseball cards are no longer made, which, if you listen to the dire reports, might be sooner than you'd like to think. That doesn't mean these books can't be fun or informative in the interim.

This one, for example, is an excellent starting point for those who still wish to get into this increasingly expensive hobby.

Working backward from 1984 to 1886, *The Complete Book* examines each set produced during the year. And it doesn't just focus on the big boys like Topps, Donruss, and Fleer, but also on the dozens of regional issues, many of which are just knock-offs of the established sets with their own logo on them, as well as cereal boxes inserts (does anyone remember Kellogg's 3-D sets?). The editors give the backstory for each set along with their pros and cons, noteworthy cards, and value at the time of the book's publication.

Although *The Complete Book* is nicely illustrated—especially with examples of the rarer sets—most of the photos are in black and white and therefore do not adequately show off the cards to their full potential. The book also includes a glossary of collecting terms and a list of Hall of Famers for those who wish to specialize their collecting.

Other categories: Collectibles, History

423. *Mint Condition: How Baseball Cards Became an American Obsession,* by Dave Jamieson. New York: Atlantic Monthly Press, 2010.

Many baseball fans of a certain age tell the same apocryphal story of how their mother threw out their prized collection of baseball cards that would have netted a fortune—that is, before the memorabilia market bottomed out.

What is it about those little pieces of paper that demand such attention and affection? Is it the nostalgia of our carefree days of youth?

Jamieson attempts to answer questions like these. From their earliest incarnations as premiums that came with tobacco products, to the seemingly endless and expensive varieties of the twenty-first century, the author covers the psychological, sociological, and economic factors that turned the cards that were basically giveaways with the purchase of penny gum—that tradition was later reversed, with the hard, thin slices of pinkness as the freebie in a pack of cards—into a multibillion-dollar industry.

424. *Sayonara Home Run! The Art of the Japanese Baseball Card,* by John Gall and Gary Engel. San Francisco: Chronicle, 2006.

American kids weren't the only ones who were nuts for baseball cards. It was a rite of passage for Japanese fans as well.

Gall and Engel's book is an excellent one on many levels. They explain the cultural similarities and differences in the hobby between the two nations. Baseball cards have been on the American scene since the late 1800s; Japan, on the other hand, began their production just prior to World War II. Other major differences are depicted in glorious color and black-and-white illustrations. While Topps was Japan's main source for decades, many companies eventually came to share the honors.

The "art" in the title is a most apt description; Japan has it, hands, down, over the United States. The country's variety of cards offers an array of colors and styles that go beyond simple head shots and action photography.

Among the numerous Japanese varieties were basic cards with statistics; menko masks, which were designed to be worn in an attempt to emulate a favorite player; and game cards, which were similar to the inserts that came with Topps brand and served as a stand-alone amusement.

The authors don't rank the sets in any way but rather present this small paperback coffee-table edition — a specialty of Chronicle Books — to illustrate how two nations honor their shared national pastime.

Other categories: Collectibles, International

425. *The T206 Collection: The Players and Their Stories,* by Tom Zappala and Ellen Zappala. Portsmouth NH: Peter E. Randall, 2010.

If you're lucky enough to own a complete set of the T-206 series — more than five hundred cards — then you're be sitting a nice bit of change. The Honus Wagner card alone garnered almost $3 million at a recent auction. Owning this book might be the next best thing and as close as most of us will ever get to possessing the real thing.

In celebration of the one hundredth anniversary of the set, the Zappalas, a husband-and-wife writing team, compiled profiles of each player featured on the cards, along with full-size, full-color reproductions. Unlike Topps and the other companies that followed, the T-206 was produced with the reverse side featuring not statistics but advertising by several tobacco companies. In fact, the Wagner card is so rare because he feared kids would buy or steal tobacco to obtain his likeness. He didn't want to be responsible for setting them on the wrong path, so he had the company remove his card from production, thereby making it a rarity.

The authors divide the players into groups, including the thirty-eight players who would eventually be inducted into the Baseball Hall of Fame. From there they discuss the athletes who just missed elite status; "The Uncommons," as opposed to the "commons" designation for your everyday roster fillers, who get a chapter of their own; Minor Leaguers; and perhaps, the most interesting chapter, "The Bad Boys of Baseball," featuring gamblers and other reprobates.

The final chapter offers insight into how cards are graded for value, which, while not necessarily worth the cover price of the book, is certainly a useful tool for any serious collector wanting to jump into the T-206 pool.

ESSAYS

426. *Damn Yankees: Twenty-Four Major League Writers on the World's Most Loved (and Hated) Team*, edited by Rob Fleder. New York: Ecco Press, 2012.

Fleder, the former executive editor of *Sports Illustrated* (who was also responsible for the *"Sports Illustrated" Baseball Book*) assembled his own literary All-Star team for this collection. The roster of writers includes the likes of Roy Blount Jr., Dan Barry, Jane Leavy, Charley Pierce, Will Leitch, Colum McCann, Daniel Okrent, Frank Deford, Bill James, and Tom Verducci, among others.

Not everyone is enamored of the Bronx Bombers, which is refreshing. Some take issue with the team for being too good, too cocky, or too conservative (they were among the last teams to sign a black player). Blount, Pierce, and Leitch, being outsiders to the metropolitan area, can be expected to be a bit on the negative side, while Leavy—a Mantle fan since childhood—writes about her favorite player's home run relationship with a Red Sox pitcher. McCann recalls how he indoctrinated his Irish father into the ways of the national pastime via the Yankees. And Nathaniel Rich sticks up for *his* favorite New York team, the Mets, as he discusses the almost symbiotic relationship between the rivals' fans and whether the word *schadenfreude* is really appropriate.

Some contributors, merely by dint of *being* writers, have had problems with the team, just as players who might be heroes to others have different feelings toward the media. Kudos to all the participants for sharing their personal feelings on the topic.

427. *Fathers Playing Catch with Sons: Essays on Sport (Mostly Baseball)*, by Donald Hall. San Francisco: North Point Press, 1985.

Hall, who was appointed poet laureate of the United States in 2006, published this gentle, honest collection of observations about the game's overriding theme of companionship that comes from the shared team goal.

The title essay stems from his 1973 experience sitting on the Pirates bench during spring training. This led to his friendship with Dock Ellis, with whom he collaborated on the iconoclastic pitcher's memoirs, which in turn developed into book-review assignments and additional essays. An excerpt from *Dock Ellis in the Country of Baseball* also appears in *Fathers Playing Catch*.

Other baseball essays include a paean to Fenway Park—the Red Sox seem to be a popular subject among the literary set—and a bittersweet commentary on the concept of old-timers games.

Despite his status, Hall is never haughty or highfalutin'; he's just one of the guys when it comes to sharing his thoughts on baseball.

Other category: History

428. *Top of the Order: 25 Writers Pick Their Favorite Baseball Player of All Time*, edited by Sean Manning. Cambridge MA: Da Capo Press, 2010.

Manning asked a bunch of his friends and associates to weigh in on their favorites. This is interesting on a couple of levels. First, the breadth of contributors runs an amazing gamut, from professional writers to former athletes to just plain folks.

Then there are the choices themselves. Actor Michael Ian Black picked Mookie Wilson because as a young student he thought it was the politically correct thing to do and it would differentiate him from his classmates. It should come as no surprise that Roger Kahn would select Jackie Robinson, one of his own *Boys of Summer*. Iconoclast Jim Bouton goes to Steve Dembowski, a college player who had a unique talent for getting hit by pitches. And Scott Raab, a writer for *Esquire*, thinks Tony Horton, one of the first players recognized as suffering mental-health issues during his playing days, deserves our understanding and support. This was something Raab and his cronies did not understand earlier, when they were booing the former Red Sox and Indians first baseman, who was gone from the Majors by the time he was twenty-six. The favorite player doesn't even to be real to qualify: Carrie Rickey, a film critic for the *Philadelphia Inquirer*, chooses Crash Davis, the hero in the feature film *Bull Durham*, as her guy.

The eclectic combination of writers and subjects offers a good cross-section, and one could easily imagine a second, all-new edition could be forthcoming.

Other categories: Anthology, Auto/Bio/Mem, History, Sportswriting

FOOD

429. *Chicago Cubs Cookbook: All-Star Recipes from Your Favorite Players*, edited by Carrie Muskat. Chicago: Triumph, 2010

I get a tremendous kick out of anything that take players away from the comfort zone of the ballpark and the locker room. Seeing them in these fish-out-of-water situations can offer lots of entertainment, and it puts the athletes in a humanizing light.

That's part of the charm of books like *Chicago Cubs Cookbook*. Are these recipes actually from the players? Perhaps, although a couple of participants merely glom something off the menu of their favorite restaurants. The items include everything, from appetizers and desserts, from the tables and or imaginations of Cubs players past and present, including such fan favorites as Fergie Jenkins, Ryne Sandberg, and Lou Pinella. Nutritional values have thoughtfully been omitted, although some, like Mike Bielecki's protein Thai noodles, make the pretense of being healthy. On the plus side, the book has a comb binding for ease of use.

Collections like this one are often created to raise money for a particular organization or charity. In this case, it's the Dempster Family Foundation, founded by former pitcher Ryan Dempster, a member of the Cubs at the time the book was published.

430. *Dodger Dogs to Fenway Franks: The Ultimate Guide to America's Top Baseball Parks*, by Bob Wood. New York: McGraw-Hill, 1988.

The bad news: many of the ballparks included in this twenty-plus-year-old appraisal are no longer in existence. The good news: Wood evokes a lot of memories, and *Dodger Dogs* serves as a guide for future customer-service business models.

Wood traveled to twenty-six Major League ballparks — which, at the time, was all of them — and graded them in several categories, including layout, seating, quality and variety of food, stadium employees, and general atmosphere. Not surprisingly, the gustatory component has changed greatly over the years. Venues have opened their culinary doors to healthier options, featuring more than the traditional peanuts, popcorn, and Cracker Jack that weren't even on the radar twenty-five years ago.

In addition, since the book was published a few new teams have come along and several new stadiums have replaced old ones; only the Dodgers — whom Wood picked has having the best overall park — Royals, Cubs, Red Sox, and Athletics remain in their old homes, albeit with new, corporation-sponsored names: the Toronto Blue Jays, Seattle Mariners, San Francisco Giants, and Houston Astros — all of which have moved into new facilities since 1989 — received the lowest marks at the time.

Amenities have changed as well. Fans no longer go to the ballpark just to watch the game. Now teams have to provide interactive features and amenities such as playgrounds, swimming pools, gift shops, and about 327 different food kiosks.

Here's hoping Wood has a revised edition in him. You have to keep those team owners on their toes, and this shows that someone is indeed watching.

Other categories: Business, Classic

MEDIA

431. *Baseball: The Writers' Game,* edited by Mike Shannon. South Bend IN: Diamond Communications, 1992.

I have always been fascinated by the creative process, so I take every opportunity to learn about how great minds operate, how they agonize over each word, until they reach their goal.

If there's a Hall of Fame for contemporary baseball authors, Shannon has collected most of them in this volume. The fifteen writers herein have published dozens of the books included in the book currently in your hand. They include Donald Honig, Robert Creamer, Peter Golenbock, Bill James, Roger Kahn, Charles Einstein, Lawrence S. Ritter, and John Thorn.

Some, like James and Honig, are incredibly prolific. Others, like Daniel Okrent, Jim Brosnan, and John B. Holway may not have the same output, but their contributions are no less impressive. Each profile lists the significant books by each writer published until the time *The Writers' Game* was written. A special tip of the hat went to Lonnie Wheeler. His name by itself might not be as familiar as the rest, but he's a highly respected guy who has been turning the ramblings of athletes into solid narrative for decades now.

Other categories: Anthology, Sportswriting

432. *Baseball Books: A Collector's Guide,* by Mike Shannon. Jefferson NC: McFarland, 2007.

As one who collects baseball books, I was excited to come across Shannon's most recent offering. After reading it, however, I find myself depressed, knowing that I will never be a true completist. I will never acquire every title, not even just the ones deemed to be important. There's never enough money, time, or space, nor would I even want to even if all the planets were properly aligned.

After reading *A Collector's Guide* I learned that I haven't treated my books with the proper respect. They're split between the attic and the basement, contrary to Shannon's advice. I know he's right about the atmospheric conditions; the heat and humidity can't be good for them. Unfortunately, there's no place else to put them. Unless my family moves out . . .

Shannon, the cofounder and editor in chief of *Spitball* magazine and the author of *Diamond Classics: Essays on 100 of the Best Baseball Books Ever Published* (McFarland, 2003) presents his book in two main sections: first, the hows and whys of collecting, and second, a substantial price guide detailing what one should expect to pay for various titles.

Of particular interest is his suggestion in "Which Baseball Books to Collect," which includes a number of other publications that feature lists of the best and most essential titles.

Other category: Collectibles

433. *The Best of "Baseball Digest,"* edited by John Kuenster. Chicago: Ivan R. Dee, 2006.

The word *best* is bandied around way too much, especially when it comes to sports. Even with all the sabermetric statistics, can we say with certainty that Babe Ruth or Willie Mays was *the* best player ever?

In the case of *The Best of "Baseball Digest,"* we'll have to accept Kuenster's considered opinion. The longtime editor culled more than a hundred articles from the thousands that have appeared since the magazine's debut in 1942. The roster of contributors comes from a large talent pool, giving readers the chance to discover regional journalists from all over the country that they might not have otherwise.

Baseball Digest has been a marvelous conglomeration of scintillating writing on a wide variety of topics with a sprinkling of amusing anecdotes, challenging puzzles, and other surprises. For example, the March issue, which heralded the new crop of rookies, and the April offering, with its thousands of facts, were always my favorites).

Other categories: Anthology, Auto/Bio/Mem, History, Sportswriting

434. *Center Field Shot: A History of Baseball on Television*, by James R. Walker and Robert V. Bellamy Jr. Lincoln: University of Nebraska Press, 2008.

The things we take for granted when we watch a ball game on TV. Take camera angles, for example. Back when the first black-and-white broadcast transmitted a meeting between the Brooklyn Dodgers and the Boston Braves in 1951, there were two cameras in use, both behind home plate at different heights. These days, there are about ten per regular-season game, with almost twice that amount used for marquee events. But it's more than just the number of cameras that's changed; there are also special effects, instant replays, slow motion, and even 3-D.

Walker and Bellamy trace the contentious relationship between TV and baseball — two of my favorite pastimes — in this lively account. Among many revelations that will undoubtedly come as a shock to younger readers, club owners originally looked at television as the enemy. They feared that if fans could watch the game in the comfort of their own homes, they wouldn't come out to the ballpark and spend money on tickets, souvenirs, and food. While this is certainly true for some consumers, the national pastime has enjoyed increased attendance almost annually (allowing for strike-shortened seasons) since the mid-1960s. In addition, broadcasting rights have amounted to beaucoup bucks for the franchises. Minor League baseball, on the other hand, did suffer because of television. It turns out that many fans favored watching big leaguers on their Philcos rather than bush leaguers at the local stadium. This led to a drastic reduction in affiliates throughout the 1950s.

In addition to local stations, networks began airing the biggest games of the week to national audiences — including the World Series and the All-Star Game — giving fans living hundreds of miles away from the closest Major League team the thrill of seeing players they had only read about.

To offer a real inside look, the authors also discuss the production aspects of the televised game.

Other category: History

435. *Hammering Hank: How the Media Made Henry Aaron,* by Mark Stewart and Mike Kennedy. Guilford CT: Lyons Press, 2006.

The astute reader will notice the two possible meanings of the title. Used as a noun, *Hammering Hank* reflects Aaron's nickname, bestowed upon him as one of the great power hitters in the game. Employed as a verb, it mirrors the actions of the press, which, if they didn't actually hammer at the ballplayer, certainly did little to promote him as a future Hall of Famer, especially early in his career. Throughout his career Aaron played for a team that was mostly considered small market. As such, he labored in the shadows of contemporaries Willie Mays and Mickey Mantle, both of whom were brought along by the New York press. He also wasn't exactly thrilled by his team relocating from the comparatively accepting environment of Milwaukee to play in the Deep South, segments of which still seemed to be fighting the Civil War.

As Aaron approached the career home run record, it created a challenge for the media. Not since Jackie Robinson had an African American athlete been so prominent on a national level. How would they handle this assault on what some unenlightened fans considered a "white record?"

Much of *Hammering Hank* is taken directly from previous books and newspaper and magazine accounts about and by Aaron, and it follows the progression of his career as reported by the press. It's more than another treatise of a long line of stories about journalistic bias; it's an indictment of the media and how it did — or did not do — its job.

Other categories: Ethnicity, History, Sportswriting

436. *Jerome Holtzman on Baseball: A History of Baseball Scribes*, by Jerome Holtzman. Champaign IL: Sports Publishing, 2005.

In this volume Holtzman pays tribute to those who went before him, such as Grantland Rice, Red Smith, Jimmy Cannon, and Shirley Povich, among others. The beetle-browed, cigar-chomping Chicago legend was personally acquainted with several of the gentlemen he writes about, and he notes the gradual transition from the purple prose of the "gee whiz" school of sportswriting that fawns over the athletes to the "aw nuts" style, popularized by the new breed of reporters in the antiestablishment 1970s. Unlike many of his generation, Holtzman embraced this change instead of clinging to the philosophy that everything was better in the old days.

He also gives a nod to figures who are often overlooked for their contributions, such as the men who developed the statistics we've come to take for granted. Holtzman was credited for making the save an official measure of bullpen success, which in turn led to the concept of the closer. All the while, he shares his strong opinions on the game as well as issues pertaining to his profession.

Holtzman, the first official historian for Major League Baseball, was himself inducted into the writer's wing of the Baseball Hall of Fame in 1990 after more than fifty years of service to the two major Chicago daily newspapers.

Other categories: Classic, History, Media

437. *"Sports Illustrated": The Baseball Book*. New York: Sports Illustrated, 2011.

It sometimes seems unfair that publications like *Sports Illustrated* can simply dip into their rich archives at any time and effortlessly publish award-winning writing and photography. On second thought, perhaps that's oversimplifying. With so many years of great writing and photos, it actually might be difficult to pick out the best of the lot and cram it into less than three hundred pages of words and pictures: after all, *Illustrated* is half of the magazine's title.

The text represents some of the best baseball writing from the last fifty-plus years, including several contributions from *SI*'s own staff, including Tom Verducci, Robert Creamer, Frank Deford, and Rick Reilly, as well as other noteworthy scribes such as Roger Kahn, Leigh Montville, and George Plimpton.

Highlights of the book—which features essays on Mickey Mantle, Roberto Clemente, Reggie Jackson, Stan Musial, Ted Williams, and Vladimir Guerrero, among many others—includes a decade-by-decade recap and an artistic rendering of the magazine's all-time All-Stars.

If you're going to give a book, give big, I always say, and this is a perfect gift. Originally published in 2004, it was updated to include the decade of the 2000s. *The Baseball Book* isn't an ordinary tome to be read; it's meant to be savored, so you might consider saving it for the off-season.

Other categories: Anthology, Coffee Table/Gift, History, Sportswriting

438. *Voices of the Game: The Acclaimed Chronicle of Baseball Radio and Television Broadcasting—from 1921 to the Present*, updated edition, by Curt Smith. New York: Simon and Schuster, 1992

Smith has a passion for the spoken word (he served as a speechwriter for President George H. W. Bush) and has tremendous joy and respect for the men and women who served to bring the games into America's living rooms, kitchens, porches, and bedrooms. One of the enduring memories of many baby boomer fans is staying up past bedtime, listening to the game via a transistor radio tucked under a pillow, or walking through the old neighborhood at World Series time and hearing the game coming through almost every window.

Smith traces the history of baseball broadcasting from the first radio transmission on Pittsburgh's KDKA in 1921 through the 1990s—just short of ESPN's *Baseball Tonight* and the MLB Network—paying homage to those who wove the stories and lit the imaginations. Having no precedents to follow, the pioneers of the industry had it especially tough, meeting each challenge and making the profession easier for those who followed. In that regard, it must have been both thrilling and frightening. Television supplemented radio in the early 1950s, creating a different set of problems: now the audience could see the action and didn't need as much exposition.

The best in the business—such as Vin Scully (still chatting away for the Dodgers well into his eighties), Mel Allen, Red Barber, Curt Gowdy, and many others—did the job with an even hand (no "homers" allowed), with dignity, and with a command of the English language. There will, however, always be a place for famous manglers like Dizzy Dean and Jerry Coleman.

A good broadcast team can stick around for a long time. As a Mets fan, I had the good fortune to grow up listening to Lindsey Nelson, Bob Murphy, and Ralph Kiner, the longest-tenured trio in Major League broadcast history.

As evidence of how much the coverage has changed over the past century, between the chapters Smith includes some of the most famous calls made from the booth.

Other category: Media

Also by the author: *America's Dizzy Dean* (1978); *Pull Up a Chair: The Vin Scully Story* (2009); *The Storytellers* (1999).

MOVIES AND PLAYS

439. *The Baseball Film in Postwar America: A Critical Study, 1948–1962*, Ron Briley. Jefferson NC: McFarland, 2011.

If you like your cinematic criticism a bit on the academic side, you'll enjoy Briley's look at some key issues in America since the end of the Second World War and how they were reflected in the baseball movies of the period.

The country still needed its heroes, as was reflected in the oft-belittled biopic *The Babe Ruth Story*, in which William Bendix gives the worst athletic performance this side of Anthony Perkins in *Fear Strikes Out*, which Briley includes for its message of following one's own heart and not living for the desires of others. Other general issues include civil rights (represented by *The Jackie Robinson Story*, which actually starred the ballplayer); the Cold War (*Strategic Air Command*, featuring Jimmy Stewart as an All-Star ballplayer who once again answers the call of his country, a la Ted Williams in Korea; upward mobility (*The Pride of St. Louis*, a biopic about Dizzy Dean, a hero of Depression-era America); and the plight of injured veterans seeking to return to some semblance of normalcy in civilian life (*The Stratton Story*, another Stewart vehicle).

Of course, if you're smart, as Briley certainly is, and you work hard enough, any critic can make unconnected theories fit his overall thesis.

Other categories: Academic, Essays, History

440. *Baseball Monologues*, edited by Lavonne Mueller. Portsmouth N H: Heinemann, 1996.

Admit it: there's a little bit of the thespian in you, a part of you that would love to be out on stage, the audience hanging on your every word. How do you get there? You audition. What do you use to audition? Well, since you are obviously a literate baseball fan, why not keep it in your comfort zone?

From drama to comedy, you can find just about anything among the nearly forty pieces included here to fit the mood. You can be a real player, a fictional one, or a manager, a fan, a wife, a girlfriend, an owner, or a disillusioned youth. In short, there are parts for all different types, so you future Tony winners don't have to worry about being forced to use something that doesn't quite fit.

Even if you have no such plans, *Monologues* is worth a look, if only to see just how much baseball theater is out there.

441. *Mr. Deeds Goes to Yankee Stadium: Baseball Films in the Capra Tradition*, by Wes D. Gehring. Jefferson N C: McFarland, 2004.

Gehring, a film professor at Ball State University and a columnist for U S A *Today* magazine, highlights eight classic and not-so-classic movies about the national pastime, which he compares with some of the characteristics of the famed director Frank Capra.

From *The Pride of the Yankees*, we get Lou Gehrig as the everyman hero, the regular Joe who accomplishes great things. *The Stratton Story*—which starred Jimmy Stewart, a Capra favorite, in the title role—represents characters who had to overcome adversity, also a Capra trademark. Other movies offered for comparison include the original *Angels in the Outfield*; *The Natural*; *Bull Durham* and *Field of Dreams*, two Kevin Costner gems; and two of the films, *The Rookie* and *Frequency*, feature the earnest Dennis Quaid. Like most of Capra's oeuvre, these movies share certain qualities of patriotism, love of family, pride in one's work, and a desire to overcome the pitfalls life can often cast in your path.

Like a lot of critical pieces, some of Gehring's narrative can get a bit daunting when he speaks in technical terms, but if you love baseball *and* Capra films, this is a great volume.

442. *Reel Baseball: Baseball's Golden Era, The Way America Witnessed It—In The Movie Newsreels*, by Les Krantz. New York: Doubleday, 2006.

Prior to baseball on television and the highlight-driven 24–7 sports cable programs, the only way fans got to see their favorite players in action aside from attending a game was through newsreels, which were part of the extras screened at the movie theaters from the 1930s through the 1960s. Those living west of Saint Louis who could come up with the price of admission were able to see New York Yankee slugger Babe Ruth trotting around the bases (or *mincing*, which was the word often used to describe his peculiar gait) or Bob Feller firing his fastball at an ill-prepared batter. For most fans, this was their only opportunity to see recaps of the World Series or players like Joe DiMaggio and Hank Greenberg in the military service.

Krantz offers the stories behind nearly fifty famous events and personalities in this coffee-table edition, including Willie Mays's famous catch in the 1954 World Series, Bill Mazeroski's walk-off home run against the Yankees in 1960, and Roger Maris's record-setting sixty-first home run in 1961. Nongame clips include the first induction ceremony at the Baseball Hall of Fame, and a tribute as fans pay their last respects to the Mighty Babe during his funeral in 1948.

An accompanying DVD, narrated by Joe Garagiola, contains background for twenty-four events and personalities featured in the book.

Other categories: Coffee Table/Gift, History

Also by the author: *Yankee Classics: World Series Magic from the Bronx Bombers, 1921 to Today* (2008); *Yankee Stadium: A Tribute; 85 Years of Memories: 1923–2008* (2008)

MUSIC

443. *Baseball and the Music of Charles Ives: A Proving Ground,* by Timothy A. Johnson. Lanham MD: Scarecrow Press, 2004.

Oddly enough, Ives (1874–1954) was working in the insurance business rather than as a musician, which is where a good portion of his talents lay. He was also a gifted athlete and felt conflicted, as many young boys do, about the tension between following his parents' wishes to study music — his father was a bandleader in the Civil War era — and just being a kid. Fortunately for him and his fans, he managed to do both.

Johnson, a music theory teacher at Ithaca College, combines his analytic skills in parsing the musical compositions with their equivalent baseball inspirations such as the Chicago Cubs of Tinkers, Evers, and Chance, and Mike Donlin of the New York Giants, to name just two.

This book is for music students perhaps more so than the average baseball fan. Johnson gets quite technical in his descriptions of chords and tempos chosen to represent the action on the field. But if you are indeed a music aficionado *and* a baseball fan, Johnson has provided you with an exciting way to celebrate both passions.

444. *Baseball's Greatest Hit: The Story of "Take Me Out to the Ball Game,"* by Andy Strasberg, Robert Thompson, and Tim Wiles. Milwaukee: Hal Leonard, 2008.

This trio put together a fascinating study of Americana to mark the hundredth anniversary of one of the most performed songs in the land. Each writer brings his own expertise to the project: Strasberg has one of the largest private collections of memorabilia about the song; Thompson, a music professor at SUNY Purchase, is the founder and director of the Baseball Music Project; and Wiles is the director of research at the Baseball Hall of Fame, as well as the editor of a few books of baseball poetry.

There's a thorough history on Albert von Tilzer and Jack Norworth and how they came together to write the music and lyrics, respectively. But it's the ancillary material that makes this book more than just a recap of the song's history.

Other topics include a look at how each Major League team observes the song during the seventh-inning stretch, a timeline of "Take Me Out to the Ball Game," a discography of just about every recording of the tune, and a list of more than one thousand pieces of baseball sheet music on file with the Library of Congress.

The book includes a CD that offers several renditions of the iconic song.

445. *Rhythms of the Game: The Link Between Musical and Athletic Performance,* by Bernie Williams, Dave Gluck, and Bob Thompson. Milwaukee: Hall Leonard, 2011.

Williams, a six-time All-Star and four-time Gold Glove winner, parlays his extensive experience as a jazz musician to link music with the national pastime.

The former Yankee favorite also has two musical CDs to his credit and takes his music just as seriously as he did baseball. He studied with Gluck and Thompson at SUNY Purchase to produce this part theory, part instructional, part self-help book. He shows how many of the attributes that go into making a someone superior athlete are the same as those that make someone a great musician: focus, dedication, preparation, and practice.

Williams sprinkles in a few anecdotes about some of his old teammates, opponents, and experiences, but make no mistake: this is no memoir meant to regale readers with tales of on-field heroics (or off-field kibbitzing). Williams is firmly committed to his second act, although still holding on to the first.

Despite the similarities between the two disciplines, one qualm I had was the issue of control: a musician has much more over his environment than a batter facing a pitcher with a ninety-five-mile-per-hour fastball. While there are undoubtedly variations in music, I doubt they compare with those in elite-level sports.

POETRY

446. "Casey at the Bat: A Ballad of the Republic Sung in 1888," by Ernest L. Thayer.

447. *The Annotated "Casey at the Bat": A Collection of Ballads About The Mighty Casey,* second edition, edited by Martin Gardner. Chicago: University of Chicago Press, 1984.

448. *The Night Casey Was Born: The True Story Behind the Great American Ballad "Casey at the Bat,"* by John Evangelist Walsh. New York: Overlook Press, 2007.

449. *Casey on the Loose,* by Frank Deford. New York: Viking, 1989.

Originally published on the opinion page of the *San Francisco Daily Examiner,* Thayer's classic baseball poem is as much a staple of baseball pop culture as "Take Me Out to the Ball Game."

But had it not been for the overdramatic renditions by DeWolf Hopper, a famous actor of the day—he filmed an experimental talkie version in 1923—it is questionable whether the thirteen-stanza work would have enjoyed as many printings as it had.

Casey is a story of ego, pride, expectations, and how the mighty can be brought low. Unfortunately, in the original writing, there is no redemption; that only comes in the revisionist works. It has been parsed, analyzed, parodied, novelized, and turned into movies, but it has mainly been republished as a children's picture book. There are slight variations in the names of Casey's teammates and a few other minor word changes; what makes or breaks an individual version are the graphics.

Some illustrators, such as the prolific C. F. Payne, base their characters in the early stages of the game. Others, like Joe Morse, give the principals a stark inner-city feel. Famed sports artist Leroy Neiman gave "Casey" a more contemporary look in his adaptation.

There are also a few titles that examine the poem from linguistic and historical backgrounds.

The Annotated Casey at the Bat contains more than two dozen forms, either directly based on the poem ("Casey on the Mound," "Casey 20 Years Later") or featuring Casey's wife, daughter, or son. Some are merely based on the theme, like Ray Bradbury's "Ahab at the Helm." There's even an updated hippie version, "'Cool' Casey at the Bat," courtesy of *Mad* magazine.

The Night Casey Was Born concentrates on DeWolf Hopper's role in popularizing the poem and spreading it across the country through his dramatic readings. Walsh delves into Hopper's standing as one of the premier performers of his era and meshes that with the subtleties of form and flow and how the actor made it his signature piece.

In *Casey on the Loose*, veteran sports journalist Frank Deford blends fact and fantasy to expand on his 1988 *Sports Illustrated* backstory of the events leading up to Casey's failure, including gambling, a boxing match with John L. Sullivan, and the things we are tempted to do for love.

Taken together, the aforementioned titles are an impressive overview of one of the most cherished pieces of American folklore.

450. *O Holy Cow! The Selected Verses of Phil Rizzuto,* edited by Tom Peyer and Hart Seely. Hopewell NJ: Ecco Press, 1993.

In every broadcast booth there's a colorful character—usually a former player—who can't seem to get the words out of his mouth quickly enough to keep pace with his brain. But was there anyone like Phil Rizzuto? The Hall of Famer Yankee shortstop spent more than thirty years behind the mike for his beloved Bronx Bombers.

The Scooter was famous for his tangents about Mrs. Marconi's stromboli, or a great movie he saw. And all that in the middle of a Yankee rally where he might forget the batter, the count, or the score—nowadays, we might attribute this to ADD.

Peyer and Seely compiled literary mixtapes of some of Rizzuto's greatest hits in a regular feature in the *Village Voice*, a popular New York alternative weekly. The poems were excerpted from Rizzuto's game accounts, which are described with the particular situations at the moment of his inspirations. More than a few might make the reader wonder if Rizzuto wasn't overdue for his reservation at the Old Shortstop's Home.

Some of the selections are quite poignant, such as "Poem No. 61," which recounts Roger Maris's historic moment, and "Prayer for the Captain," which followed the death in 1979 of Thurman Munson.

This collection of ninety-four poems reflects Rizzuto's ability to change trains of thought with frightening speed then scramble to get back onto the track.

An example:

> A little disconcerting,
> Smelling that pizza
> And trying
> To do a ball game (96).

Other category: Auto/Bio/Mem

451. *Shakespeare on Baseball,* compiled by David Goodnough. New York: Barricade, 2000.

2B or not 2B. That is at least part of the answer. In this reference volume Shakespeare scholar Goodnough uses lines from works by the bard to explain various baseball concepts and situations from the sublime — for Hank Aaron's 715th home run, he pulls the line "Aaron, thou hast hit it!" from *Titus Andronicus* — to the ridiculous: "Fastidious winning manager doused with champagne: "I could well wish courtesy would invent some other custom of entertainment," from *Othello.*

Sure, it's a cutesy little bit of fluff, but give credit to the editor for knowing enough Shakespeare and baseball to keep the project from seeming like too much of a reach. All in all, *Shakespeare on Baseball* is, to quote Osric in *Hamlet,* "a very palpable hit."

12

Reference

These books come in very basic forms, either as encyclopedias or lists of statistics, with a few hybrids—like Total Baseball *—thrown in. One problem is that they are constantly in need of revision, especially when it comes to the stats, which makes purchasing the updated versions of those thick tomes impractical. On the other hand, they serve as valuable research tools from which readers can glean both the form and substance of bygone days.*

452. *The 100 Greatest: Baseball Games of the 20th Century Ranked,* by Joseph J. Dittmar. Jefferson NC: McFarland, 2000.

This is another one of those topics that's sure to engender fevered discussion. The author explains in his introduction that his take on the one hundred greatest games was based on a combination of "drama/excitement and game importance." There are no milestones like three thousand hits or three hundred wins (those are games he addresses in his *Baseball Records Registry*); no lopsided games, which as he so properly noted have meaning for fans of the winners, but not so much for the losers. No, to make it into his century mark, these games must truly be significant.

Of course, the highest rated consist of the moments we've heard about for years, such as the "shot heard 'round the world" and Carlton Fisk's home run in the Game Six of the 1975 World Series. But how, some will argue, could Don Larsen's World Series perfect game not make the top ten? And where's Joe Carter's Series-ending home run for the Toronto Blue Jays in 1993?

Even with the author's caveats, readers will scratch their heads over some of the selections, especially when it comes to those prior to the expansion era. While Dittmar does a good job of setting the scenes and relaying the sense of drama, a deeper explanation as to why a particular game deserves such attention would have been helpful.

One other change I might have made would be to list the games in descending order to increase the drama. If you're going lead off with number one, you might as well include a table of contents for easy navigation.

Other categories: Analysis, History

453. *The Ballplayers: Baseball's Ultimate Biographical Reference*, edited by Mike Shatzkin. New York: William Morrow, 1990.

454. *Baseball: The Biographical Encyclopedia*, from the editors of *Total Baseball*. Kingston NY: Total Sports Illustrated, 2000.

The Ballplayers is another massive reference book that came out in the last few years of the twentieth century, before such information was readily available on the Internet and smartphones, thereby rendering the printed page just about obsolete. There's little doubt that the edition you're now holding will eventually be available as some sort of e-book. It is also the type of book that you don't need to read in its entirety to enjoy, which is perfect for short attention spans.

The Ballplayers—which utilized the services of more than 75 contributors for its 1,200-plus pages—contains more than 6,000 players plus about another thousand Negro Leaguers and non–Major Leaguers, writers, executives, manages, umpires, those who played prior to 1900, and others who have had an impact on the national pastime. Requirements for inclusion differ: for example, fewer at bats for active players, more for retired athletes. Naturally, someone like Hank Aaron will merit major real estate, but even relative unknowns like Bo Diaz or Bots Nekola—a pitcher for a couple of seasons who garnered more fame for discovering and signing Carl Yastrzemski, Rico Petrocelli, and Ben Oglivie for the Red Sox—get some love.

A decade after *The Ballplayers* was published, Total Sports released a similarly thick volume, *Baseball: The Biographical Encyclopedia*. This one is a bit more exclusive, with only 2,000 entries, including every Hall of Famer, every batter with 2,500 or more hits or pitcher with 200-plus wins; MVP and Cy Young Award winners; World Series–winning managers; and LCS and Series MVPS. Several of the figures included span multiple categories. Then the editors added some of the key personalities in the game, including broadcasters, executives, and players who enjoyed special moments in the sun. Aesthetically, the end product is slightly nicer than *The Ballplayers*, printed on glossy papers with thumbnail photos of the individuals.

Other categories: Auto/Bio/Mem, History

455. *Baseball by the Books: A History and Complete Bibliography of Baseball Fiction*, by Andy McCue. Dubuque IA: William C. Brown, 1991.

McCue, a former president of the Society for American Baseball Research and chair of the organization's bibliography committee, lists several hundred books, beginning with William Everett's 1868 title *Changing Bases* and wrapping up with some forty titles released in 1990.

The books are listed alphabetically by author and include capsule descriptions, but McCue also offers several other convenient ways to find a publication: alphabetically by title, by subgenre, and even by books that focus on Major League teams. Most of his book is straightforward and fairly dry, as lists are wont to be, but McCue injects a certain amount of humor in his introductory chapter, "From Frank Merriwell to Henry Wiggen: A Modest History of Baseball Fiction."

With so many new novels published over the last twenty years, a revision of this book would be most welcome.

Other category: Fiction

456. *Baseball Desk Reference*, by Lawrence Lorimer with the National Baseball Hall of Fame and Museum. New York: Dorling Kindersley, 2002.

It's amazing how much information you can cram into a mere six hundred pages. And who better than the Hall of Fame to decide *the* most important items to include and then present it with class?

The handsome (and heavy) volume leads off with a timeline, followed by a brief history of the Hall and its members. Next up is a glossary of terms and objectives of the game.

The bulk of the *Desk Reference* features profiles of each franchise and more than seven hundred profiles of the leading position players and pitchers since the inauguration of the modern game, which has been defined as 1893, when the mound was set at its present distance of sixty feet six inches from home plate. You'll also find lots of statistics and records, as well as fundamental information about the Minor Leagues, the Negro Leagues, and baseball as played in foreign lands.

Another chapter highlights baseball in pop culture and feature films, collectibles, songs and poetry, and there's even a ten-page section on reading suggestions, most of which can be found within *501 Baseball Books*.

Although this volume is more than a decade old, much of the information is still pertinent, and it would make a valuable addition to any fan's library.

Other categories: History, Pop Culture, Statistics

457. *Baseball Field Guide: An In-Depth Illustrated Guide to the Complete Rules of Baseball*, revised and updated, by Dan Formosa and Paul Hamburger. Cambridge MA: Da Capo Press, 2008.

Let's face it: any rule book is, by virtue of its intent, practically a legal document and therefore should almost be expected to come off as a bit boring. Oh sure, it's mandatory for umpires, and managers and players should—but don't always—know the rules, but that still doesn't exactly make for compelling reading.

That's where the *Baseball Field Guide* comes in. It's kind of an almanac, but without all the little factoids that usually comprise such volumes. While offering practical instruction on many of the finer points of the game, BFG goes even further, making the rules actually readable, informative, and entertaining. For example, fans think they know what constitutes a check swing, but the authors actually get into the question of how much is too far. Colorful diagrams help by aiding the explanations.

There are separate sections dealing with running, batting, pitching, fielding, equipment specifications, and the responsibilities of official scorers, umpires, managers, and coaches. My favorite chapter is "Misbehavior," which addresses how those who engage in such poor manners should be handled by the men in blue.

The book is nicely designed with an unusual trim—it's taller and narrower than the average paperback—that makes for a crisp look.

Other category: Rules/Umpires

458. *The Baseball Necrology: The Post-Baseball Lives and Deaths of Over 7,600 Major League Players and Others*, by Bill Lee. Jefferson NC: McFarland, 2003.

The beauty of this encyclopedic work is how it brings in the great equalizer: death. Every player—from the most mediocre to the highest Hall of Famer—has that common factor of being an ex-player far longer than an active one.

Lee—not to be confused with the former Major League pitcher—undertook an incredible project to uncover the information for all those entries, which he basically boils down to how long the individual was in the Majors, his postbaseball career, the circumstances of his death, and place of internment, if applicable. No flowery eulogies, no statistics: just an honest and humbling appraisal.

Of course, by now there have been scores of additional players who have gone to that great ballpark in the sky.

Other categories: Auto/Bio/Mem, History

459. *The Baseball Novel: A History and Annotated Bibliography of Adult Fiction*, by Noel Schraufnagel. Jefferson NC: McFarland, 2008.

An excellent overview of the genre, *The Baseball Novel* is limited to serious works, which separates it from McCue's *Baseball by the Book*, which covers just about every title up until its publication.

Schraufnagel, a former English professor, offers capsule summaries for some four hundred titles, dating back to the first mention of the game by James Fennimore Cooper in his *Home as Found: Sequel to Homeward Bound* (1838) through Peter Schilling Jr.'s *The End of Baseball* (2008). Some, such as the mysteries, for which he thoughtfully provides a separate list, are baseball through and through; some only include the game as a tangential plot device.

Among the helpful appendices, which make life easier for readers seeking to zero in on specific themes, are books inventoried by ethnicity, gender, class, and race; science fiction; mysteries; the author's opinion on each year's best baseball novel; and a somewhat redundant chronological list of all titles.

Other categories: Fiction, Pop Culture

460. *The Baseball Rookies Encyclopedia: The Most Authoritative Guide to Baseball's First-Year Players*, by David Nemec and Dave Zeman. Washington DC: Brassey's, 2004

Here's a thought: in the first year of professional baseball, everyone was a rookie.

Nemec and Zeman trace the chronology of freshmen since 1872 up to the 2002 season. Each year focuses on one main story with additional highlights from some of the great starts and great stalls. Some first-timers go on to great careers, but the majority of players do not. Many highly touted rookies fail to live up to the hype, which is frequently built up by a floundering ballclub to give their fans something to look forward to — David Clyde, anyone? For every Willie Mays or Mickey Mantle who goes on to a Hall of Fame career, there's a Hurricane Hazle or a Super Joe Charboneau. Those who excel in their inaugural campaign would do well to look out for the "sophomore slump." Like they say in the investment commercials, past performance is no guarantee of future earnings.

The *Encyclopedia* contains lots of interesting filler to keep things moving along. A few more nice features include rookie records for each franchise and an all-rookie All-Star team.

Other categories: Analysis, History, Statistics

461. *The Baseball Timeline*, by Burt Solomon. New York: Dorling Kindersley, 2001.

Solomon first published *The Baseball Timeline* in 1997, a commendable effort to record the highlights of the national pastime since its birth in 1845. It's nothing fancy, mind you: a paperback edition with a simple double-column layout on recycled paper. But it was a useful reference for the baseball researcher or casual fan, in that the format made it easy to look up meaningful anniversaries.

In 2001 Dorling Kindersley transformed *Timeline* from an ugly duckling into a beautiful swan. This literally heavyweight revision, produced "in association with Major League Baseball," is everything the advertising industry had in mind when it invented the phrase "new and improved." Most of the material is identical to the previous version published by Avon, but the new arrangement is worth the additional cost. The massive volume of over 1,200 pages includes photos and illustrations of players and events absent in the first go-around.

Solomon does a superb job, citing birthdays, trades, noteworthy games, and what he terms the "best of each season," including league leaders and major award winners. He also underscores the fact that baseball is part of the American fabric by offering a smattering of headlines for major events from each year, such as "Truman Defeats Dewey," for a broader context.

Extra information is sprinkled throughout *Timeline*, including trivia; changes to the league, rules, and equipment; quotes; and other historical notes.

Other categories: Coffee Table/Gift, History

462. *The Baseball Uncyclopedia: A Highly Opinionated, Myth-Busting Guide to the Great American Game,* by Michael Kun and Howard Bloom, Cincinnati OH: Emmis, 2006.

Is the *Uncyclopedia* a refreshing change from the heavy, staid tomes that focus on stats or snapshot biographies? Is it an iconoclastic look at some of the long-held opinions on the national pastime? Why not have both in a single volume?

The authors would no doubt take exception to the premise of my book, which is that because baseball is a metaphor for life, it touches many aspects. As Kun writes in an entry addressing just this issue: "I have four words for every writer and broadcaster who insists on employing 'baseball-as-a-metaphor-for-life' whenever discussing the sport: Please stop it. Really" (360).

Ouch.

Among the other topics the *Uncyclopedia* considers: "Fish, Raw: Sushi Does *Not* Belong at a Ballpark"; and "Jackson, Shoeless Joe: Joe Jackson Is Not in the Hall of Fame Because Kevin Costner Made *The Postman.*"

When selecting entries for this book, I certainly considered Kun and Bloom's assessments about the state of baseball literature, which, they claim, consists primarily of: "Books about the Yankees. Books about the Red Sox. Books about the Yankees *and* the Red Sox. Books about players who played for the Yankees. Books about players who played for the Red Sox. Books about players who played for the Yankees *and* the Red Sox. And, depending upon where you live, a book or two about your local team" (53).

Very entertaining, thought-provoking, perhaps a bit aggravating—just what I want in my baseball readings.

Other categories: History, Pop Culture

463. *Baseball Uniforms of the 20th Century: The Official Major League Baseball Guide*, by Marc Okkonen. New York: Sterling, 1991.

When Okkonen first published this colorful coffee-table edition, I wonder if he could have envisioned a day when only one set of home and away uniforms would be passé for so many teams. While some organizations — most notably the Yankees — still cling to that century-plus-old tradition, others have spent a lot of time at the design board, coming up with a constant flow of combinations of tops and bottoms whose use is determined by a number of factors, rather than just where the team is playing on a given day. The 1966 Kansas City Athletics were the first team to deviate from the norm, with three distinct looks.

Okkonen, who specializes in uniforms and old ballparks, has illustrations available via Baseball-Reference.com, which uses his faceless suited figures to represent the attire worn by every player.

He discusses the trends in baseball attire, including caps, vest-and-undershirt combinations, patches (often to mark anniversaries, deaths, or special events), and accessories. He also analyzes the various logos, color schemes, and other unique characteristics — remember the shorts the White Sox wore briefly in 1976, or the Astros' horizontal rainbow-striped jerseys?

The book's main section depicts the teams in each league on a year-by-year basis. Granted, many remain the same for long periods, but it's fascinating to see how quickly they change from the end of the 1960s through 1991, where *Baseball Uniforms* leaves off.

The original edition was just over 270 pages; I imagine a revised edition could be twice that. It would still be a welcome update, if a tad cumbersome to produce.

Other categories: Coffee Table/Gift, History

464. *Bill James Presents* STATS *Inc. All-Time Baseball Sourcebook*, edited by Bill James, John Dewan, Neil Munro, and Don Zminda. Northbrook IL: STATS, 1998.

This doorstop of more than 2,600 pages was published just once in an attempt to compete with the *Total Baseball* series.

What sets it apart from similar tomes is the breadth and breakdown of data previously unavailable to the nonprofessional. Rather than listing the individual records of every player, which can be found in other books and online at websites like Baseball-Reference.com, the *Sourcebook* offers batting and pitching averages listed by decade, age, and time span. And these are just a few of the sections.

There is also an extensive franchise area where you can find out all manner of data on your favorite team, along with almanac-like capsules of interesting factoids.

The *Sourcebook* contains box scores from every All-Star and post-season game, along with registers and statistical summaries of each participant. The editors also give you their collective assessments on ninety of the greatest games ever played and wrap things up with a look at the history of the amateur draft.

The Internet has made books like this prohibitively expensive to publish—not to mention obsolete—but there's a still a special place on the bookshelf for them.

Other categories: History, Statistics

465. *The Book of Baseball Literacy*, third edition, by David H. Martinez. Self-published, 2011.

The word *literacy* here means making fans and nonfans aware of a number of the most important people, places, and things involved in the national pastime.

Martinez, a SABR member and former broadcaster, offers more than seven hundred entries on such items in eight general categories, including players and managers (only the top of the heap here); executives, media, and others (ditto); teams, leagues, and other groups (both current and defunct, Major, Minor, Negro, foreign, and women's); dates and events (various World Series, strikes, and other prominent proceedings); places (ballparks, mostly); folklore, literature, and diversions (a catchall category); records, statistics, and awards; and rules, general terms, and baseball business.

Baseball Literacy is a great starting point for newbies to the game.

Other categories: History, Pop Culture

466. *Daguerreotypes of Great Stars of Baseball*, edited by Paul MacFarlane. Saint Louis: Sporting News, 1971.

This paperback was similar in principle to the annual *Baseball Register* published by the *Sporting News*, but much more narrows in scope.

The prologue to the 1971 edition—there were eight editions published between 1934 and 1990—lists the requirements for inclusion, which made for a pretty exclusive club. Batters needed a lifetime .300 batting average with at least ten years of Major League service, 2,000 hits, or 200 home runs. Pitchers needed at least 175 victories, 4,000 innings, or 2,000 strikeouts. Every Hall of Fame inductee also makes the cut. "The standards were chosen to weed out the merely good player and include the genuine standout whose feats will stand—or have stood—the test of time," MacFarlane explains (2).

Like *TSN*'s *Register, Daguerreotypes* included information about trades, injuries, records held, and statistical categories in which the player led.

Other categories: History, Statistics

467. *Diamond Classics: Essays on 100 of the Best Baseball Books Ever Published*, by Mike Shannon. Jefferson N C: McFarland, 1989.

Another book that could use an update, *Diamond Classics* consists of an alphabetical listing of the author's selections. As editor of the estimable *Spitball* magazine, a literary baseball periodical, Shannon is particularly qualified to opine on the subject.

The criteria is simple: the book has to be "relatively available"; it has to be "of interest to the average reader"; it has to be well-written, containing "indispensable information or analysis"; or it has to tell an unforgettable story.

Among those he feels fall into these categories are the usual titles that populate top-five or top-ten lists, as well as a few surprises, such as *Joe, You Coulda Made Us Proud*, an autobiography-memoir by the Yankees' underachieving first baseman, Joe Pepitone; *Sandlot Peanuts*, a collection of baseball-themed cartoons featuring Charlie Brown and the rest of gang; and *Mighty Casey: All-American*, an updated version of Martin Gardner's *Annotated Casey at The Bat*.

Like many readers, Shannon has his favorites and includes several titles from authors like Tom Boswell, Donald Honig, Roger Kahn, Robert Creamer, and Charles Einstein, as well as each volume of the American Baseball and Fireside Book of Baseball series.

Diamond Classics goes into more detail than one normally finds in books like this. Shannon leads off each entry with excerpts of reviews, both pro and con, from other sources, followed by some backstory and his own comments. All this is fascinating, but it might actually run counter to his purpose: after reading the recaps, you might feel you don't need to read the books themselves, which would be a mistake for the majority of the titles he analyzes.

Other categories: Academic, Pop Culture

468. *The Dickson Baseball Dictionary*, third edition, by Paul Dickson. New York: W. W. Norton, 2009.

When I'm asked about the one book I would want if I were stranded on a desert island, I respond: "The dictionary. It's got all the other books in it." This is not an original line; I heard it on an episode of *M*A*S*H*.

But if I had to pick one baseball title, I would have to give this one extra consideration. *The Baseball Dictionary* is a must-have not just for lovers of the game, but for lovers of language as well.

Dickson enlisted the assistance of hundreds of contributors for the ten-thousand-plus definitions entries that appear within its one-thousand-plus pages. Some of the terms are still in use from the game's earliest days; others have gone by the wayside as new words and phrases pop into use. In that regard, *The Baseball Dictionary* is also a colorful etymology of American culture, as items from other walks of life insinuate themselves into the game's vernacular. For example, the "Linda Rondstadt fastball" is named after a singer who was popular mostly in the seventies and eighties. It's defined as: a "nickname for a fastball that 'Blue Bayou.' Not be confused with the 'Peggy Lee Fastball' ('Is that all there is?')." (Ms. Lee was a popular crooner from the 1950s and on.) There are also plenty of photographs and illustrations that serve to reinforce the concepts.

Dickson does not rest on his laurels; he is already preparing for the next edition.

Other categories: Coffee Table/Gift, Pop Culture

469. *The Gigantic Book of Baseball Quotations*, edited by Wayne Stewart. New York: Skyhorse, 2007.

The *"Gigantic"* in the title is no exaggeration here. Stewart has collected nearly seven hundred pages of material from players, baseball executives, and celebrities.

Topics include classic quotes, such as Jacques Barzun's standard, "Whoever would understand the heart and mind of America had better learn baseball," which appears ad nauseam in many a baseball book; humor; the media; hitters and hitting; pitches and pitching; fielders and fielding; managers and managing; the World Series; and "wacky quotes. Stewart deems Babe Ruth worthy of a section all to himself.

I have a couple of nitpicks, though. Although the editor lists all of the men and women who contributed their thoughts for posterity, there's no index that would lead to you what Humphrey Bogart, for example, said about the game: "A hot dog at the ballpark is better than a steak at the Ritz." There also doesn't seem to be any kind of order to the quotes within each chapter. But perhaps that's part of the charm. *Gigantic* is not meant to be read in a linear manner, but instead, like the sport, enjoyed at leisure.

Other category: Pop Culture

470. *The Great Encyclopedia of 19th Century Baseball,* by David Nemec. New York: Donald I. Fine, 1997.

Reminiscent of *The Bill James Historical Abstract,* Nemec focuses solely on the thirty-year period between 1871 and 1900. This massive volume combines team records with individual records, a difficult undertaking given the rapid evolution of statistics in those days combined with changing reporting methods. While striving for accuracy, Nemec concedes that such an elusive goal, especially given the relative lack of sophisticated record keeping of the era, is problematic.

Like other books of this kind, Nemec follows a relatively established format. The bulk is a chronology that includes team and league information followed by rosters that seek to be as complete as possible. Admittedly, there is lot of information missing, including several holes, such as a lack of the "height-weight, bats-throws" variety.

Single-season leaders are divided into two era: 1871–92 and 1893–1900, when the pitching mound was relocated to its present distance of sixty feet six inches from home plate, but career leaders are all lumped together. I guess if one wanted to be truly accurate these days, such books would have to consider expansion, night ball, as well as the dead- and live-ball eras, not to mention inflated numbers reached during the steroids years.

Other categories: History, Statistics

471. *How to Do Baseball Research,* edited by Gerald Tomlinson. Cleveland OH: Society for American Baseball Research, 2000.

Even if you have absolutely no plans to do a baseball project of your own, this how-to guide is worth perusing if just to get an appreciation of all the work that goes into preparing your favorite book. Of course, many of the recommendations contained therein are applicable to other subjects as well.

It's quite complete for a small book of less than 170 pages. There's a chapter on working with librarians, and another on Larry Lester's list of traveling essentials, which includes such helpful hints like making sure to have lots of coins for parking meters or photocopy machines; bringing pencils, since many archives don't allow the use of pens; and having mints and such for long periods without food and striking up conversations in libraries. Hey, just because it's research doesn't mean it has to be completely isolating. Other chapters include how to find information about specific components of the game, such as the Minors, the Negro Leagues, photographs, and so on.

One caveat: Since the book was published more than a decade ago, the breadth of information available on the Internet has expanded tremendously. That said, the chapter on "Using the Computer for Baseball Research" still offers some relevant tips.

472. *The SABR List and Record Book: Baseball's Most Fascinating Records and Unusual Statistics*, edited by Lyle Spatz/Society for American Baseball Research. New York: Scribner, 2007.

With so many books containing more or less the same basic information, you have to find that volume that offers a different spin, something out of the ordinary. This SABR publication meets the challenge.

One helpful feature is the player index, where you can quickly find out what records your favorite player set, for better or worse. At a glance, you can see who the heavy hitters were — even if they were pitchers — by how many entries they have. Babe Ruth, for example, leads with 112. Barry Bonds had 107 at the time of publication, just a year before he retired.

To eliminate a small degree of controversy, many of these records, events, and items — and there are more than 740 of them — are grouped by time period, with separate categories for events after 1893, when the mound was moved to its present distance.

Most of the records are standard righty, lefty, and overall marks, but some are even more interesting due to the difficulty in finding the information, such as pitching triple crowns (leading the league in wins, strikeouts, and earned run average) or pitchers who completed all of their starts in a single season, or five teammates with the most years together (the record stands at twelve, by Gates Brown, Bill Freehan, Willie Horton, Mickey Lolich, and Mickey Stanley of the Detroit Tigers, from 1964–75).

It's just those types of nuggets that have come to represent the attention to detail and love for the game that is SABR's hallmark.

Other categories: History, Statistics

473. *The San Diego Padres Encyclopedia*, by David Porter and Joe Naiman. Champaign IL: Sports Publishing, 2002.

One of the few books about the San Diego franchise, the *Padres Encyclopedia* is a good choice and serves as an example of a well-done team encyclopedia.

Books like these are for die-hard fans, collectors, or serious students of the game. The standard lineup includes a history of the franchise, biographies of key personnel, including players, managers, and executives, and, of course, statistics. Other information—an all-franchise team, "this day in team history," trades, and the like—depends on the size of the book and the age of the organization. The older the franchise, the more data available.

The Padres' relatively brief existence allows deeper examination, while a similar book on, say, the New York Yankees would of necessity contain shorter chronologies and profiles to accommodate its longer history; otherwise you're looking at a thousand-plus page tome. That's fine for some fans, but it could also put the book out of most readers' price range

Another consideration is the name associated with the project. Do you pair a former star with a highly recognized, established writer, sports journalist, or broadcaster? Or do you try to get someone closer to the franchise involved—more familiar perhaps, but with less buzz? In the case of the Padres, the publisher settled on an academic and a freelance writer, respectively.

Other categories: History/Team, Statistics

474. *The Team-by-Team Encyclopedia of Major League Baseball,* by Dennis Purdy. New York: Workman, 2006.

This 1,100-plus-page user-friendly volume includes lots of nuggets for each franchise. After a very brief introduction, the statistics begin with a list of yearly finishes and managerial records. A brief section of "Franchise Highlights, Low Points, and Strange Distinctions" follows, and then the fun really begins: a list of special achievements includes every award winner, every All-Star, every Hall of Famer who spent time on the club, every league leader, every pitcher who threw a no-hitter, and more, followed by a list of primary pitching staffs and starting lineups. There are also the top ten career and single-season batting and pitching leaders. The chapters conclude with brief profiles of significant members of each team.

475. *Total Baseball,* by John Thorn, Pete Palmer, Michael Gershman, et al. New York: Warner, 1989.

The bulk of this massive reference book consists of pitcher and batter registers, with additional sections of statistics—these vary slightly from one edition to the next—heretofore unavailable in one volume. For example, the seventh edition, published by Total Sports Publishing, includes a relatively small section on situational statistics. There's also a postseason register; a year-by-year wrap-up for each league; all-time leaders lists; annual team rosters, which consist of regulars, key utility players, and primary starting pitchers and relievers; rosters for managers (with win-loss records), coaches, umpires, and owners; key executives for each league and franchise; even a roster of announcers. There are also brief sections on important baseball quotes, top amateur draft selections and, finally, baseball firsts.

Most of the aforementioned items do not change from one edition to the next, although they are updated. What justifies the purchase of each new edition are the excellent essays. The topics range from general historical overviews to much more narrow themes, such as baseball and the Civil War, baseball families, the top one hundred players, regular-season-ending tiebreakers in the form of postseason playoffs prior to divisional play, and the evolution of baseball records, among others. And that's just in the seventh edition.

Don't expect an updated edition any time soon, if ever. For one thing, they've become prohibitively expense to produce and to purchase; the most recent was published in 2004 and carried a cover price of almost $70. Even the first edition was almost $50, pretty dear for a baseball title in 1989. And, quite frankly, the information, both statistically and narratively can easily be found online in a much more economical fashion, in terms of both affordability and statistical accuracy.

Total Baseball, which debuted in 1991 as an answer to the Macmillan encyclopedia, became the official reference volume of Major League Baseball starting with the fourth edition.

Other categories: History, Statistics

13
Statistics

In the beginning, there were statistics. And the fans saw them, and they were good. Over time, however, they took on a life of their own, almost a case of the tail wagging the dog (especially in fantasy baseball). The books in this section are a combination of the history and development of statistics and their place in baseball, as well as more complex works going into the new generation of sabermetrics.

One of the first books I ever bought was Earnshaw Cook's Percentage Baseball (Waverly Press, 1964; reprinted by the MIT Press in 2003). I didn't understand it when I was ten, and I still don't get it today. But that's just me; I have trouble balancing the checkbook.

Over the past thirty years or so, a new generation of statistics has led to the creation of dozens of books trying to explain what the heck these new formulas mean.

There is a faction of sabermetricians who try to show their superiority by inventing all sorts of formulas so complicated they seem accessible only to MIT grad students. But as sportswriters and broadcasters increase their references to these new metrics, outfits like Baseball Prospectus, perhaps realizing the scope of the market, are trying to make these concepts more comprehensible to the numerically challenged.

476. *Baseball Between the Numbers: Why Everything You Know About the Game is Wrong,* edited by Jonah Keri. New York: Basic, 2006.

Why is the sky blue? Why is the grass green? Why is Mario Mendoza so important?

Baseball Between the Numbers, brought to you by the folks at

Baseball Prospectus (BP), might only be able to answer the last question with authority, but it will be a doozy.

There are a lot of aspects of the game fans take for granted, whether because they feel they should know them implicitly or out of embarrassment that they should have to ask. So to have their cherished beliefs challenged is a humbling experience.

BP, which puts out an excellent annual print publication as well, released this analysis to answer some of those questions. In Mendoza's case, it was his ineptitude that led to the creation of the sabermetric VORP, or "value over replacement player."

Some of the questions are event or player specific: "Did Derek Jeter Deserve the Gold Glove?" "Is Alex Rodriguez Overpaid?" "Was Billy Martin Crazy?" Others are more general: "Are Teams Letting Their Closers go to Waste?" "Can a Team Have Too Much Pitching?" Each is answered in a comprehensive and patient manner, as a teacher would explain to a student, by writers for the popular BP website, including Steven Goldman, Nate Silver, and Dayn Perry. Several of these writers have graduated and moved on to websites of their own.

Other category: Classic

477. *Beyond Batting Average: Baseball Statistics for the 21st Century*, by Lee Panas. Lulu.com, 2010

478. *Encyclopedia of Baseball Statistics from A to ZR*, by Eric Blabac. Bloomington IN: iUniverse.com, 2010.

Murray Chass, who spent some forty years as a baseball writer for the *New York Times*, famously criticized the new wave of baseball statistics and their advocates, castigating them for being the product of a bunch of nerds who were more interested in the fantasy aspects of the national pastime. Many new-age bloggers and others firmly in the fantasy-baseball demographic passed him off as a "dinosaur."

The problem is that many of these numbers do get a bit esoteric.

I mean, who comes up with some of this stuff? For example, in *Beyond Batting Average*, Panas introduces his readers to the concept of "batting runs," which is a type of "linear weight system" that he calculates as follows:

$$BR = 0.047 \times 1B + 0.77 \times 2B + 1.04 \times 3B + 1.40 \times HR + 0.31 \times BB + 0.34 \times HBP - 0.28 \times \text{outs}.$$

Easy for him to say.

Nor can you find out exactly *why* the equation is thus constructed. Why does is a hit by pitch 0.03 higher than a base on balls when both have the same result? Further complicating the issue is the author's assertion that there are slightly different variations depending on the source of the formula.

Blabac deserves credit for at least trying to simplify his information with cogent narrative and alternatives for batting, fielding, and pitching stats designed to reach similar conclusions. It's kind of like online mapping sites: you can take the proffered route or drag the line to go in a different direction. Either way, you should get to the same destination.

And BBA is actually the simpler of the two titles. Blabac, who has master's degrees in statistics, applied mathematics, and business administration, includes almost four hundred pages of equations and charts in his *Encyclopedia*, but with fewer explanations than Panas. It reads almost like a college textbook. Consider this one if you're a real numbers lover.

Nevertheless, he deserves props for rounding up information via some of the most popular purveyors of baseball calculus, including Baseball Prospectus, the *Hardball Times*, *Total Baseball*, and various Bill James publications.

Other category: Analysis

479. *Flip Flop Fly Ball: An Infographic Baseball Adventure,* by Craig Robinson. New York: Bloomsbury, 2011.

Like the proverbial fallen tree, if statistics are constantly presented via boring spreadsheets, pie charts, and bar graphs, can the regular fan benefit from them?

Robinson, a British expatriate, discovered baseball relatively late in life, but he has taken to it with a passion that shows in his inquisitive investigations into some of the questions that have rendered fans sleepless for years. For example, if Alex Rodriguez's $33 million salary were paid in pennies, how high would they reach? They would be 3,178.3 miles high, he explains, represented by a very tall line extending from a very small Earth. What the heck happened to the complete game? And what should the relationship be between going to a ballgame and participating in the wave? Items fall into both the "I always wondered about that" and the "I never thought of that" categories, as Robinson attempts to find the connection between totally disparate issues.

The colorful, well-conceived diagrams, an outgrowth of his website, flipflopflyin.com, are supplemented with Robinson's essays of discovery as he travels across America, meeting news friends and sampling various team cultures in his new favorite pastime. Granted, not every one of the 120 illustrations is exceptional—there are a few too many maps offering pedestrian information that isn't improved by a pretty presentation—but major props to him for his imaginative expression. If schools employed this kind of material in teaching just about any subject at the elementary or secondary level, I would imagine a lot of grades would improve.

Other categories: Analysis, Classic, Pop Culture/Art

480. *The Hidden Game of Baseball,* by John Thorn and Pete Palmer. New York: Doubleday, 1984.

This was the first book focusing on statistical analysis for a general audience and the one that put Thorn and Palmer on the sabermetric map.

The authors sought to dispel the use of traditional metrics, such as batting average and pitching wins, as an adequate measure of ability and success. Instead, they advocated a linear-weights system, deeming certain situations to be more important than others, throwing it all together, and coming up with their new definitive conclusion. Their system has since fallen out of favor as *the* statistic of choice, but they did open the door for subsequent math fiends to search for an optimal combination that could give that authoritative answer to the eternal question: Who is the best player of all time?

About half the book is commentary, and the rest goes back in time to reassess historical stats and update them, rearranging some long-held conventions.

Other categories: Analysis, Classic, Commentary, History

481. *The Numbers Game: Baseball's Lifelong Fascination With Statistics,* by Alan Schwarz. New York: Thomas Dunne, 2004.

Schwarz, a sports reporter for the *New York Times* who most recently has specialized in stories dealing with the long-term mental-health issues of former pro athletes, delved into the history of statistics in the national pastime and wrote one of the most engaging examinations of its kind.

This is not a typical book with line after line of ERA, BA, SA, OBP, WARP, VORP, and other metrics ad nauseam. Instead he pays tribute to the men who bucked tradition, going up against baseball lifers who didn't need cold numbers to know how their players were doing. Little did they comprehend what would come to pass, how these formulations and accounts would enhance the enjoyment of the fans, bolster both players and management at the negotiating table, and serve as filler for broadcasters during those lopsided games, interminable rain delays, and pitching changes.

One thing I really appreciate is Schwarz's acknowledgment of men like Alan Roth, the Montreal-born employee of the Brooklyn Dodgers who first popularized the use of statistics by the front office as a tool to improve the team, and the Elias brothers, Al Munro and

Walter, who practically took their material door-to-door to newspapers back in the early 1900s. They would eventually go on, with the help of Seymour Siwoff, to create the Elias Sports Bureau, which provides so many essential—not to mention entertaining—facts and figures on Major League Baseball.

The Numbers Game should be required reading for every fan, not just those interested in the fantasy world.

Other categories: Analysis, Auto/Bio/Mem, History, Pop Culture

482. *Who's Better, Who's Best in Baseball? "Mr. Stats" Sets the Record Straight on the Top 75 Players of All Time,* by Elliot Kalb. New York: McGraw-Hill, 2005.

Another in a long line of comparative baseball literature designed to promote debate and conversation, Kalb makes his a bit more entertaining than most authors, who take themselves and their subject too seriously. In writing about Satchel Paige, who comes in surprisingly high at number fifteen, Kalb invokes the lyrics of "That's Life," one of Frank Sinatra's signature songs. He explains why the reedy Negro League pitcher is, at various stages of his legendary career, a puppet, a pauper, a pirate, a poet, a pawn, and a king.

Sure, there are plenty of statistics, but the fun part is when Kalb puts a Ty Cobb head-to-head with an Oscar Charleston (whom the racist Cobb would never deign to play with or against in real life). And when those tête-à-têtes become too blasé, the author offers a better analogy. Sandy Koufax or Warren Spahn? Feh! How about Koufax and author J. D. Salinger, another top-flight performer in his field and famous for his demands of privacy? Roger Clemens or Pedro Martinez? What about Clemens and that other famous rocket man, John Glenn?

Similar books are frequently updated when modern-day players inch up the milestone trail, but *WBWB* stands on its own merely for the amusement factor. But just for the hell of it, Kalb's top five players are Barry Bonds, Babe Ruth, Willie Mays, Hank Aaron, and

Walter Johnson, with Carlton Fisk bringing up the rear at number seventy-five.)

Is this the final word? Of course not. There will probably never be a definitive ranking on which everyone can agree, but getting there is more than half the fun.

Other category: Popular Culture

483. *The World of Sports Statistics: How the Fans and Professionals Record, Compile, and Use Information,* by Arthur Friedman with Joel H. Cohen. New York: Atheneum, 1978.

Although this one isn't wholly about baseball, the majority of it considers the fascinating relationship between statisticians, teams, and broadcasters.

Friedman frankly addresses the arduous work involved in compiling, typing up the data in an age before having a personal computer was as common as having a television, and distributing the information (does anyone out there remember mimeo machines?) in a timely manner.

But it's Friedman's anecdotes that make this more than a run-of-the-mill report of what some might consider a boring job. Stats not only make the game more enjoyable, but they can also have far-reaching impacts on a player's livelihood in terms of salary or even the ability to keep his job.

The author—who worked for most of the New York–based pro sports teams—was a bit prescient in discussing which statistics he considered to be overrated and which should be given more respect; he advocated a runs-created formula well before it became de rigueur.

Yes, the material is dated, but they still teach about the colonial days in school, don't they?

Other categories: Auto/Bio/Mem, Pop Culture

14

Umpires and Rules

According to legend, when trying to sort out a difficult play in a ballgame, Hall of Fame umpire Bill Klem once declared, "It ain't nothing 'til I call it," which probably didn't go over too well at the time.

The men in blue take all sorts of abuse as they simply try to do their jobs: that is, interpret and enforce the laws of the game as per the rule book. These statutes have been the subject of discussion and debate since the game's forefathers set them down more than 150 years ago. It's amazing how many remain to this day: three strikes and you're out, nine innings to a regulation game, and 90 feet from base to base—a couple of feet in either direction would change the scope of the sport.

Numerous books pay homage to these arbiters, who never have a home game and seldom have a day off. At least half the players and fans will be unhappy with whatever decision they make, and their work is constantly scrutinized. A good umpire goes through a game anonymously; it's usually when he screws up that people learn his name.

Others titles in this chapter concentrate on the history and analysis of the rules themselves and offer hours of philosophical edutainment as they examine and dissect challenging situations that would make Solomon scratch his head. Neither category will be boring to the curious fan.

484. *As They See 'Em: A Fan's Travels in the Land of Umpires,* by Bruce Weber. New York: Scribner, 2009.

It looks so easy that anybody can do the job. Until it's not. An umpire can make 999 calls correctly, but make one flub and everyone knows your name. Just ask Jim Joyce, who admittedly blew Detroit Tiger pitcher Armando Galarraga's perfect game in 2010 on the penultimate call.

But when you think about it, being a Major League umpire is even harder than making it to the big leagues as a player. Do the math. There are hundreds of players, but fewer than seventy-five men in blue. The training has to be almost Marinelike in culling out the few good men.

Weber, a writer for the *New York Times,* does a George Plimpton, embedding himself in the rigorous training program, where he takes classes, breaks bread, and shares stories. His fellow pupils have a deep love and respect for the game and decided this was their chance to make a career out of it. And for such devotion, Weber is *their* fan and tries to make fans of his readers.

Of course, knowing that you're really just pretending for the sake of writing a book might detract from the overall seriousness of the project. But Weber threw himself into his assignment, and the result is an honest and in-depth report on the men in blue who, in reality, are just like the ballplayers over whom they officiate, sharing the common dream of working professionally in the national pastime.

Other categories: Auto/Bio/Mem, History, Pop Culture

485. *Baseball Scorekeeping: A Practical Guide to the Rules,* by Andres Wirkmaa. Jefferson NC: McFarland, 2003.

Many fans pride themselves on their knowledge of baseball's rules and their ability to keep a neat and greatly detailed scorecard. If you fall into this category and enjoy the minutiae inherent therein, this one is for you.

To be accurate, however, the title is a tad misleading. You will not find instructions or anecdotes on how to actually keep score in the casual fan sense. In fact, one does not necessarily need an intimate knowledge of the rules to keep a good scorecard. This volume isn't for the layperson. Wirkmaa provides an almost legal document for those who wish to understand, and perhaps take on, the responsibility of serving as an official scorer, the person with the final say in how the statistics will be recorded for posterity. It's not an easy situation but, in some respects, it's also not as complex as one might expect.

On more than one occasion when I worked as an in-stadium game reporter for STATS Inc., the official scorer was, shall we say, "out of position" during a play and had to query members of the media for a consensus before making his decision. Hey, we're only human.

486. *The Best Seat in the House, but You Have To Stand! The Game as Umpires See It*, by Lee Gutkind. New York: Dial Press, 1975.

Books about umpires range from oral histories to individual autobiographies, biographies, and memoirs. But just as there are teams of players with different personalities and quirks, there is also the Major League umpiring crew, which normally consists of four individuals (six in the postseason). In *Best Seat*, Gutkind chronicles the 1974 season he spent embedded with the quartet of Harvey Wendelstedt, Nick Colosi, Art Williams, and crew chief Doug Harvey, as they battle the teams—and sometimes each other, as they movie blurbs might say—during the course of a typical campaign.

Players take some comfort in getting to spend half the season at a home base, even if it's not their off-season abode. The umpires have no such solace; they are always away, always the visitors, which can put an extra burden on their domestic situations. Gutkind does not sugarcoat or seek sympathy on that account. His is an honest, sometimes sad, sometimes funny documentary of what the profession involves and the dedication it takes to get to the game's top level.

Just as players don't make it on talent alone, neither do the umpires. There are politics involved and personality clashes. The nature of the profession demands a bit of stubbornness, which is not always the best quality to have if you want a long career.

Other categories: Auto/Bio/Mem, Classic, History/Event

487. *The Cheater's Guide to Baseball*, by Derek Zumsteg. Boston: Houghton Mifflin, 2007.

Similar in intent to Gutman's *It Ain't Cheating If You Don't Get Caught*, Zumsteg's book offers a bit more in the how-to category, including how you, as a fan, might be able to influence the game through the time-honored tradition of heckling.

It would be interesting to attend a game with Zumsteg. I imagine watching him point out the potential ways to put a little something over on the opposition would be quite entertaining. He starts his *Guide* slowly with a section on "Cheating for Beginners," which includes such subtleties as careful groundskeeping, which consists of wetting down the base paths for teams with swift runners and keeping the infield grass high to help your bunters; delaying the game if your team is ahead or behind, depending on the circumstances and the weather; and the most little league stunt of all: the hidden ball trick.

From there the lessons become more advanced. The author provides history lessons and practical details on how to doctor the ball and the bat. He then wraps up with the truly heinous manipulations: gambling—he calls the Black Sox scandal "the worst thing ever to happen to baseball"—and the steroids scourge.

Unlike Gutman, Zumsteg doesn't get heavy into the philosophical aspect, although it's basically implied that we should all do the right thing.

Other categories: History, Pop Culture

488. *It Ain't Cheating If You Don't Get Caught: Scuffing, Corking, Spitting, Gunking, Razzing, and Other Fundamentals of Our National Pastime,* by Dan Gutman. New York: Penguin, 1990.

There are few things more embarrassing for a player than getting caught with his hand in the proverbial cookie jar. Sammy Sosa's bat once exploded on a swing, sending tiny rubber balls flying from the hollowed-out core, a flagrant violation of the rules. Same for the pitchers who are, infrequently, found to be using a foreign substance they apply to the ball to alter its path to the plate. And it wasn't all that long ago that Derek Jeter, the Yankees' poster boy for sportsmanship and fair play, deked an umpire into believing he'd been hit by a pitch, to the consternation of both his fans and detractors.

Gutman's book could be called a primer on cheating. He breaks his chapters down into innings to describe the whys, whats, hows, and whos of getting away with some chicanery. Of particular interest for ethicists is his take on "The Morality of Cheating: Would Jesus Throw a Spitball?" while historians will appreciate "Great Moments" in cheating.

Not that Gutman condones any of this behavior. We should hope not, since he's also a prolific writer of baseball books for young readers.

Other categories: History, Pop Culture

489. *The Joy of Keeping Score: How Scoring the Game Has Influenced and Enhanced the History of Baseball,* by Paul Dickson. New York: Walker, 1996.

Dickson has published several titles that belong on every serious fan's bookshelf. But where you have the thick and workmanlike *Baseball Dictionary* and the serious *Baseball: The President's Game,* you also have the petite and charming *The Joy of Keeping Score.*

This book is both practical—with its brief but detailed how-to pointers—and entertaining, with an A-to-Z primer on the methodology and lore that accounts for most of the information. Topics run from the practical (proofing your scorecard to make sure it's correct, and a timeline of rule changes) to the anecdotal (which First Families were diligent in logging their games) to the international ("Scorekeeping in French"). There are a few examples of scorecards from notable events, but they and the other nostalgic illustrations would be better served in a larger publication; *Joy* measures less than eight inches by eight inches.

If you're looking for a stocking stuffer for scoring fans of any age, you've found a good one in Dickson's modest offering.

Other categories: Analysis, History, Pop Culture

490. *You're the Umpire: 130 Scenarios to Test Your Knowledge of Baseball,* by Wayne Stewart. New York: Skyhorse, 2010.

Most devoted fans think they know the game inside out, but how many truly know the rules? Heck, a lot of managers and players don't even know them. Can *you* recite the infield fly rule? Stewart, the author of more than twenty baseball titles, has come up with a fun and educational little book that tests fans on a number of basic and not-so-basic situations.

Three sections consider "Routine Calls" that seem too obvious until you realize you're stymied: If a batted ball hits the foul line, is it fair or foul? From the section "Basic Situations": What's the call if a shortstop's throw pulls the first baseman off the bag, but the runner fails to touch the base? And from "Obscure Rules and Situations": What if an outfielder playing in Wrigley Field touches a fly ball that then gets stuck in the famed ivy?

Stewart uses actual players, past and present, which makes it easier to visualize the myriad situations. Thankfully, he never gets so technical that the average fan can't follow the logic.

The oddly baseball-shaped book is amusing in its quirkiness and makes for an appealing gift.

Other categories: Analysis, History, Pop Culture

15

For Young Readers

It's never too early to introduce children to reading, and there's lots of quality literature for any age. So if you want to start guiding your kids to the national pastime, there's no time like the present. Now if only Major League Baseball could just do something about those late starting times . . .

491. *Baseball from A to Z*, by Michael P. Spradlin, illustrated by Macky Pamintuan. New York: Harper, 2010.

The perfect first book for baseball-loving parents to introduce their toddlers to the game, *Baseball from A to Z* teaches some of the important concepts in a colorful manner, with funny yet heroic figures representing various players and plays, the defensive positions, the geography of the ball park, types of hits, even mascots.

Adults should consider taking this to the stadium when it's time for baby's first game. It's difficult to say if the book would make the event more real for the tyke, but it is a good way to keep him or her involved.

492. *First Pitch: How Baseball Began*, by John Thorn. Santa Barbara CA: Beach Ball, 2011.

Just as Geoffrey C. Ward and Ken Burns did with adult and children's versions of the 1994 companion to their *Baseball* documentary, Thorn published this colorful primer for young newcomers to the game as sort of a junior version to his *Baseball in the Garden of Eden*.

In both books, albeit with varying degrees of sophistication, Thorn — who was named the official historian for Major League Baseball in 2011 — seeks to dispel the myth that the national pastime was the creation of a single person (Abner Doubleday) and to give proper credit to a group of gentlemen for developing the game as we now know it. Thorn also touches on the differences between the versions played in New York and Massachusetts, which eventually combined into one standard game. The nineteenth century illustrations and photographs are a wonderful visual introduction to the era as well.

Will small children be that interested in the early history of baseball? Hey, you have to start somewhere.

Other category: History

493. *Home Is Everything: The Latino Baseball Story*, narrative by Marcos Breton, photography Jose Luis Villegas. El Paso TX: Cinco Puntos Press, 2002.

By now most baseball fans are aware of the difficulties facing many Latino ballplayers. For every one that has found success in the United States, hundreds have foundered and returned to their native countries disillusioned.

Breton and Villegas present both sides of the coin in their colorful book for young adults, which follows the arc of Miguel Tejada, one of the more successful Latino players, as his journey begins on the hardscrabble fields of the Dominican Republic. While he was one of the lucky few, his progress was challenged by the culture shock that he, like so many who came before, had to endure. The early years in the Minors were a combination of joy and frustration for the young Tejada. He experienced the language barrier, isolation from his teammates, and the general feeling of being a stranger in a strange land.

It was ultimately worth it, though; Tejada has enjoyed an All-Star career, and the book is as much about his triumphs as anything else.

Home is Everything, which is presented in English and Spanish in the same volume, also recalls some of the great Latino players, such as Orlando Cepeda (who contributed the book's preface), Roberto Clemente, and Luis Tiant, as well as others whose reputations were built more in their own countries than in the States.

Other categories: Auto/Bio/Mem, Ethnicity, History, International

494. *The Jackie Robinson Story*, by Arthur Mann. New York: Grosset and Dunlop, 1963.

They don't make 'em like this anymore, which is precisely why it's important to read a book like *The Jackie Robinson Story*.

Mann, who worked for the Brooklyn Dodgers as an assistant to Branch Rickey, penned this optimistic, uplifting biography of the first African American to cross baseball's unofficial color line. The original version was published in 1950, just three years after Robinson's Brooklyn debut.

The target audience is definitely young people, and as such Mann refrains from relating some of the uglier incidents Robinson was forced to endure early in his career; this was part of his agreement in signing with the Dodgers. Ben Chapman, the Philadelphia Phillies manager who gave Robinson such an obscenely difficult time in that first year, is mentioned, but with the details toned down. Mann describes other incidents as well, including how some Dodgers declined to play with their new teammate. Mann uses the term *Negro* when referring to African Americans, which further dates the book, although it does hearken back to a kinder, gentler style of writing than one would find today. Whether that's better or not is up to the reader to decide.

The Jackie Robinson Story was updated in 1951 and 1956 before its final version, which included Robinson's induction into the Hall of Fame.

Other categories: Auto/Bio/Mem, Ethnicity, History
Also by the author: *Baseball Confidential: The Secret History of The War Among Chandler, Durocher, MacPhail, and Rickey* (1951); *The Real McGraw* (editor, with Mrs. John J. McGraw, 1953); *Branch Rickey: American in Action* (1957)

495. *The Journal of Biddy Owens*, by Walter Dean Myers. New York: Scholastic, 2001.

The Journal of Biddy Owens is a work of historical fiction about a seventeen-year-old African American who lands a job as batboy for the Birmingham Black Barons, one of the legendary teams of the Negro Leagues whose ranks included some of the greatest players of all time—regardless of color—such as Satchel Paige, Buck Leonard, and Willie Mays.

Owens keeps track of the excitement of the season, the fans, and the players, both on and off the field. Although the Barons are headed for pennant, it's not all fun and games. There's pressure from within, as personalities clash despite shared goals. The bigger pressure, however, comes from areas beyond their control in the pervasive racism the team endured as they traveled from town to town for the next game: separate drinking fountains, separate cars on trains, and substandard housing arrangements: all were par for the course in the era of Jim Crow.

Journal is also a story of the difficulties in the Owens household. When World War II ended, blacks faced the brunt of layoffs when returning veterans sought to reclaim their former jobs. Against this backdrop Biddy is caught between the end of childhood and the beginning of manhood.

The book is part of the My Name Is America fiction series for nine- to fourteen-year-olds, which looks at historic events from the perspective of young members of various ethnic groups.

Other categories: Ethnicity, History, Negro Leagues

496. *Lipman Pike: America's First Home Run King*, by Richard Michelson with illustrations by Zachary Pullen. Ann Arbor MI: Sleeping Bear Press, 2011.

Michelson, an award-winning children's author, tells the story of the first Jewish professional ballplayer, Lipman Pike, who made his debut for the Troy Haymakers in 1871. Like many children of immigrants, young Lipman wanted to establish himself as an all-American kid, and the way to do that was through baseball.

Michelson's message of old world traditions versus new world struggles are told in a way that young readers can understand, while Pullen's illustrations charmingly convey the nineteenth-century styles. Books like this have the ancillary benefit of teaching kids not just about sports, but about other cultures as well.

Other categories: Auto/Bio/Mem, Ethnicity, History

497. *The Lucky Baseball Bat,* by Matt Christopher with illustrations by Robert Henneberger. New York: Little, Brown, 2004.

Christopher was one of the most prolific writers of juvenile sports literature, with more than one hundred titles to his credit covering just about every popular sport. He published almost fifty titles of baseball fiction alone, as well as biographies for young readers.

As is the case with most of his books, Christopher combines a kid's enjoyment of games with life lessons and sportsmanship. In *The Lucky Baseball Bat*—which was originally published in 1954 and rereleased in a commemorative fiftieth-anniversary edition—young Martin wonders if he can continue his high level of play without the use of his favorite piece of lumber.

Life was so much simpler back in the day. The problems of kids in the 1950s are a far cry from some of the topics that currently appear in books for that age group. In those days, young people were taught to be polite to strangers. Now they're warned about the dangers of child abuse and kidnapping. Sad.

Other category: Fiction

498. *Samurai Shortstop,* by Alan Gratz. New York: Dial, 2006.

There are hundreds of novels for young adults about growing up and playing baseball in the United States. While several of them are pretty good, there is a decided lack of material about kids from other cultures who also have a mania for the game.

Gratz seeks to amend that oversight with *Samurai Shortstop*, the tale of late-nineteenth-century Japan as it moves from a feudal to a modern society. Sixteen-year-old Toyo Shimada must fight for family honor and his own identity as a star baseball player in his new school, all the while butting heads with traditional narrow-minded teachers and classmates.

Gratz plays up the concept of *wa*, the discipline of the Japanese athlete to put the team above all else, making the search for identity in the face of Toyo's family's opposition and demand for obeisance all the more stressful.

Samurai Shortstop was included among the American Library Association's top ten best books for young adults in 2007.

Other categories: History, International

Also by the author: *The Brooklyn Nine* (2009) follows nine decades of one family's connection with baseball—from the sandlots in the mid-nineteenth century to the Negro Leagues to the Brooklyn Dodgers in the mid-twentieth century. That one was picked as one of the ALA's top ten sports books for youth.

499. *We Are the Ship: The Story of Negro League Baseball,* by Kadir Nelson. New York: Jump at the Sea/Hyperion, 2008.

Nelson, an African American artist, pays tribute to the pioneers of black baseball in this award-winning overview.

The paintings of the old Negro Leagues' central characters are dramatic, endowing the subjects with strength (Josh Gibson), youthfulness (Judy Johnson), dignity (Turkey Stearnes), heroism (Jackie Robinson), and general marvel (Satchel Paige).

Writing in the first person, Nelson portrays a player passing along stories to his young charges. One can easily envision an elderly veteran of the Negro Leagues talking to a group of children at his feet. He speaks of the bad—the discrimination, mistreatment, poor conditions—as well as the good: the camaraderie, the pride in achievement. It is a bittersweet voice.

Examples of Nelson's images can be viewed on his website, KadirNelson.com. *We Are the Ship* received *Spitball* magazine's CASEY Award in 2008.

Other categories: Award Winner, History, Negro Leagues

500. *Who Invented the Game?*, by Geoffrey C. Ward and Ken Burns, with Paul Robert Walker. New York: Knopf, 1994.

Consider this a junior version of the companion book for Burns's watershed documentary.

The two collaborators pare down the intricacies, following the same format of nine innings to mark the chapters, which divides the history of the game into neat compartments. Unfortunately, the title question is never really answered. The opening page recounts the traditional belief that Abner Doubleday concocted baseball. "This story has been told to five generations of American children," the authors declare, "but it is not true" (6).

From there the book follows a fairly thorough though brief history of the national pastime, from the first rumblings of codified rules and organized competition between teams in the mid-nineteenth century through Kirk Gibson's dramatic walk-off home run in the 1988 World Series.

Just like its big brother counterpart, *Who Invented the Game?* is neatly illustrated, highlighting many of the premier ballplayers and serving as a good general introduction for the younger reader.

Other category: History

501. *You Never Heard of Sandy Koufax?*, by Jonah Winter and Andre Carrilho. New York: Schwartz and Wade, 2009.

When Sandy Koufax declined to pitch the opener of the 1965 World Series because the game fell on Yom Kippur, the most solemn holiday on the Jewish calendar, it created quite a stir. Unlike Hall of Fame slugger Hank Greenberg, who sat out of an important day in the 1935 season for the same reason, second- and third-generation Jews had become more assimilated into American society. There was not the same pressure as there was in their parents'—and grandparents'—day to follow the strict tenets of their religion.

Since Koufax retired in 1966 at the age of thirty after five dominant seasons, younger generations, even more removed from the synagogue and observant life, have grown unfamiliar with what his actions meant to Jews at the time. Winter wrote this slim, gorgeously illustrated picture book to bring this modest hero and role model to a new audience. Even though neither the author nor illustrator is Jewish, their goal is still to teach youngsters certain values, chief among them the need to set priorities and realize what's truly important in the grand scheme of things.

Other categories: Auto/Bio/Mem, Ethnicity, History

Also by the authors: *Roberto Clemente: Pride of the Pittsburgh Pirates* (2005); *Fair Ball!: 14 Great Stars from Baseball's Negro Leagues* (2002); *Beisbol!: Latino Baseball Pioneer and Legends* (2002).

Index